Chassidus, Kabbalah

and

Meditation

Written by

Reb Moshe Steinerman

Edited by Elise Teitelbaum

ilovetorah Jewish Outreach Network

ilovetorah Jewish Publishing

First Published 2018

ISBN: 978-1-947706-03-3

www.ilovetorah.com

moshe@ilovetorah.com

Editor: Elise Teitelbaum

Co Editor: Rochel Steinerman

Cover Art by Boris Shapiro

Book Format By: Rabbi Benyamin Fleischman

Graphic Art by Reb Moshe Steinerman

Dedication

In memory of my father, Reb Shlomo Zavel ben Yaakov zt"l, my father-in-law Menachem ben Reuvain zt"l and all the great souls of our people

I grew up in a house filled with the *Torah* learning of my father, who studied most of the day. Although there were no Jews in this remote part of Maryland, my father was a man of chesed to all people and was known for his brilliance in *Torah* scholarship.

I want to say a special thank you to the Nikolsberg Rebbe and the Biala Rebbe for their encouragement and blessings. Most of all, I offer thanks to my wife, Rochel, for her faithful support.

Dedicated to my wife Rochel and to my children Shlomo Nachman, Yaakov Yosef, Gedalya Aharon Tzvi, Esther Rivka, Yeshiya Michel, Dovid Shmuel, Eliyahu Yisrael may it bring forth the light of your neshamos.

Dear Reader,

IloveTorah Jewish Outreach is a non-profit organization; books and *Torah* classes are available at low cost. Therefore, we appreciate your donation to help Rabbi Moshe Steinerman and ilovetorah.com to continue their work on behalf of the Jewish people. We also ask that you pass on these books to others once you are finished with them.

Thank you,

Reb Moshe Steinerman
www.ilovetorah.com
Donations
www.ilovetorah.com/donations

About the Author

Rabbi Moshe Steinerman grew up as a religious Jew on the hillsides of Maryland. During his teenage years, Reb Moshe developed his talent for photography, while connecting to nature and speaking to *HaShem*. He later found his path through Breslov *Chassidus*, while maintaining closeness to the *Litvish* style of learning. He studied in the Baltimore yeshiva, Ner Yisrael; then married and moved to Lakewood, New Jersey. After settling down, he began to write *Kavanos Halev*, with the blessing of *Rav* Malkiel Kotler *Shlita*, Rosh Yeshiva of Beis Medrash Gevoha.

After establishing one of the first Jewish outreach websites, iloveTorah.com in 1996, Reb Moshe's teachings became popular among the full spectrum of Jews, from the unaffiliated to ultra-Orthodox. His teachings, including hundreds of stories of tzaddikim, gained popularity due to the ideal of drawing Jews together. Reb Moshe made aliyah to Tzfat in 2003, and returned thousands of English-speaking Jews to Judaism, through his many Jewish videos, audio shiurim and outreach Torah learning website. His learning experience includes the completion of both Talmud Bavli and Yerushalmi as well as other important works.

In 2012, Reb Moshe, with his wife and children, moved to Jerusalem. Some of his other books are <u>Kavanos Halev (Meditations of the Heart), Tikkun Shechinah, Tovim Meoros (Glimpse of Light), Pesukei Torah (Passages of Torah), Yom Leyom (Day by Day), Pathways of the Righteous, A Journey into Holiness, and The True Intentions of the Baal Shem Tov.</u>

Special thanks to Rabbi Benyamin Fleischman for making the books into print-ready format and to Elise Teitelbaum for helping to edit the books.

Rabbinical Approvals/Haskamah

Approval from the Baila Rebbe of New York, Miami, Betar - Israel

הובא לפני גליונות בעניני קירוב רחוקים לקרב אחינו בני ישראל אל

אביהם שבשמים, כידוע מהבעש"ט זיע"א שאמר "אימתי קאתי מר

לכשיפוצו מעינותיך חוצה" ואפריון נמטי"ה להאי גברא יקירא מיקירי

צפת עיה"ק תובב"א כמע"כ מוהר"ר משה שטיינרמן שליט"א אשר כבר

עוסק רבות בשנים לקרב רחוקים לתורה וליהדות, וכעת מוציא לאור

ספר בשם "חסידות קבלה והתבודדות" וראיתי דברים נחמדים מאוד וניכר מתוך

הדברים שהרב בעל המחבר - אהבת השי"ת ואהבת התורה וישראל

בלבבו, ובטחוני כי הספר יביא תועלת גדולה לכל עם ישראל.

ויה"ר שיזכה לבוא לגומרה ברוב פאר והדר ונזכה לגאולתן של ישראל

בב"א.

בכבוד רב:

אהרן שלמה חיים אליעזר

בלאאו"ר בלילה"ה אב'יאלא

Rabbi M. Lebovits

Grand Rabbi of
Nikolsburg

53 Decatur Avenue
Spring Valley, N.Y 10977

יוסף יחיאל מיכל
לעבאוויטש
ניקלשבורג

מאנטי - ספרינג וואלי, נ.י.

בעזהשי"ת

בשורותי אלו באתי להעיד על מעשה אומן, מופלא מופלג בהפלגת חכמים ונבונים,
ירא וחרד לדבר ה', ומשתוקק לקרב לבות ישראל לאביהם שבשמים,
ה"ה הרב **משה שטיינערמאן** שליט"א בעיה"ק צפת תובב"א

שעלה בידו להעלות על הספר דברים נפלאים שאסף מספרים הקדושים, בענין אהבה
אחוה שלום וריעות, לראות מעלות חברינו ולא חסרונם, ועי"ז להיות נמנעים מדברי
ריבות ומחלוקת, ולתקן עון שנאת חנם אשר בשביל זה נחרב בית מקדשינו
ותפארתינו, וכמשאחז"ל (רש"י. ויקרא רבה פ' מ) על ויחן שם ישראל, שניתנה תורה באופן
שחנו שם כאיש אחד בלב אחד.

וניכר בספר כי עמל ויגע הרבה להוציא מתחי"י דבר נאה ומתוקן, ע"כ אף ידי תכון
עמו להוציאו לאור עולם, ויהי רצון שחפץ ה' בידו יצליח, ויברך ה' חילו ופועל ידי
תרצה, שיבר[ך] על המוגמר להגדיל ולהאדירה ולהפיצו בקרב ישראל, עד ביאת
גוא"צ בב"א

א"ד הכותב לכבוד התורה ומרביציה.
י"ט חשון תשס"ו

Rabbi Abraham Y. S. Friedman
161 Maple Avenue #C Spring Valley NY 10977
Tel: 845-425-5043 Fax: 845-425-8045

רב דביהמ"ד אמרי שפ"ר קאמאדא
וראש כלל הא"י

בעזהשי"ת

ישפות השם החיים והשלו', לכבוד ידידי מאז ומקדם מיקירי קרתא
דירושלים יראה שלם, זוכה ומזכה אחרים, להיות דבוק באלקינו, ה"ה
הר"ר משה שטיינרמאן שליט"א.

שמחתי מאוד לשמוע ממך, מאתר רחוק וקירוב הלבבות, בעסק
תורתך הקדושה ועבודתך בלי לאות, וכה יעזור ה' להלאה ביתר שאת
ויתר עז. והנה שלחת את הספר שלקטת בעניני דביקות בה', לקרב
לבבות בני ישראל לאבינו שבשמים בשפת אנגלית, אבל דא עקא
השפת לא ידענו, ע"כ לא זכיתי לקרותו, ע"כ א"א לי ליתן הסכמה פרטי
על ספרך, ובכלל קיבלתי על עצמי שלא ליתן הסכמות, ובפרט כשאין
לי פנאי לקרות הספר מתחלתו עד סופו, אבל בכלליות זכרתי לך חסד
נעוריך, האך הי' המתיקות שלך בעבדות השם פה בעירינו, ובנועם
המדות, וחזקה על חבר שאינו מוציא מתחת ידו דבר שאינו מתוקן,
ובפרט שכל מגמתך להרבות כבוד שמים, שבוודאי סייעתא דשמיא
ילוך כל ימיך לראות רב נחת מיוצ"ח ומפרי ידיך, שתתקבל הספר
בסבר פנים יפות אצל אחינו בני ישראל שמדברים בשפת האנגלית
שיתקרבו לאבינו שבשמים ולהדבק בו באמת כאות נפשך, ולהרבות
פעלים לתורה ולעבודה וקדושה ודביקות עם מדות טובות, בנייחותא
נייחא בעליונים ונייחא בתחתונים עד ביאת גואל צדק בב"א.

כ"ד ידידך השמח בהצלחתך ובעבודתך

בס״ד

RABBI DOVID B. KAPLAN
RABBI OF WEST NEW YORK
5308 PALISADE AVENUE • WEST NEW YORK, NJ 07093
201-867-6859 • WESTNEWYORKSHUL@GMAIL.COM

דוד ברוך הלוי קאפלאן
רב ואב״ד דק״ק
וועסט ניו יארק

י' שבט ה'תשע"ז / February 6, 2017

Dear Friends,

Shalom and Blessings!

For approximately twenty years I have followed the works of Rabbi Moshe Steinerman, Shlit"a, a pioneer in the use of social media to encourage people and bring them closer to G-d.

Over the years Rabbi Steinerman has produced, and made public at no charge, hundreds of videos sharing his Torah wisdom, his holy stories, and his touching songs. Rabbi Steinerman has written a number of books, all promoting true Jewish Torah spirituality. Rabbi Steinerman's works have touched many thousands of Jews, and even spirituality-seeking non-Jews, from all walks of life and at all points of the globe.

Rabbi Steinerman is a tomim (pure-hearted one) in the most flattering sense of the word.

I give my full approbation and recommendation to all of Rabbi Steinerman's works.

I wish Rabbi Steinerman much success in all his endeavors.

May G-d bless Rabbi Moshe Steinerman, his wife, Rebbetzin Rochel Steinerman, and their beautiful children; and may G-d grant them health, success, and nachas!

With blessings,

Rabbi Dovid B. Kaplan

Table of Contents

Prologue

Introduction by Rabbi Perets Auerbach

The Infinite Presence blows existence away and completely sweeps it off its feet, leaving room for nothing else.

Divine Love, infinitely expansive, expresses through the first and last act of giving from above Time & Space.

The Divine Presence constricts and creates a stage for reality. An empty vacuum wins the audition and everything that was, is and will be performed within. The star of the show is the Streak of Light, blitzing the vacuum and etching out everything.

The whole *seder hahishtalshilut* [chained cascading order of realms] results in interwoven rings progressing from Above to below. An elaborate infrastructure of interlocking souls, worlds, and angels are all molded after the supernal human archetype,[1] all the way down to metaphysical forces and the material plane. "From my flesh, I gaze at G-dliness." (Iyov 19:26) "All beneath is like Above" – look at the bottom and fathom the top...[2]

The heart yearns for its Source with a longing that knows no limit, so intense, that it leaves place for nothing else. Take the whole picture into consideration. Constrict and create a vacuum inside for positive traits to manifest within, which channel into positive action. You are in the Divine Image, a mirror of the lower world.[3] Stay linked and always meditate on the Divine Presence – a perfect reflection from below to Above.

Life is one great sweet meditation, intricate yet simple, involved yet straight. The Light of the Supernal Emanator fills all worlds and surrounds them, above and beneath them, infusing and enthusing, pervading and permeating, transcending yet imminent. "Creation is full; it shines of His Glory." (Yeshayahu 6:3/Yechezkel 43:2)

"The world stands upon three things:

---

1 Eits Chaim Beginning
2 Zohar
3 Likutei Moharan 49

Torah, Devotion, Practicing Kindness."[4]
Expand the mind learn *Torah*.

Activate discipline – contract in the devotion of introspection.

Integrate--practice kindness: Right/Left/Middle mechanics of Extension/Constriction/Fusion.

Universal Mechanics of Development/Refinement/Synthesis - The basic modus operandi of the three triads of Divine Attributes – which fuel and animate everything there is.

Learning Kabbalah is good but know that it is only laying groundwork. It is practice, spring training, for the real thing. When there is *'kabbalah* [reception]' of true inspiration, it flows from on High to Heart. It warrants serious labor in purifying from selfishness and ego to become Divine and G-dly, completely loving and giving.[5] This lets the Presence in and fuels absolute enlightenment.

Illumination graces earth, even before the body of the sun surfaces on the horizon. On the way to *Mashiach,* super-consciousness starts to unleash itself.[6]

May the knowledge and paths, outlined in this compilation, aid truth-seekers in their quest for the real thing!

Words that come from the heart, enter the heart. May we all learn to truly love each other, and practice giving from simple pristine altruistic benevolence. Thereby, manifesting our mutual unity, and bringing down the ethereal gift of Higher Awareness, the Divine Kiss of Prophecy, heralding when, "The universe will be filled with Divine Knowledge like water covers the Sea," (Yeshayahu 11:9) - speedily in our days, *amen.*

---

4 Avos
5 Derech HaShem
6 Midrash

Introduction

I must begin by telling you that I do not claim to be a master in Kabbalah, nor do I seek to turn the masses to these higher teachings. Those who find themselves seeking such things, should evaluate their lives, before continuing on such pathways. It is known that those who fill their mind with thoughts from the higher worlds, many times experience more trials in their lives. This is because they draw more attention to themselves from people in this world and from the angels above. Should their study of Kabbalah be completely *lishmah*, seeking spiritual purity and to elevate the world, their devotion is invaluable. The only reason I sought these higher studies for myself was that I found myself at the bedside of a very sick man who couldn't read, speak, or find comfort in this world, having lost all his physical abilities. My father, Reb Shlomo Zavel Ben Yakov zt"l, lay helplessly seeking comfort that only Torah could provide, with a thirst only the Kabbalah could quench.

I feel that few who teach, or print Kabbalah books today, understand what they are speaking about. I worry for those who learn such books, which only trap them into more thirst for higher worlds but give little ground to stand on. My intentions are to not give you a course on deep Kabbalah, but rather a pathway to be in tune with your actions, surroundings and that, which is unknown to you. Some of the secrets I will reveal to you have never before been taught to the masses. There are some that haven't been spoken in English. Some ideas are my own *chiddushim* and thoughts. After years of personal experience with heads of *yeshivos*, *chassidic rebbes*, and *baalei teshuvah*, and having spoken with thousands of irreligious Jews, *Hashem* has shown me the need to bring certain holy teachings to light. I do not believe it is right to teach straight Kabbalah to those unprepared, nor did the holy *rabbis*, such as the Ramchal, the Baal Shem Tov, Rebbe Nachman and Rav Aryeh Kaplan. As much as they chose to reveal, they hid far more. What they chose to put in print contains far more secrets than the reader perceives. The only one who understands the nature of man in this generation can bring these lights down in a way that will be helpful instead of harmful, *chas v'shalom*. Bearing these things in mind, with the help of *Hashem*, I will bring teachings to you that have been opened to me through years of Kabbalistic study and practice. I hope that these teachings will bring new vitality to your souls.

A sealed barrel is filled with more gems than a barrel with holes. I recommend that you prepare yourself, by studying the complete texts of both Mishna and Talmud before embarking too deeply on your Kabbalistic journey. At the very least, make a commitment and priority to complete these foundational works of Judaism.

After a person has learned *Ma'aseh Bereshis*, the *Ma'aseh Merkavah* teaches him how to go from level to level in advanced meditation, what Names to recite, and how to engage this persona in a dialogue.

Although the Talmud advises against teaching the *Ma'aseh Merkavah* publicly, this prohibition refers to the tradition that was given by word of mouth from master to students, from generation to generation. Anything outside of that tradition can only be an introduction to the *Ma'aseh Merkavah* and therefore is not included in the prohibition.

In the same way, the Italian community of Lattes allowed the printing of the Zohar. They were asked on what basis they authorized the printing of this text, dealing as it does with *Ma'aseh Bereshis* and *Ma'aseh Merkavah*. The answer was that since it was available as a book, or even as a manuscript, it was permissible to print it. The prohibition only applies to the secret oral tradition. (Yitzchak Yehoshua ben Yaacov Bonet de Lattes, Introduction to the Zohar first edition, Mantua 1558)

My mother asked me, "Why are you writing another book? Aren't there already too many books in the world that nobody is reading?"

I explained to her, "When I write my books, it is a legacy for my children and grandchildren. When I leave this world after 120 years, I will not just leave behind a memory of some good times, or a few concepts that can be remembered about me, but rather I will leave behind guidelines for how I came close to *Hashem* for them to also follow. Besides this, is it better that a person should study Torah all his life in *yeshiva* and not pass along his study to others? There might be many authors and some of those will only have twenty or thirty readers, while I might have 20,000 people drawn to my works. Either way, it is my purpose to give this blueprint of my soul to others."

My holy friends, a blueprint is just one dimensional, whereas a person sees in three dimensions. You can read the blueprint of my soul through my works, but only if you were to get to know me personally, can you ever experience the complete version of me. That is why even though *tzaddikim* have left us gems from their treasure unless we were in their generation directly hearing Torah from their precious lips, we are missing some pieces to the important puzzle of life.

You can read the greatest teachings in a book, but you must experience a living version of Torah as well. Yossei, the son of Yoezer of Tzreidah, would say: "Let your home be a meeting place for the wise; dust yourself in the soil of their feet, and drink thirstily of their words." (Ethics of the Fathers, Ch. 1)

"Unlike other teachings of Torah, Kabbalistic concepts are infinite, ten *Sefiros* of Nothingness. Their end is embedded in their beginning and their beginning in their end." (Sefer Yetzirah 1:7) If you want to come close to *Hashem*, the key to accomplishing this is to constantly make new beginnings and to renew your fear of *Hashem* always. Understand, before you attempt any action, what will be the end result. When you start something in life, visualize the steps that will be taken in order to complete this action, and start things you can complete.

The understanding of Kabbalah requires a lot of patience. It takes a lifetime of study and devotion. More than just Torah concepts, it is a lifestyle in and of itself. It is about connecting to *Hashem* at every moment, becoming a living vessel of holiness.

At first, you might turn this Holy Light switch on and off, depending on how you feel that day, but this is only because you're not truly connected to the *Shechinah* at all times. A person who is truly a *ba'al Kabbalah* doesn't detach himself from light. He is a living and breathing reflection of the Upper Worlds and *Sefiros*. *Shefa* is flowing through his body and soul, continuously. People who see their presence are drawn closer to *Hashem* and the *Torah*. Everything they do, from the moment they rise until they retire at night, is done for the sake of *Hashem*. Their sleep can also be part of their devotion and attachment to Hashem.

The purpose of this *sefer* is so the average person can have a manual, with which to connect to the higher worlds, in order to find the encouragement to perfect their souls. We learn in the Talmud about Rabbi Yochanan, who would not walk more than four *amos* without wearing *tefillin* and being connected to *Hashem*.

The concept of a continuous connection to *Hashem* was common in the days of our previous masters. However, in today's generation, we are very far from this idea. But there really isn't any reason we cannot reconnect to *Hashem* and the *Shechinah*, as the holy masters once did.

In this *sefer,* we will speak about concepts you're already aware of, while opening them up for you, so you can utilize them more strongly. We will speak about concepts like the *mikvah*, *d'vekus*, names of *Hashem*, *yichudim*, all with the goal of awakening our souls. With the right tools, we too can connect to *Hashem* at all times.

Lesson 1: Wonderment

I assume that, like myself, you wonder what spiritual lights and revelations are available, should we pursue them. The truth is, that what lies ahead is a never-ending stream of knowledge. It is also interesting to note that this will affect each person differently. *Hashem* created each person's *neshamah* and mind to be unique. No two people think alike. Therefore, each person's revelations and understanding of the spiritual realms comes out differently. Of course, there are basic guidelines. It is certainly possible to see things incorrectly. This is why it is important to study the *Sefiros*, and the basic works of Kabbalah, through which one acquires understanding and vision. Along the way, you must have a spiritual guide to show the correct pathways. The true methods of Kabbalah are hidden among the righteous. You must first prove yourself worthy, and also pray to find a *rebbe*.

In today's world, there is a danger. You may be forced to seek out your own path in these matters, for few can teach them today. Very holy people can but may have neither time nor strength to teach us common folk. Even if they do open a pathway for you, due to your unpreparedness in wisdom and spiritual purity, you may experience many dark days after the revelations of light. Why would a *rebbe* take upon himself such a responsibility for your soul? Therefore, you must take upon yourself to separate from evil and *bitul* Torah immediately. Otherwise, why have you come here? Why do you wish to enter a cave from which you may not return?

Slowly but surely, you will become a container to hold these great lights. It is entirely up to you if you are truly devoted to changing yourself. Kabbalistic revelations aren't like other goals in life. They cannot just be grabbed. Many have entered with a measure of holiness and left with nothing. So please, be sincere in your desire to come close to *Hashem*, do not take it lightly.

I understand that you're thirsty and seek more wisdom, but are your intentions pure? Many people who are thirsty take a drink that is unhealthy or not really what will quench their thirst. Some drinks contain salt, caffeine, sugar and other additives that not only don't quench your thirst, but make you thirstier, providing no benefit for your body. The Torah is a vast ocean of ideas and concepts to draw you closer to *Hashem*, but you need a spiritual dietitian to lead you on the right pathway.

One thing we know for sure, is that the Torah is required for every Jew's healthy spiritual diet.

Lesson 2: The Key to Kabbalah

Few people fully grasp the concept of what it means to have true *ahavas* Yisrael. I have been lying to myself a very long time, thinking, "Since I have written so many pages of Torah and spoken to so many people, I must have great *ahavas* Yisrael." In truth, though, I have not even begun to understand what it means to be self-sacrificing for my fellow Jew.

Thinking back over the years, I can come up with many situations where I passed by someone who could have used more kindness. There are widowers I didn't invite for *Shabbos* meals or reach out to in order to make sure they had their basic necessities. Young *bachurim* who needed help to come study in Israel, but I didn't manage to secure a *yeshiva* and home for them. Yes, I was faced with a difficult task, but did I really try everything within my ability to help them?

For example, there is a Jewish man in the Ukraine who wished to reconnect to his Jewish roots, by coming closer to *Hashem*. He sits there today because I was not successful in getting him a visa to learn in Israel, even though he very much wanted to learn in *yeshivas* Aish HaTorah. To this day, he has never experienced a *Shabbos*, yet we continue to speak together. The visa department told me they would grant him a visa only if I was willing to pay $5,000 and take full responsibility for him, should he do anything wrong. I did not have the money for this, but if I truly had *ahavas Yisrael*, I would have found a way. This is only one example of many missed opportunities.

There is a conservative *shul* in Indiana that was looking for a new *rabbi* and someone asked if I would consider the job. I declined since I didn't feel it was best for my growth to go to a small town with few Jews. Today, this *shul* has no religious Jews and a reform *rabbi*. How many people might I have brought back to the Torah if I had at least found them a religious replacement?

When it came to our holy *rabbis*, for example the late Rabbi Shlomo Carlebach, would not think twice when it came to the *mitzvah* of helping out a fellow Jew. Whenever a situation presented themselves, these *tzaddikim* immediately rose to the occasion and fulfilled the needs of any Jew.

This is why the heavens were open to them; it was not because of deep understanding and great wisdom. Rather, it was the love of their fellow that opened all the gates to the secret chambers of the *Sefiros*.

A *chassid* of the current *gaon*, the Nikolsburger Rebbe *shlita*, asked him, "How is it that the *rebbe* can see everything a Jew has done from the moment he was born till the current time?" The *rebbe* responded, "When you see every Jew with an eye of *tova*, goodness, this is how you attain *ruach hakodesh*, divine spirit."

My dearest friends, I know you long for the hidden light, and THIS IS TRULY THE KEY TO IT. Here is the secret to coming close to Hashem. Once you begin to have a true love for another Jew, yearning to give to him, all the *Sefiros*, the four worlds, the Holy Names, everything will be set before you as a fully set table.

The Holy Names can help when you're already there with *Hashem* and want to keep yourself attached and elevated. If you're still stuck within your own body and problems, youre connected to yourself rather than *Hashem*. Therefore, the Kabbalah and Holy Names really can't help you draw closer to *Hashem*.

A Kabbalist seeks perfection of the soul only because it is the will of *Hashem*. He isn't just interested in his own advancement but also the achievements of all Jews around him. He doesn't live within the closed box of his body but rather lives outside of it. The idea of *tikkun*, correction, cannot come about through only his actions. He is not able to fix the world himself. He must uplift others and reach out to them.

Lesson 3: Entering the Pardes Through the Back Door

In memory of Rav Yitchak Kaduri zt"l, written on the night of his passing…

It is the dream of every scholar to one day be worthy to feel the *Pardes*, Divine Orchard or Paradise.

"Four rabbis ascended into the Orchard: Ben Azzai, Ben Zoma, Acher, and Rabbi Akiva. Ben Azzai gazed and died; Ben Zoma gazed and became demented; Acher became an apostate; Rabbi Akiva departed in peace." (Chagigah 14b)

This has always been a heartbreaking lesson for me. Who could compare themselves to these scholars mentioned? However, all hope is not lost, for two reasons.

1. I know of *tzaddikim* today who have entered and left the *Pardes*, in peace. (not that I advise this)

2. The Baal Shem Tov has given us another way!

Noticing the importance of a mystical experience, even for the common Jew, the Baal Shem Tov taught the following: "When one recounts the praises of the *tzaddikim*, it is as if he engages in the mysteries of the *Ma'aseh Merkavah*." (Shiv'chei Baal Shem Tov 158)

So, if this is the case, why did so many holy *rabbis* strive to experience the *Merkavah* through the most difficult way, climbing the worlds, *Asiyah, Yetzirah, Beriyah, Atzulos*, when they could have simply read over stories of the *tzaddikim*? Can it truly be so easy for me to have such a mystical experience?

The same arousal one experiences by climbing the *Ma'aseh Merkavah*, one feels through a truly good story of *tzaddikim*, but he should choose his stories wisely. Not all stories have this power to draw you to such high levels, but rather it takes a special story that speaks to your individual soul.

This past *erev Shabbos,* I prepared for myself many high combinations to meditate on. Thank *Hashem*, I had tremendous pleasure from them, but it wasn't until early *Shabbos* morning, when I had little strength left to continue, that I realized the greatness of this teaching of the Baal Shem Tov. Not having the strength to continue my deep study, I picked up a storybook about Rav Dovid of

Lelov and the holy Seer of Lublin. I instatntly felt as moved by the stories as by the deep meditations. I realized that every person can feel a truly mystical experience as Rabbi Akiva did, through simple methods as well as advanced ones. As you read in previous chapters, I find this to be true in all aspects of Kabbalah. Everything that can be attained through complicated methods must also have a simple method paralleling it. In this case, one can experience the deepest Kabbalah, the *Pardes*, through the stories of our sages.

By telling stories of *tzaddikim*, a person attains an expanded consciousness, and through this, they are purified. Rebbe Nachman explains, "I myself was greatly motivated to serve *Hashem* through stories of *tzaddikim*." It was through this that the *rebbe* attained the great levels that he did (Rebbe Nachman's Wisdom #138). By hearing a moving story about *tzaddikim*, one is then motivated to model himself according to their good deeds. The *rebbe* also said, "No matter how deeply one is sleeping (spiritually), one can be awakened by stories from ancient times" (Likutey Moharan 60). Rebbe Nachman of Breslav says that a good story has the ability to touch a person and light a fire within him.

The Baal Shem Tov taught, "Every day a person should tell one of his friends a story about the deeds of a *tzaddik*." (Divrei Shalom). By telling stories of *tzaddikim*, you draw the light of *Moshiach* into the world. Telling these stories over also chases away much darkness and suffering. (Sefer Hamidos)

Lesson 4: Without Balance, You Don't Have a Thing!

"If I ascend to Heaven, You are there; and if I make my bed in Hell, here You are." (Tehillim 139:8)

Probably the greatest secret of *avodas Hashem* is how to balance your life; how to run and return after a spiritual revelation or fall.

Let's say a professional sportsman misses scoring a goal. He is trained to immediately get up and play defense. If he waits too long before recovering, or making an effort to get up, the other team can score. Should he attempt to score, thereby allowing the defensive team to collaps on him, what does he do? He adjusts his play, but no matter what, he doesn't simply hand over the ball to the other team. Now if he plays a balanced game, with speed and passing abilities, he is able to maneuver or change positions when needed. Should he lack a broad range of understanding, he constantly puts himself and his team in jeopardy.

In the same way as this professional athlete, we must build a strategy and be willing to work hard, even after our failures. Throughout life, you will make mistakes and have to get back up. Things will get hard and may hurt so badly that sometimes it will feel like you're all alone. Yet, *Hashem* will be there in this lowest place.

It is imperative that you build for yourself a skill set and a foundation to fall upon. The athlete realizes that he is having a bad day. What does he do? Instead of attempting to score by himself, he passes the ball and helps his teammates to succeed. He must continue even though nothing is working out because if he quits, the results will be far worse.

The Rambam teaches that a person should take the straight path, meaning the middle temperament of each character trait. He says, "Every man whose traits are intermediate and equally balanced can be called a 'wise man'." (Hilchos Da'os, 1:4)

This teaching is so important because often spiritual people tend to be unbalanced, so unbalanced that they draw attention to themselves and seem to be like a ping-pong ball in everything they do. Bouncing around from one idea to the next without any real structure. This may not be completely unavoidable, due to the unique nature of the spiritual being, but one should certainly attempt to control it. Maintaining balance is everything in the *talmud chacham's* service of *Hashem*.

One thing that those who are beginners to Kabbalah don't understand, is that learning elevated levels of Torah draws heavenly attention to a person, good attention and also bad attention. Therefore, if a person has any weakness or imbalance, the *klipah* uses this opening to attack.

It is a principle that a person who learns *Chassidus* or Kabbalah also learns the Shulchan Aruch. He must learn to be a master in the art of running and returning, something that can be done only with the study of *halacha*.

Rebbe Nachman teaches: (Psalm 139:8) The expertise of running, "If I ascend to Heaven, You are there." Then the expertise of returning, "and if I were to make my own grave, You are there." The straightforward meaning of all this is that the person who would like to walk the pathways of repentance must gather up his fortitude and continuously strengthen himself in the ways of *Hashem* - whether in a status of spiritual ascent or descent, corresponding to "If I ascend to Heaven... and if I were to make my own grave." In other words, even if he is encountering an ascent and a high spiritual level, he must not linger there nor be satisfied with this. Rather, he must be expert at this, knowing and believing that he must go further and further. This is the proficiency of running, an aspect of ascent, which corresponds to "If I ascend to Heaven..."

The opposite is also true. Even if, *Hashem* forbid, he falls to wherever he falls - even into the lowest Hell - he must still never give himself over to despair, but constantly seek and search for *Hashem*. No matter where he is he must strengthen himself with all the means at his disposal, for *Hashem* is to be found even in the deepest levels, and there too it is possible to attach oneself to Him. This corresponds to "and if I were to make my own grave, You are there," the expertise of returning, for it is impractical to walk the pathways of repentance unless one possesses both these types of expertise.

Rebbe Nachman was very precise in referring to this concept by the term *boki*. For it is indeed an incredibly great expertise when a person knows how to exert himself and toil continuously in the service of *Hashem*, hoping all the while to reach a higher spiritual level, and yet not allowing anything to draw him down. Even if he is as he is, *Hashem* forbid, he still does not get discouraged at all, as he fulfills, "and if I were to make my own grave..." (Likutey Moharan #65)

Without a descent, there cannot be an ascent. Why don't we embrace these descents instead of fearing them or becoming trapped by them? A person has to know themselves. They need to understand how much they can stretch, before forcing their own downfall. Then, instead of an uncontrolled massive decline, they can control their own downward slide. The Gemara warns us not to test *Hashem* and think we are strong enough to handle any challenge. At the same time, though, if we approach normal life with fear we will only lose. We have to face all the challenges before us like a lion, but this too takes *daas*. There is still a time to run and a time to stand your ground. If you need to run, though, don't run out of fear, but rather, as a strong person with *daas*. The fears of the world all too often steal the good energy from us. We must not let them.

The holy Baal Shem teaches us that, if something in the world draws your attention, think of its true source, *Hashem*. When we fall, the biggest problem in getting up is fear of the negative power in the thing that has caused us to stumble. This fear is an aspect of *avodah zara*, worshiping idols. We return to *Hashem* when our *daas* has been restored. Without *daas*, we remain lost.

The way not to lose *daas* in the first place is to control your fall with an organized plan in place for those low moments. When you have this, you become a master at running and returning. You become a very powerful *neshamah* and servant of *Hashem*. Before long, your low moments will be rare. If only we would think ahead, preparing ourselves with Mishna, Talmud, and *halacha*, in order to stand our ground. The study of Talmud and *halacha* should be your main study.

These are the type of things you need to put in place before attempting very high spiritual levels. You must wake up early in the morning to study and pray before others. Watch your eyes and heart from immoral behavior. Have set times in which to study Torah and pray, both day and night. You must keep away from people who waste time and go after impurities. Be clean in your dress and wash your body in the *mikvah* often. You must make sure that you do some form of kindness to others regularly. Your relationship with *Hashem* must be intact where you feel you can talk to Him in *hisbodidus* at any time. Staying away from anger and depression is a must. Realize that *Hashem* provides for all of your needs and even your accomplishments come from Him. Therefore, you should have no pride or thought in your mind that you deserve more than you have. These are the pathways needed in order to serve *Hashem* and pursue high levels of spiritual attainments.

Lesson 5: The Sense of Bitul; Loving Your Fellow Jew

A *tzaddik's* humility leads to *ahavas Yisrael.* "When a person sees only the good in himself, he will end up seeing the flaws in others; however if he is low in his own eyes, he will love all Israel." (Seer of Lublin)

One of the greatest mistakes people make is judging others. The Talmud teaches us that when you judge other people, you end up sealing your own fate with this same judgment. However, more than this, when you don't look for the good in others and the world, you impair your own soul.

You're obviously here, reading this Kabbalah manual, in order to perfect yourself and to reach higher levels than those around you. The pathway you have chosen is for the good of your soul because most people of the world don't care about their true fate. So, as you grow in *Yiddishkeit,* and your understanding of Kabbalah, you will be taking on a big responsibility. You could actually seal another person's fate for good or bad, so strong can your understanding of Kabbalah reach.

The stronger your mind will become, the more difficult this task will be. When Rabbi Shimon and his son left the cave after many years of seclusion, they looked at the world with stern judgment because they couldn't comprehend why someone would not be involved in Torah study at every moment.

If you study the Kabbalah and you don't reach this level of total *d'vekus* at all times, you missed the point of it all. And what really is *d'vekus*? Didn't we just get done learning that Kabbalah is about fixing the world, not being in 'la la' *d'vekus* land thinking only about ourselves?

My friends, I have news for you. You don't have exclusive rights to your soul, you're only borrowing it from *Hashem.* We are told there are thirty-six hidden *tzaddikim* in each generation. Probably many of them are Kabbalists, but even these hidden people don't live their life in total seclusion. Usually, there is some special *chesed* they are also doing, something simple, yet profound.

When you borrow an item from your friend, the *halacha* teaches that you have to care for that item as if it is your own, maybe even with more care. Let's face it, most of us treat our souls with disdain. I was once traveling to Chevron and struck up a conversation with the passenger next to me. He asked me during our talk, "Have you ever asked your soul for forgiveness?"

Everything in the world, every word, has some form of *shoresh*, root. The Jewish people all come from the same root and our branches and leaves are all connected. When we do something good or bad, it affects all of us.

Therefore, when you see other Jews making a mistake, that person too is you. In fact, it could very well be your fault that he isn't stronger in his *Yiddishkeit*. Can I ask you, how many Jews did you reach out to today or teach a passage of Torah to? Should you only study and not give to others? What gives you the right to not be thinking about every Jew as you study Torah, and include them in your every action and *mitzvah*? Do you even know what *ahavas Yisrael* is? Emulate Avraham Avinu, with selfless acts of chesed, to bring others closer to Hashem.

"Who shall ascend the mountain of the L-rd? And who shall stand in His holy place?" (Tehillim 24:3) We try to enter the holiest gates with ulterior motives. With anger, uncontrolled passions, pride, and desires for materialism, you stand at the gate and say, "Lift up your heads, O' ye gates, and be ye lifted up, ye everlasting doors that the King of Glory may come in."

Know the King and Master of the World. Put Him first in your life and heart. If *Hashem* gives you a punishment or reward, do you love Him the same, knowing that His Will is only good?

In previous generations, they didn't just teach people Kabbalah. They first made sure the people were properly prepared. It was an embarkment onto an entirely new way of life and thinking. I wonder if even the best of us would pass their entrance exam. When Reb Chaim Vital came before the Arizal, do you think he didn't already know all of the Talmud and Tenach, backward and forwards? Before Raish Lakish would discuss Torah with his teacher and comrade, Rabbi Yochanan, he would study the Mishna forty times in preparation.

If I were to give you preliminary requirements before reading my book on Kabbalah, would you still continue? I would ask you the following: What are your motives in wanting to learn Kabbalah? Do you spend most of your time in the study of Talmud and *halacha*? Are you involved in *chesed* projects? Do you attend the *mikvah* regularly?

Should you come to me, openly admitting you don't eat kosher food, don't fully keep *Shabbos*, don't wear a *kippah* and *tzitzis*, should I then be willing to teach you something that you are not spiritually prepared for?

Let's just pretend that I was a top official of a King, and you asked me to accompany you through the castle, so you could glance at his treasures and maybe even meet the King Himself.

I would have to be crazy to take you with me. Not only would the King toss you out, but He also would remove me from His castle. So why are you here learning Kabbalah and why would you want to endanger us both?

When an initiate wanted to learn Kabbalah, the first thing the society asked him was, "are you stoic?" Rabbi Abner related, "A sage once came to one of the meditators and asked to be accepted into their society. The meditator replied,

'My son, blessed are you to *Hashem*. Your intentions are good. But tell me, have you attained stoicism or not?'

"The sage said, 'Master, explain your words.'

"The meditator said, 'If one man is praising you and another is insulting you, are the two not equal in your eyes?'

"He replied, 'No my master. I have pleasure from those who praise me, and pain from those who degrade me. But I do not take revenge or bear a grudge.'

"The other said, 'Go in peace my son. You have not attained stoicism. You have not reached a level where your soul does not feel the praise of one who honors you, nor the degradation of one who insults you. You are not prepared for your thoughts to bind on high, that you should come and meditate (*hisboded*). Go and increase the humbleness of your heart; learn to treat everything equally until you become stoic. Only then will you be able to meditate.'" (Shaarey Kedushah, 4th part)

This story related to us by Rabbi Chaim Vital, in which a sage who was turned away from learning the secrets of Kabbalah, should really make us think twice before delving into a world that may have detrimental repercussions for those whom are not ready. What then can be said of us who travel these uncharted waters without preparation? There will come a time when we will have to answer to this question. "Who may ascend the mountain of *Hashem*, and who may stand in the place of His holiness? The clean of hands and the pure of heart, who has not borne my soul in vain, and has not sworn deceitfully. He will bear *Hashem's* blessing and righteousness from the *Hashem* of his deliverance. This is the generation of those who seek Him, the seekers of Your Presence." (Tehillim 24: 3-6)

Even though we must adhere to these warnings and take them to heart, Dovid Hamelech reminds us that we are seekers. Explorers who will stop at nothing to attain our goal of coming close to *Hashem*. To do this, we must exemplify the characteristic of being *bitul*, nullification. There are a few ways to achieve *bitul*, and only when all of them come together, do you become a complete person. It is not enough to think of yourself as nothing compared to *Hashem*. You must also think yourself lower than every Jew in the world. There must be no difference between insults and praise, sweet foods or bitter.

Rabbi Isaac of Acco writes in the name of Rabbi Moshe, a disciple of Rabbi Joseph Gikatalia:

If a person's heart compels him to rectify his traits, perfecting his personality and deeds, he should pursue humility to the ultimate degree. He should, "be insulted but not insult, hear himself scorned but not respond." The Divine Presence will then immediately rest upon him, and he will not have to learn from any mortal being, for the spirit of *Hashem* will teach him. (Reshis Chachmah, Anavah, 3, 119d)

We found this in the books of the Kabbalists who were worthy of the way of truth:

One of the great rectifications for one who wishes to know *Hashem* is that he should be among those who are "insulted but do not insult." This should be true even with people of whom he is not afraid and before whom he has no shame, such as his wife and children. Even if members of his household insult him, he should not answer, except to correct their ways. Inwardly, he should feel no anger, but his heart should always be joyful, while, attached to *Hashem*.

"My angelic master taught me this: Do not worry about anything in the world, other than that which will influence your worship of *Hashem*. With regard to all worldly things, everything should be the same as its opposite.

This is the mystery of the words of the sage, who asked an initiate who wished to involve himself in unifications (*yichudim*), 'Have you attained stoicism?' If a person does not see that good in the physical world is exactly the same as evil, it is impossible for him to unify all things." (Rabbi Joseph Caro, Maggid Mesharim, BeShalach p.57a)

Pride, even the slightest thought of it, is a very grave matter. Any ulterior motive derives from pride. Every thought is a complete structure. With pride, therefore, one causes a serious blemish above and "repels the feet of the *Shechinah*," as is written, "Everyone who is proud in heart is an abomination to *HaShem*." (Proverbs 16:5; Tzava'as Harivash 92)

Why you we physically nothing?

Somewhere on this globe is a little dot, probably four to seven feet tall, 90 to 300 pounds of flesh and bones. Somewhere here is YOU!

The world continues only in the merit of those who disregard their own existence (Chullin 89a).

Well if the picture doesn't convince you, read some of these statistics!

THE EARTH
Estimated Weight 6 x 10 to the 24th kilograms

Current Population approximately 7.6 billion
Surface Area 510.1 million sq. km
Land Area 148.94 million sq. km
Ocean Area 361.9 million sq. km
Ocean's Greatest Depth: Mariana Trench, Pacific Ocean 10,994 meters
Tallest Mountain in the World: Mount Everest 29,029 meters
Nepal/China

Now if this is the case in the physical realms, how much more is it the case in the spiritual realms, where there is no time or space? When we compare our physical size to this vast world and universe we live in, it is impossible to not grasp how insignificant we are. Shlomo Hamelech teaches that this realization is the holiest and greatest goal of every man. It connects us to our source, *Hashem's* vision, and light. When we think we are something, we separate ourselves from *Hashem* and the Jewish people. Only when we realize our nothingness, and that we are only something in respect with being a link in the chain of the Jewish people, are we able to connect to the highest of lights, the light of the World to Come.

When a person is so humble that he is literally nothing, he can attain both Torah and greatness at the same time. Otherwise, it is hard for the two to dwell together (Likutey Eitzos, Pride and Humility).

Dovid HaMelech Said, "I am a worm and not a man." (Tehillim 22:7)

Avraham Avinu said, "Behold, now, I desired to speak to my L-rd although I am but dust and ash." (Genesis 18:27) Even while communicating with the Almighty he still feels that he is "but dust and ashes."

All this being so, why do we struggle so much with pride? *Hashem* says: "I and the proud person cannot be together." (Sotah 5a) Therefore, the only way to come close to *Hashem* is to rid oneself of pride. We can begin to do this by seeing the light in our fellow Jews.

The Seer of Lublin said, "According to our sages, even Jewish sinners are as full of *mitzvos* as a pomegranate is full of seeds. Why a pomegranate? Because one drinks only its inner nectar and discards the peel. So too, with a Jewish transgressor: his sins are only external, whereas his essence is wondrous indeed." (A Chassidic Journey p.12)

The Me'or V'Shemesh, Reb Kalonymous Kalman, wrote, "A person beholds the world according to his inner character. A *tzaddik* cannot see evil in others because the light and goodness of *Hashem* shines in him. Wherever he looks, he sees only good." (Chassidic Journey p. 39)

Reb Dovid and Reb Yitzchok of Vorki were once staying in a small village and decided to visit the Jewish families there. When they reached the house of a certain unscrupulous, public sinner, Reb Yitzchok tried to keep Reb Dovid from entering. "*Rebbe*," he told him, "that man is truly wicked!" Reb Dovid paid no attention and pointed to the *mezuzah* on the door. "How can you say he is wicked? See, he has a *mezuzah*." (A Journey Into Holiness p.46)

So next time you go to the Kabbalists and ask to join in on their learning, be ready to say, "I am nothing! I am the lowest Jew in the world." Next time your spouse serves you a meal with too much spice, know that it is also sweet. When your friend insults you, know he is praising you. If your friend throws a snowball at you, smile and thank him. Enjoy life in a stoic way, in the way of *bitul*.

If you want to study the Kabbalah and become a Kabbalist, make working on your *middos* the priority. The Ramchal understood that the introduction to Kabbalah is fixing one's character, and therefore he wrote *sefer* Mesilas Yesharim (The Path of the Just), which is not only a preparation for Kabbalah; it is the Kabbalah. Rabbi Pinchas ben Yair said: "Torah leads to watchfulness; Watchfulness leads to Alacrity; Alacrity leads to Cleanliness; Cleanliness leads to Abstention; Abstention leads to Purity; Purity leads to Piety; Piety leads to Humility; Humility leads to Fear of Sin; Fear of Sin leads to Holiness; Holiness leads to Prophecy; Prophecy leads to the Resurrection of the Dead." (Avodah Zara 20b)

Lesson 6: The Real Chassidus of the Baal Shem Tov
Has it Been Forgotten?

When the Baal Shem Tov created the *Chassidic* movement, it was essential to the future of Judaism. He saw there was a huge void in the Jewish communities and it had to be filled. Immediately, to heal thousands of lost souls, he set out with the determination to change the world. He dispersed great scholars to teach Torah to people from all walks of life, regardless of their learning abilities. With the perspective that Torah could be fulfilled by all people, not just those with a gifted mind, he decided to wake up Jewry. Somehow over time, *Chassidus* went through many new leaders and followers. Over time it has become a movement that felt it needed to separate from the world, in order to protect *chassidim* from being exposed to spiritual harm. Not to say that this is the case in all branches of *chassidus* today, but the movement generally isn't as open-minded as in the times of the Baal Shem Tov and the Maggid. We have reached a junction where *Chassidus* is not seen in the light that it should be, even by *chassidim* themselves.

The real light of *Chassidus* is outreach, teaching Torah to the regular Jews The water carrier, the postman, the janitor or the handyman. You see, at the time of the Baal Shem Tov and even today, nobody thinks that a simple Jew's learning is as great as that of a *talmud chacham* or *tzaddik*. This was the point of *Chassidus*. Some say the point was to spread joy and spirituality in Judaism; this may be so, but it wasn't the core reason, it was to simply reach out and awaken the simple folk.

I was once speaking with the *Rosh Hayeshivah,* Rav Malkiel Kotler *Shlita,* and during the conversation, he excused himself that he hadn't finished reading my book Kavanos Halev (which he later finished and approved). He said to me, "Moshe, my life is entirely about teaching *Torah*. It is the air I breathe, and I try to teach Torah every moment I can." You see, Rav Malkiel's entire life revolves around the *mitzvah* of teaching Torah *lishmah*.

The Baal Shem Tov saw in his time that nobody believed the simple man's

Torah was worth anything. They thought only the students who proved to have quick minds and be brilliant were supposed to learn. This would leave the masses uneducated and ignorant of both *halacha* and the spiritual growth that the Torah will nurture. Meanwhile, the other Jews were supposed to just keep the basic commandments. But this is not the Torah from Sinai! The Torah from Sinai is for every Jew to learn, even if he is not the wisest and doesn't know how to read Hebrew. Even if the Jew doesn't know how to pray, the Besht saw that his prayer was also holy and important to *Hashem*, maybe even holier than the prayer of someone who does know how to pray. This, my friends, is the foundation of *Chassidus*, but it goes even further.

During the time of the Baal Shem Tov, his most inner circle of followers consisted of very great *tzaddikim*. They too, were on the level to perform miracles and wonders. Guess who the Ba'al Shem Tov sent out for his mission, to teach the simple Jewish folk, the Torah? It was the holy Toldos Yaakov Yosef, the Maggid of Mezritch and a dozen other great and brilliant *rabbis*. Can you imagine the *gadol hador* sitting down and teaching a tailor how to read the *alef beis*? That is true *Chassidus*.

If you look at *Chassidus* today, you see many isolated, holy and pure people. Most do not know how to reach out to others. This is because they are so pure and excluded from a worldly life that they don't really know how to approach the simple Jew. This is a mistake. Every Jew should cry to *Hashem* to be holy enough and smart enough to understand the needs of other Jews and be able to approach them in the loving way of true *Chassidus*. Nobody today is higher than the holy Maggid of Mezritch, but even he managed to go out and show the love of *Yiddishkeit* to the simple Jew.

I am not convinced that the main reason for *Chassidus* was light and joy alone. Rabbi Akiva taught that the love of one's fellow Jew commanded in the Torah in the well-known verse, "You shall love your neighbor as yourself," (Vayikra 19:18), is the "great, all inclusive, principle of the Torah." When approached by the convert with the request "teach me the whole Torah while I stand on one foot," the sage Hillel the Elder replied: "What you hate, done to you, do not do unto others. This is the entire Torah on one foot; the rest is commentary, go and learn."

The Ba'al Shem Tov taught that true *ahavas Yisrael* is to love, from the depth of one's heart, a Jew "who one has never seen." This implies that one's love of Israel is based upon the identity of souls, irrespective of any conscious ground for friendship.

Rabbi Shneur Zalman of Liadi said that the love of Israel is, in fact, the consummation of the love of *Hashem*, for when loving Israel "one loves what one's beloved loves [for *Hashem* loves Israel, as is said 'I love you, says G-d']." In love of Israel, one should be conscious that every Jew possesses a uniquely holy quality, unparalleled by any other Jew (this in addition to the essentially the root of love that we are all one and sibling "children of G-d" – "no matter what").

This is why we have *Chassidus* today. In order to bring back to the forefront the aspect of loving one's fellow, as himself, and taking care of another Jew. I am certainly disappointed in some aspects of *kiruv* today. One truly has to learn how to better himself in reaching out to others. It is one of the most difficult things to learn. The people today are smart. You need to anticipate their questions and concerns. What is really important? Being real and true. People can read right through a person if they are a hypocrite. If you are sincere when you do your outreach, there are no bounds to your success. Many are lonely, spiritually unfulfilled and searching. It takes the loving heart of *Chassidus*, the real *Chassidus*, to take them in.

When I was in Tel Aviv for a doctor's appointment, every non-religious Jew was staring at me. Almost as if they almost never saw someone like me walking around these parts. I was put there to make a *kiddush Hashem*.

Everyone thinks that the non-religious Jew doesn't care, but they too have an inborn curiosity and good nature. Their souls are simply confused by the worldly life that surrounds them, but this doesn't mean that inside this person isn't one of the greatest souls of the generation.

Chassidus teaches us to embrace that person and seek out his good points, to find a way to open your heart to him and talk about *Hashem* in a non-intrusive way. You would be surprised how people are open to taking on more spirituality, if only someone showed them some warmth.

Today, when the non-religious people hear or see *chassidim*, they automatically label them as having a cold personality. How we came to such a point, when we started on a plateau from the Baal Shem is beyond me. Let us give some credit here, though. Some of the largest *chesed* organizations were started by *chassidim*. Some of the biggest *ba'alie tzedakah* today are dressed in a long coat and *peyos*. Many *rebbe*s I know personally reach out in the same way as in the times of old. Surrounded by them are Jews nobody else wants to be around; they are loud, sometimes with learning disabilities, yet the *rebbe* takes them in as his own children.

So, it isn't that *Chassidus* doesn't have this light still within it, but it's just that it lost the aspect of *kiruv* as one of its focal points. A person shouldn't feel ashamed or embarrassed to walk into a *chassidic tish* or synagogue dressing differently. He should rather be given a seat near the head table. That is what the Baal Shem Tov would have done.

So why is *Chassidus* such an important aspect of Kabbalah? It is because a *rebbe* is someone who draws down the highest *divrei* Torah from Kabbalah and simplifies it for the common man. That after all is what a teacher is all about. He brings what is otherwise incomprehensible and manages to teach it over simply to his students. The greater the *rebbe*, the more he is able to make what is deep, simple. What is deep? What will wake up the slumbering minds of those distant from *Hashem*? The Kabbalah taught in an everyday, useful way.

If you read *Chassidic* books like the Noam Elimelech, Likutey Moharan, and others, you will see that they are basically *mussar* books, many times based on the *parsha*, that draw Kabbalistic concepts into everyday life. The teachings are warm, they are comprehensible, and they speak directly to one's soul.

Chassidus, in general, puts a lot of emphasis on prayer, more so than the *litvish* way of life. The *Chassidic* Jew can be found in the synagogue for hours, praying and lengthening his prayers. For the *Chassidic* Jew, whose *rebbe* taught him that he is just as important as the greatest of scholars, if he couldn't study deeply, he would pray deeply. Prayer, after all, draws a person near to his Creator and therefore, *kavanah* in prayer and blessings really connect to the newly religious *chassidim*.

If you found a proper *minyan* of *chassidim* today, which does take a bit more searching, you won't be able to pray anywhere else. Every word is heartfelt, drawn out and said with passion. This is *Chassidus*. Serving *Hashem* with love, passion, fervor, excitement, and joy.

So many people don't really understand what a *tish* is. They visit the *tish* gathering, only to feel no connection to it at all. They dismiss it as something meaningless or a silly waste of time. What they don't understand is that the whole idea of Judaism is one of unity. The *tish* unifies all the *chassidim* and *rebbe* as one soul. Together they draw closer to *Hashem*. With the *chassidim* beside him, the *rebbe* is able to soar above in his mind, further than he could alone. He is now like a general with his troops beside him, ready to push away all resistance.

Beginner *chassidim* would relate to the *tish* as simply watching someone of flesh and blood elevate himself above. To those who are also experienced in meditation, they soar along with the *rebbe* to great heights, sometimes right beside him and other times on their own path. The environment itself is one of total *kedusha* and holiness. It is a launching pad for flights that go beyond time as we regularly know it.

The *rebbe* makes *kiddush*, everyone takes a sip, and they are joined in his holiness. Then he breaks the bread, his eyes sparkling with sincerity and holiness. Just looking into his eyes alone is a *tikkun* for regular souls who can't reach these high levels. Joining in the fish that goes around the table, know that this is not a simple festive meal. The fish has within it a soul that appears to the *rebbe* for a *tikkun*, you join him in this event and you taste this now elevated soul along with him. Then there is the singing of *zemiros*. People joining together, in seeking spiritual elevation through song and meditation. If you want to know who the real *chassidim* are at the *tish*, look around the room for those whose eyes are shut in concentration along with the *rebbe's*. Those are the ones who understand the *tish* and are rising with the *rebbe*. Join them both and rid yourself of the material.

I asked Rabbi Friedman, *the gabbai* of the Nikolsberg Rebbe, how often is it normal to phone the *rebbe*? Having been given his private number, since I have known him for decades. The *gabbai* responded, "Everyone is different. It depends on what you need, ask your mother." My mother calls without hesitation, whenever she has a question for the *rebbe*, she is on the phone seeking her answer. For me, I always felt it's best not bother the *rebbe* if it is something I have already asked previously, or if it's something that might answer itself if I am more patient. The point is that every *chassid's* connection to the *rebbe* is unique. There is no rule book when being a *chassid*.

Sometimes, your connection with a *rebbe* is for a brief period, during your time of need. Other times, it can be like that of Rav Noson, the student of Rebbe Nachman of Breslov. Rav Noson authored most of the Breslov material we have today, as he transcribed it from the *rebbe*.

You have Rebbe Shimon bar Yochai, whose students wrote most of the Zohar under his tutelage, and some after his death. The Arizal had Reb Chaim Vital whom he said that "I came down to this world, only to teach Reb Chaim the spiritual secrets of the Torah.

Rabbi Noson Maimon used to be the *gabbai* for my *rav*, Rabbi Michal Dorfman *zt"l*. He literally was his right-hand man and was glued to him at all times. He knew what Rav Michal would answer before he even gave my questions to the *rav*. Before this, Rabbi Maimon would follow his father-in-law, Rabbi Aryeh Rosenfeld *zt"l*, in the same way. Then after both holy *rabbis* passed away, he followed around another great master in Breslov *Chassidus* until he also passed.

Why did he exert himself so much to cater to these *tzaddikim*? Because he understood that their holy actions would rub off on him. He knew that by helping *tzaddikim* and serving them, it is similar to serving *Hashem* and bringing an offering in the Temple. Today, I wonder if I should follow his pathway and follow him, but I am too busy writing these *divrei* Torah for all of you.

I have gotten to know many *gabbaim* over the years, and I can tell you that it is a very special job. Nobody really knows the *rebbe* like the *gabbaim*. Therefore, while many people try to draw directly to the *rebbe*, many times I have done my best to make a strong connection to the *gabbaim*. Because of this, I know many holy secrets, that only they were privileged to hear. They would even hide these events from other *chassidim*, but as the *gabbai's* friend, I would be privileged to keep the secret.

For instance, one such *gabbai* was on his way with the *rebbe* to visit the Tush Rebbe *zt"l*, whom I also had the privilege to visit. Traveling from New York to Montreal is usually a seven to eight-hour drive, but it only took them two hours due to *kefitzas haderech*. The road became shorter in the *zechus* of the *rebbe*.

People think that the *rebbe* enjoys the extra respect he is given by the *gabbai* and *chassidim*. I found this wasn't the case, when I was the *gabbai* a few times for the Biala Rebbe of New York. Having served him the entire night, as soon as we left the wedding hall he sped up his walking speed and opened the car door himself. Earlier, he had motioned to me every time he required my assistance. He would nod his head, even for me to open the door, but when there was nobody looking, the show of *kavod* was over. The *rebbe* not only didn't enjoy the attention, but he actually despised the *kavod*. It had nothing to do with his on respect, but what his position stood for. When we show honor to a *tzaddik* it is for both the *tzaddik* and the *Torah* that they have incorporated into their very being.

Here is an original story I have for you, from a close friend of mine, who was a student of the *gadal hador*, Rabbi Chaim Pinchas Scheinberg *zt"l*. Once the *rav* walked into the *bais medrash* of Yeshivas Torah Ore, and all the students stood up for the *rabbi,* but the *Rosh Hayeshivah* said, "Sit, sit."

"Of course, we all waited for him to take his seat," said Rabbi Benyamin Fleischman. "After the *shiur,* I approached the *Rosh Hayeshivah* and told him, 'the Mishneh says, a shy person cannot learn.'

"He nodded his head to give me permission to ask [a question].

"'Why does the *Rosh Hayeshivah* tell us to sit?'

"He asked me, 'why do you stand?'

"I responded, 'the *Rosh Hayeshivah* is a living representative of the Holy Torah. When a Torah is brought into the room, we stand to honor it and the Torah. I am standing to honor *Hashem's* Torah the *Rosh Hayeshivah* teaches us.

"He said, 'You can stand.'

"I said, 'now I am even more confused.'

"The *Rosh Hayeshivah* smiled and said, 'Most people stand for me. I am unworthy of that. They should sit. You [however], are standing in honor of the Torah; that is worthy of standing. You can stand!'"

So, let's return to my original point. Being a *chassid* of your *rav* or *rebbe* is not a simple matter. For everyone, it is different and requires a lot of humility. A willingness to get your feet wet and for some, waking up at unusual hours of the night just to walk the *rebbe* to the *mikvah*. To spend every waking minute that you can, and to find some private time with him. One's connection to the *rebbe* or *rav* is at the forefront of the *chassid's* mind. It is an integral part of *Chassidus*.

So how is a *chassid's* *kavanah* different from that of a regular Jew? Well, this isn't something that is set in stone that a *chassid* is so-called "better" at *kavanah* than a non-*chassid,* but as a general rule, a *chassid* is supposed to add extra *kavanah* whenever possible to his *mitzvah* observance.

When he washes his hands before his meal, he does so emphasizing joyous thoughts and extra concentration. According to the Baal Shem Tov, he should draw out the letters with his mouth, as if not wanting to let them go. He can, therefore, soar above along with the letters. The *chassid* may even attempt to visualize the letters on fire and draw Kabbalistic concepts into his *kavanah*.

A *mitzvah* done without a joyous heart, to the *chassid* is almost a lost *mitzvah*. The *chassid* is to place all his heart and love for *Hashem* into all his actions. This love should then reflect on others around him and inspire them to service of *Hashem* as well.

So, these are the main points of *Chassidus*. Have they been completely lost in our generation? Well, that is not for me to determine. Every generation has different requirements in their service. Their goals are the same but sought out differently.

It pains me that Breslov *Chassidus* isn't like it was during the time that Rav Michel Dorfman *zt"l* was still alive. My heart is so full of things I can't explain when it comes to this. Uman for me was a place that 2,000 of us came to from around the world to join hands in unity. Today it is an event that draws 40,000 people. For me, it isn't the same anymore, but that is because the idea of Uman and the *rebbe* is in my heart, without such a need for a physical connection.

The Baal Shem Tov once said that he was willing to go to *Gehennom* just to save another Jew from being connected to evil. He didn't just say this, he actually gave his soul to save a Jew he hadn't even met previously. The *rebbe's* job is to constantly elevate everything in this world. I used to be so close to some *rebbeim* that they would call me on the phone occasionally. I miss this strong connection, as it was something special.

I think everyone needs a *rebbe* or *rav* who will notice when he doesn't show up to synagogue and is willing to lower himself to pick up the phone and check up on his *chassid*. Rabbi Moshe Feinstein *zt"l* would actually call his congregants up on the telephone, when he noticed they were absent from *shul* for a few days. What a *rabbi!* I would do anything to have this today.

There were other *rebbes*, whose drawing close was by pushing away. By showing the *chassid* rejection, the *chassid* would evaluate his life and realize he had to do more *teshuvah*, in order to be near the *rebbe*. Chabad *chassidim* would prepare themselves for months before visiting their *rebbe* in the town of Lubavitch, so great was this encounter to them. But for us, we take for granted how easy it is to approach *tzaddikim*. Do you know how many days it would take a *chassid* to travel by horse and buggy to visit his *rebbe?* The harshness of travel would leave him thirsty, hungry and exhausted.

So, are any of us real *chassidim*, compared to the *chassidim* of the old generation? We complain about the *rebbes* not having the same smoothness in *ruach hakodesh* and insights as their predecessors, but it is we, the *chassidim*, who have changed. The *rebbes* are still doing much outreach, *kavanah* in *avodas Hashem*, but we are trailing tremendously behind them.

I know many *chassidim* who don't wear all the clothes with the *chassidish* look. In their heart, they are secretly *Chassidic* and follow the main concepts of *Chassidus*. They have a *rav* in their life, but to them, this *rav* takes on a role as a *rebbe*. *Chassidus* is far more than a way of dress and dancing around a *rebbe*. It is a heartfelt method of serving *Hashem*.

I don't like it when people limit themselves. You really don't have to do this. Judaism is vast and it's important to take light from all holy places. Even though one should have a main *derech*, that doesn't mean to shut out and be close-minded to other ways.

As a *chassid*, I love the books from Rabbi Chaim Volozhin, a student of the famed Vilna Gaon, who was opposed to *Chassidus* in his day. I love when I can surprise people and quote Torah from the Gaon of Vilna.

The Baal Shem Tov once knocked at the door of his opponent. Knock, knock... The man answered and asked, "Who is it?"

"I am dust and ashes," responded the Baal Shem Tov.

"I too, am dust and ashes," the man responded while understanding that the visitor must be none other than the Baal Shem Tov. At that point, they became friends and were at peace.

So, my friends don't be so hardheaded. The debates between *tzaddikim* are above our understanding. It is not our place to interfere or delve too much into this.

I once heard from a friend, who owned a bookstore, that a certain *rebbe*, who was known to be opposed to Breslav, used to secretly visit his store, so he could read all the Breslav books. He explained to the store owner, that there are deep reasons why he can't have his followers reading this material, but he loves the *divrei* Torah. If I told you who this was, my friends, you would not believe me, but I can guarantee you that in the heavens above, there is perfect *shalom* between the Gaon and the leader of *Chassidus*. There may even have been a secret connection we never knew about. So, don't be so quick to judge, and open up your mind to the vast ocean of Torah available to quench your thirsty soul.

Lesson 7: Hisbodidus Meditation

Being a student of Kabbalah, I try to think beyond the spectrum of time. Time in a way is limiting and is physical. In the heavens, there are different watches and orders, and is beyond limit or time as we know it. In the dimensional planes of the heavens, we have *Yetzirah, Beriyah,* and *Atzilus.* Even Einstein said, "Time has no independent existence apart from the order of events by which we measure it." This measurement brings us into the world of *Asiyah.*

The three dimensions of our existence are not only part of our physical reality. Forward and backward, horizontal left and right, and vertical up and down all play a part in our religious experience as well.

Our tradition knows too of an entirely different dimensional triad. Not merely three aspects of space, but three modes of human experience: time, space, and person. In Hebrew, this triad is known as *olam-shana-nefesh,* literally "world-year-soul."

The more we try to understand what we cannot see or comprehend, the more we realize we don't know. The speed of light always appears to be 299,792,458 miles per second regardless of how fast you think you're traveling from the light source. The only way this can be true is that time advances relative to how fast you're traveling, compared with other things.

When a person becomes *bitul,* completely nullified of ego, and unified with *Hashem,* he begins to leave the dimensions of time. At the same time, prayer is given a schedule. Three times a day we pray the prayers organized by the Great Assembly, prayer is infinite.

Nobody has ever died from praying too much. In fact, the Rambam teaches that, in times of old, the sages would prepare one hour a day before and after prayer. They prayed for a full hour during the prayers themselves, and they certainly didn't pray just one time a day.

In the heavens, never a minute goes by that the angels aren't singing praises to *Hashem.* When one angel leaves his position, another immediately takes his place. Myriads of angels are praising *Hashem.* The praise of *Hashem* is also infinite. We can't even contemplate all the miracles wrought for us in one day, one hour and even one minute.

So, why are praise and prayer desired by *Hashem*? Well, it isn't because *Hashem* needs this pleasure, being beyond feelings as we understand them. It is rather for us.

When we hear other people pray, we too begin to desire closeness to *Hashem*. While most of us don't hear the angels in prayer, a few select might, and the righteous in the Garden of Eden most certainly do. The Talmud teaches the reward for the world to come is being able to point and say, this is *Hashem*. I'd venture to say that all of *Olam Haba* is the praise of *Hashem*. The prayers of the departed, the holy Torah academies in Heaven, the angels, all praise *Hashem* and bask in His holy light.

So, what does prayer mean to us in this world? It is the idea of closeness to *Hashem*. Prayer is faith at its source.

"If only a person were to pray the entire day." (Brachos 21a) In the times before the Great Assembly, we didn't need all this organized prayer service. People naturally felt close enough to *Hashem* to compose their own prayers. Many were constantly in meditation and prayer. Seeing that there were some who lacked this skill, the *Sanhedrin* was forced to compose the prayer books as we know them today. They organized everything for us because, otherwise, we were forgetting how to pray. We were simply forgetting our faith.

Now that we have this structured system of prayer, we need to re-establish the old time traditional prayer based on complete attachment to *Hashem* at all times. This can be done through *hisbodedus*.

For weeks I argued with a master in *hisbodedus* on the idea of timing one's prayer. The master was explaining to me how I must make sure to reach one hour a day in *hisbodedus*, as Rebbe Nachman of Breslov recommended. I debated this, explaining to him that the idea of *hisbodedus* is to become *bitul* and beyond time. Saying that my prayer session must take x amount of time isn't relevant or significant because no two prayer sessions I have are the same. Sometimes my mind is at ease and I am able to talk to *Hashem* very quickly. Other times, my *hisbodedus* takes longer and requires deep thought.

Knowing the Sages to be only *emes*, I knew there must be more that I am missing about *hisbodedus*. The idea of *hisbodedus* is to be connected to *Hashem* continuously, to read a passage in the Torah and suddenly glance above to the heavens, basking in the beauty of these gifted words. To walk down the street and be so connected to *Hashem* that one meditates on His holy names, or to sporadically speak to Him. This is the goal of *hisbodidus*. It is to connect to *Hashem* all day.

So how does one reach this level? He must begin by designating a special time and place to talk to *Hashem*. It won't be overnight that a person can train his mind to continuously yearn for *Hashem*. We have to get there with baby steps, starting with fifteen minutes a day, and then slowly growing to thirty to forty minutes. Ideally, Rebbe Nachman recommended one hour, but when you're nearing that point, you should already be connected to *Hashem* in such a way that one hour becomes two or three. Just as you shouldn't need to force yourself to do *hisbodidus* for one hour, you shouldn't need to end in just one hour. To learn more about *hisbodidus* and how to practice it, please see my book Kavanos Halev, the chapter on *hisbodidus*.

Meanwhile, understand that the true purpose of prayer and *hisbodidus* is to have a continual connection to *Hashem*. Really, that is the purpose of life and sometimes when we study Torah, and then set about our daily chores, we simply forget why we are here. While we are to achieve consciousness of *Hashem* at every moment, Satan's job is to distract us from serving *Hashem*. The telephone rings, a new bill enters one's mailbox, one has to cook lunch or run an errand.

While others may become distracted, your regular practice of *hisbodidus* will make you realize that this too is an opportunity to connect to *Hashem*. In fact, by running an errand, you can learn even more Torah while on the way. What is normally a closed door to connecting to *Hashem* becomes open through the pathway of *hisbodidus*.

It is told in the Talmud that Rebbe Shimon Bar Yochai did not have to pause from his Torah study in order to pray. The Gemara explains that this is because his Torah study was on such an elevated level that it was higher than prayer. I'd like to shed light on this by explaining to you that Rebbe Shimon's Torah study included *hisbobedus*. It included the concept of a complete and utter connection to *Hashem*, at all times. Others compared themselves to the *rebbe* but couldn't do it. They had to work, pray and study, but Rebbe Shimon was able to accomplish everything inside his *Torah* study. How did he reach such a level? Through daily *hisbodidus*. Rebbe Nachman taught that if some *rabbi* tells you that he didn't reach his high level through *hisbodidus*, don't believe him. This is because that is exactly how a person becomes a *tzaddik* and *talmud chacham*. Rabbi "Shas" Cohen *Shlita*, who finished the Talmud over 300 times, said that one of the main things that helped him was praying to *Hashem* that he be given the gift of the Torah. This is what Moshe Rabbenu did as well when trying to comprehend the Torah. He prayed in *hisbodidus* for forty days till the last day, *Hashem* just gave him the Torah as a gift. Until the fortieth day, *Hashem* kept teaching the Torah, but Moshe failed to comprehend it.

When it comes to the study of Kabbalah, how much more do you need *Hashem's* help, to give you an understanding of these deep concepts? Suddenly you look at the combinations of a *Yichud* and the understanding just comes to you. This can only take place when you're connected in *hisbodidus*. That is when your Torah study and *hisbodedus* are as one.

Lesson 8: Ilovetorah Mindfulness

Ilovetorah Mindfulness, by Reb Moshe, is a form of Jewish meditation that combines classical western and eastern meditation methods (which are diluted methods of original Jewish, Kabbalah meditation) based on Jewish Torah values and Kabbalah. The main difference between regular mindfulness and ilovetorah Mindfulness is the idea of *tikkun*, rectification. While the non-Jewish method of mindfulness would be to simply observe one's thoughts, I teach that no thought is there by accident, and so must be given a *tikkun* and be elevated back to its source. We understand from Kabbalah that man was put on this earth to elevate all of mankind and the world. Combining his knowledge in Jewish meditation, Talmud, Kabbalah, and NLP (Neuro-linguistic programming, NLP, is an approach to communication, personal development, and psychotherapy), I seek to give a new direction to mindfulness meditation.

Mindfulness is a state of active, open attention on the present moment. When you're being mindful, you observe your thoughts and feelings from a distance, without judging them as good or bad. When practicing mindfulness, one becomes aware of their "stream of consciousness", and instead of letting life pass you by, you will come to live in the moment. Thoughts come and go of their own accord. You are not your thoughts, but thoughts are given to you by both the Satan and *Hashem* to challenge you. They will come and go, and ultimately you have a choice about whether to act on them or not. The Baal Shem Tov says, "A person is where his thoughts are." By just observing thoughts that come to you, choosing only the good ones, and elevating the negative, harmful thoughts back to their source in the *Sefiros* (upper worlds), you thereby elevate them and the world. You release yourself from thought patterns before they tip you into a downward emotional spiral. This begins the process of putting you back in control of your life.

Mindfulness training may:

Improve memory and academic performance (PsyBlog). In this study, students who did attention-building exercises experienced increased focus (or less mind-wandering), better short-term memory, and better performance on exams.

Help with weight loss and a healthier diet. Mindful eating means paying attention to each bite and eating slowly while paying attention to all your senses (Harvard Medical School, Women's Health). Participants in mindfulness studies ate fewer calories when they were hungrier than the regular groups.

Lead to better decision-making. Mindfulness reduces our tendency to stick with lost causes—such as an unhealthy relationship or dead-end job—because of the time and energy already invested (BPS Research).

Lower stress and help cope with chronic health issues. Mindfulness increased the mental and physical well-being in patients diagnosed with chronic pain, cancer, heart disease, and more (Elsevier).

Improve immunity and create positive brain changes. Researchers measured brain activity before and after volunteers were trained in mindfulness meditation for eight weeks, finding positive changes in brain activity (Psychosomatic Medicine).

Other brain benefits we've seen from mindfulness meditation: Better focus, more creativity, less anxiety and depression, and more compassion for others.

BELOW ARE SOME STEPS OFTEN DONE IN MINDFULNESS TRAINING:

(a) Use a consistent posture or place of meditation.

(b) Try to distinguish between naturally arising thoughts and elaborated thinking.

(c) Focus on current feelings of the body in order to release tension.

(d) Follow your breath as an anchor for attention during meditation.

(e) Repeatedly count up and down to ten consecutive inhalations and exhalations.

(f) Label the thoughts that come to you; don't suppress the occurrence of thoughts.

KABBALISTIC MINDFULNESS, ILOVETORAH METHOD:

(a) Combine Rebbe Nachman's *hisbodidus* methods with Mindfulness.

(b) Try to gently let go of thoughts and elevate them for their *tikkun*, rectification in the *Sefiros* (Explained later).

(c) Add *emunah*, faith that all thoughts and all tests, in one's life, come from *Hashem* and are there to help us grow.

(d) Use Hypnotic Anchoring to train our subconscious (Establishing a trigger which, when activated, will trigger certain responses; this happens randomly in life, but can be suggested during hypnosis).

(e) Carefully use permitted Kabbalistic names in order to increase healing and fear of *Hashem* (like focusing on *YKVK*).

MINDFULNESS AND STRESS RELIEF

Most of us experience stress in our lives one way or another. Studies show that mindfulness can help you to stop focusing on things that cause stress. It prevents you from dwelling on negative thoughts over and over. Mindfulness can be used to decrease anxiety about the present, as well as the future. It can allow you to take a mental break from stressful thoughts, leading to better health.

The regular practice of mindfulness meditation leads to a complete change in your perspective. Mindfulness is more than a simple meditative technique. It is a way of life. After a while, you will find yourself practicing mindfulness subconsciously while gardening, listening to music and even while cleaning the house. Focus on the present and quiet the voice that offers a running commentary on what you're doing, what you've done, and what you will be doing. You can start living a life with true perspective. It truly is time to take our lives back and not over- think.

HOW TO START MINDFULNESS

Week 1
Sit in a relaxing and quiet place.

Practice taking deep breaths and counting from one to ten, then reverse the count from ten to one. Do this for ten to fifteen minutes. Pay attention to your stomach muscles while inhaling and exhaling.

Week 2
Continue your practice of taking deep breaths, but this time try doing so without needing to count.

Start to label the sensations that you feel. For instance, if you hear something, label that as a sound. If you smell an odor, label that as a smell. Should you have a thought, label that as a thought, and you can either think about this or release it, let it go. Do this with all senses, thoughts, and feelings.

Week 3
Follow the methods from previous weeks, adding new ideas to your meditation. It is okay to personalize it.

Instead of labeling only the sensations you have, begin to identify which *Sefiros* some of them stem from. For instance, anger, money, and physical pleasures derive from *Gevurah*. Make a choice of observing the sensations or releasing them back to *Gevurah*, then continue to elevate them up the ladder all the way to *Binah*. This idea can be used in the visual spectrum as well. For instance, if you see the color blue, elevate this blue item to its possible source in *Malchus*.

Week 4
Make a set time to meditate, using *hisbodidus* and mindfulness meditation together. They can go together very well, as both are founded on the principle of spontaneous thoughts and sensations.

Practice throughout the day during regular activities, to identify feelings and to just observe them or elevate them.

Advanced Methods

Once you're comfortable with being mindful, you can add numerous Kabbalistic concepts into your meditation. If you were to approach this *Yichud* without understanding mindfulness, probably you would lose hope in its ability. Now that you understand how to concentrate on your specific senses, this *Yichud* from the Arizal becomes a wellspring of enlightenment.

Begin by contemplating that your ear is the Tetragrammaton expanded as *Sag*, with the final *Heh* left out, like this:

י ו-א-ו ה-י ד-ו-י

The reason for this is that the final *Heh* descends to the nose. The expansion *Sag* [has a numerical value of 63, but removing the *Heh* takes away five, leaving 58.] This is the numerical value of *Ozen* (אזן), meaning Ear. Through this meditation, you may be worthy that your ear should hear some lefty holiness when you pray.

Then meditate on your nose, contemplating that it is the expansion of *Sag*:

ה-י ו-א-ו ה-י ד-ו-י

This has a numerical value of 63, the same as that of *Chotem* (חוטם), meaning nose. Through this, you may we worthy of sensing the fragrance of holiness.

Then meditate on your mouth, contemplating that it is the expansion of *Sag*, together with the 22 letters that are expressed by the mouth. *Sag* has a value of 63, and together with 22, the sum yields 85, the numerical value of *Peh* (פה), meaning mouth. In one's prayer, one may then be worthy of the level mentioned by Kind David, when he said, "The ruach (spirit) of *YKVK* speaks in my mouth, and His word is on my tongue." (2 Shmuel 23:2)

This is the meditation for the eyes:

If one is in the Universe of *Asiyah*, he should meditate on give simple Tetragrammations:

	ה-ו-ה-י	
ה-ו-ה-י	ה-ו-ה-י	ה-ו-ה-י
	ה-ו-ה-י	

[Each Tetragrammation has a value of 26, so the five of them have a value of 130] the same as that of *Eyin* (עין), meaning eye.

If you are in the Universe of *Yetzirah*... meditate on these same five simple Tetragrammations. Then expand them with *Alefs* to form the expansion of *Mah*.

If you are in the Universe of *Beriyah*, expand them as *Sag*. If you are in *Atzilus*, expand them with *Yuds* as *Ab*.

When you walk in the street, meditate that your two feet are the *Sefiros* of *Netzach* and *Hod*. When you look at something with your eyes, meditate that your eyes are *Chochmah* and *Binah*. Meditate in this manner with regard to every part of your body. Also, contemplate that you are a vehicle for the Highest Holiness.

This is the meaning of the verse, "In all your ways know Him." (Proverbs 3:6)

"There is no question that if you constantly make use of these meditations, you will become like an angel of heaven. You will gain an enlightenment so that you will be able to know all that you desire." (Shaar Ruach HaKodesh)

Remember that mindfulness is not just a meditative practice. It is a way of life, devoid of stress. The Hornosyple Rebbe once told me, "The trials of life are much easier than the stress that comes from overcomplicating, by living events repeatedly in our minds." We have to simply do our best in this world and not drive ourselves crazy unnecessarily.

Mindfulness is about letting go, and not allowing physical feelings to confuse you, by combining meditating on holy names, *hisbodedus,* and using main stream mindfulness methods.

As spoken previously, the goal of all *mitzvos,* prayer, and study is to be connected to *Hashem.* This means being mindful that *Hashem* is always there in all instances of your life.

How do we generally connect to *Hashem?* Through our thoughts and keeping the *mitzvos.* Yes, we pray and make a motion of the mouth, but the main part of prayer is the contemplation and *kavanah* we have in mind. Therefore, getting control of one's mind is a necessity. A loose mind leads to sinful thoughts and actions.

As an opposing view to always being mindful, you have the Kotzker Rebbe who said that one should completely place themselves inside the moment of the *mitzvos.* It isn't enough to look outside oneself to possibly habitually perform the commandments. We have to live completely inside the moment in our thoughts and our feelings. If you're an overthinker, being mindful could cause a bit more stress at times. Every technique requires balance. A wise person serves Hashem in all ways. He takes out only the beneficial parts of wisdom that benefits his particular soul.

Lesson 9: Eating with Kavanah

The holy *rabbi*, Rabbi Hirsh the "Servant" [of Rimanov], said that service of *Hashem* through eating is greater, and on a higher level of service, than that of prayer (Divrei Shmuel, p. 211, #9).

It is easy for a person to recognize those tasks in *avodas Hashem* that are most clear to him. We know that prayer, Torah study, and kind deeds are the main vehicles to draw close to *Hashem*. The simple task of eating with holiness is far from understood by the general masses, as being a vehicle of significant importance. In fact, not only is it extremely significant, but it's also the foundation of holiness. The Chasam Sofer taught that if you feel a desire for food it is really your soul that desires to lift up the holy sparks within the food, and that it is *Hashem* who has sent this desire to you. (Chasam Sofer, Yesodos b'Avodas Hashem, p. 12n)

To understand the importance of eating with holiness, we must take a step back and understand its significance. For the most part, all food has a life-force that stems from fallen sparks and *neshamos*, souls in need of rectification. Without a proper rectification, this life-force must continue to recycle over and over again within the food chain. Only when a Jew eats with holiness, is the life-force given its final rectification. Should a Jew eat only to satisfy the lust in his heart, this life-force cries out in pain from the insensitivity of his brother. It must once again continue in the food chain. So, to eat with *kavanah* is a *mitzvah bain adam lechavaro*, to love one's fellow Jew. How can we take this matter lightly, when so much is at stake?

So how can we begin to eat in the proper way? Rabbi Yechiel Michal of Zlotchov said, "Be careful to say all blessings with fear and love of *Hashem* as much as possible, especially those blessings on worldly enjoyments, because when you do not make blessings with the appropriate consciousness, the food deadens your heart and makes you forget the service of *Hashem*. Then you will fall into sin, *chas v'Shalom*." (Yeshuos Malko, p.138)

It is interesting that people blame the *Satan*, or events themselves, for leading them into the sinful waters, but rarely do they trace it back to the real source of their sin, improper eating. I would venture to say that eighty percent of sins would be avoided if people would properly devote themselves to eating. Now that is a very strong thing to say, but Rav Aharon Rott proves this point in his *sefer*, Shulchan Hatahor. It contains over 250 pages of how to eat with *emunah*, faith, and *kavanah*. It is interesting because, unlike many *tzaddikim*, Rav Rott doesn't really attack a person for desiring food, but rather he teaches you how to channel the desire. Explaining how to make it into *avodas Hashem*, service of *Hashem*.

When Rav Aharon was a young *bachur* in *yeshiva*, one of the workers there noticed that he always had what he needed. The workers found this strange, considering that his family had no means to really support him. Forcing an answer out of him, little Aharon admitted that he always *davened* to *Hashem* each day for his needs on the following day. Also, he would look up to Heaven and then put his hand in his pocket. Inside would always be the money he needed to care for his physical and spiritual needs. When he was much older, already a *rebbe* to hundreds, he said, "This is a small level compared to what I have reached now through *emunah* and eating." (Shulchan HaTahar)

Although we have no place to bring a true sacrifice to *Hashem*, hope is not lost. As long as the *Beis Hamikdash* was in existence, the altar served to atone for Israel, but now it is every man's table that atones for him. (Berachos 55) Rav Moshe Cordovero teaches us how to do this practically. He says, "If you think over words of Torah, with each and every chew, then the food you eat will be like a sacrifice. The water and the wine you drink like a libation poured out on the altar." (Hanhagos Rabbi Moshe Cordovero, #32, in YHvT, p. 12) On this matter, it also says, "It is good and appropriate that at each meal you learn something concerning the sacrifices; study the *Shas* [the Mishna or Talmud], the order of *Kedoshim*, or any other similar matter. Then your eating will be as if you had offered a sacrifice." (Derech Chayim, 3-66) The secret of eating is, during the meal of men who serve *Hashem*, a spiritual arousal rises from below to above, as a pleasing scent before *Hashem*. (Shnei Luchos ha-Bris, quoted in Kedushas ha-Shulchan, p. 29)

Wise words about eating:

1. Rabbi Yechiel Michal of Zlotchov said that it was his practice never to lean down to the food, but to sit upright, in order to bring the food to his mouth (Mazkeret Shem ha-Gedolim, p.26).

2. When you sit at the table you should meditate on being in the presence of *Hashem* and think of yourself as before the *Shechinah* in the Garden of Eden. (Reshis Chochmah, Sha'ar ha-Kedushah, chap. 4, #21)

3. It was the custom of the Baal Shem Tov, when he washed his hands for the meal, to be in an intense state of *d'vekus*. (Mishnas Chasidim, p. 379, #6)

4. The Arizal teaches that one should say Psalm 23 before *bentching*, having in mind that there are fifty-seven words in the Psalm, being the same *gematria* as the word זן, *zan*, which means nourishment.

5. The Baal Shem Tov said, "A person benefits from the life-energy in every piece of food that he eats. But when he eats, even from bodily necessity, and afterward serves *Hashem* with the life-energy his body received, he thereby fixes and repairs the sparks [in the food]. (Keser Shem Tov, p.48)

6. As mentioned above, when you eat and drink you will certainly experience enjoyment and pleasure from the food and drink. Be careful to arouse yourself every moment to ask yourself in wonder, "What is this enjoyment and pleasure, and where is it coming from?" And answer yourself, "This is nothing but the holy sparks from the Upper holy worlds that are within the food and drink." (Kedushas ha-Shulchan, p. 24)

Concerning the blessings of enjoyment (over food, etc.): At first sight, one would have thought that we are to get enjoyment only from spiritual things and not from things of this world. As the *rabbis* say, "During a meal when you see that you are starting to indulge your food lust, draw back your hand from it." Yet we see the *rabbis* ordained that we make blessings for enjoyment over material things like food, such as "Blessed are You... Who creates many living things and their needs."

The resolution of this apparent problem is that certainly we are permitted to get a spiritual pleasure, but not a physical pleasure. Regarding the pleasure, and enjoyment we derive from food, the Baal Shem Tov said that this is from the World of Pleasure. His meaning is that the pleasure in the Upper [spiritual] World is the radiance of the *Shechinah;* as the *rabbis* say, "In the future world, the *tzaddikim* will sit with their crowns on their heads and enjoy the radiance of the *Shechinah.*" (Berachos 17a)

The taste in the food and the pleasure within it is really from the pleasure of the radiance of the *Shechinah,* which is clothed in this lower world in the taste of the food. This is the matter of raising up the holy sparks. When you make blessings of enjoyment you should arouse that higher pleasure and the light of the *Shechinah* which is in that food. This is an aspect of "Taste and see that *Hashem* is good." (Tehillim 35) This means that the goodness and pleasure in everything is from *Hashem.* The life-energy and the spiritual aspect are contracted within the food. Alternatively, when you make the blessing of enjoyment over it, you can raise it up from a state of contraction to that of love. For through the life-energy that comes to you from the food, you can cling to *Hashem.* This food you eat gives you the strength and energy to say holy words of Torah and prayer. The holy people say that it is like a bee that transforms the food it eats into honey. So too, a person elevates the food from a physical pleasure to an experience of the radiance of the *Shechinah* and a spiritual pleasure. (Or ha-Ganuz l'Tzaddikim, p. 83)

Lesson 10: The Four Elements - Fire/Water/Air/Earth

Rabbi Chaim Vital teaches that, just as the world was created using four elements – earth, air, fire, and water– so too, each person was created using those same elements. For each individual, one specific element is dominant. This to a large degree, defines your essential strengths and weaknesses. Identifying your personal "element" will help reveal the area of spiritual rectification, *tikkun*, you need to achieve your own greatness and complete your soul. The main job of a person in this world is to purify all of his qualities from their bad aspects. (Shaar Kedusha)

WATER: "Streams came up from the Earth and watered the whole surface of the ground." (Genesis 2:6)

EARTH: "Then the L-rd G-d formed a man from the dust of the ground." (Genesis 2:7)

AIR: "And breathed into his nostrils the breath of life." (Genesis 2:7)

FIRE: "And the man became a living soul." (Genesis 2:7)

The Radak teaches, "The earth is full of *Hashem's* faithful care [earth element]. By a word of *Hashem*, the heavens were made [fire element]; by the breath of His mouth [air element], their entire host. He heaps up the ocean waters like a mound [water element]; stores the deep in vaults." (Tehillim 33:5-7) In these verses all four elements are mentioned, for the word "heavens" hints at the element of fire, "the breath of His mouth" is a hint to air, and earth is hinted at in both verses. (Radak on Tehillim 33:7)

The Alter Rebbe explains that, "Just as the four physical elements of fire, air, water, and earth are the foundation of all physical entities, so too is the *nefesh* (the lowest level of the human soul, most connected with our personality and physical self) comprised of the four corresponding spiritual elements." From the elements come all of the character traits.

In the Book of the Zohar, the four basic elements are mentioned in the context of the creation of Adam, the first man, referring to parallels among these elements and the four corners of the earth, the four ministering angels (Raphael, Uriel, Michael, and Gabriel), and more. (The Book of Zohar- Part 2, page 23, 2; page 254, 2; Part 3, page 225, 1)

The four elements-'*aish*' (fire), '*ruach*' (wind), '*mayim*' (water), and '*afar*' (dust)-are themselves an expression of the four letters of the *Tetragrammaton* as explained in the Zohar. (Va'era 23b)

In the ancient text of the Midrash, the four elements are mentioned in the description of their order in Creation. This appears in the chapter on gifts presented by the heads of the 12 tribes of Israel, at the dedication of the Tabernacle in the desert. (Bamidbar Rabbah, Chapter 14)

The Holy One created four cardinal directions in the world - East, West, North, and South. East is from where the light shines forth into the world. As the Holy One, blessed be He, created the four cardinal directions and four standards corresponding to them, so too did He set about His throne, four angels - Michael, Gabriel, Uriel, and Raphael. (Midrash Rabbah, Bamidbar 2:7-10)

URIEL: Element of earth

GABRIEL: Element of water

RAPHAEL: Element of air.

MICHAEL: Element of fire

Rambam provides an extensive discussion of the four basic elements and their interrelationships on the physical plane, interfacing with the spiritual plane, in the Book of Science, Laws of the Foundations of Torah. (end of Chapter 3 and beginning of Chapter 4)

The Rambam shows how, below the celestial band in which the moon orbits, there are four more bands, each a source for one of the four elements.

The Infinite Light shines to the four letters, and they shine to the four sides of the Divine Chariot, which in turn shine to the four elements and the four angels in charge of them. (Sefer Yetzirah) Eventually, it all progressively descends and cascades down to become the four elements of the universe. The uniqueness of any given name, or part of Creation drawn from a name, will be based upon its predominant element. (Rambam, Mishna Torah, Hilchos Yesodei HaTorah, Chapter Four). Physical and spiritual items are made up of the elements. Every creation is held together by elements. The elements cannot exist without the light from *Hashem* sustaining them. This light goes through the channels of the 4 Worlds: *Asiyah, Yetzirah, Beriyah,* and *Atzilus.* They also must pass through the *Sefiros.*

Each of the four elements, in all of their combinations, totals six hundred thousand. They divide into many parts, according to the permutations, each part a complete *Partzuf* called 'man' [his supernal root]. This is a term for a complete spiritual organism, composed of two hundred and forty-eight spirit limbs and three hundred and sixty-five spirit-veins.

The division is unlimited. With this, you can understand the secret of *gilgul,* which is the reincarnation of the 'parts', and the arrival of each depends on the time appropriate for it.

Rebbe Nachman Says, "When G-d reincarnates a soul, a different *ruach* is paired with a different *nefesh*." (Sichos Haran) This brings about a different elemental dynamic in the personality. It is tailor made for the tests and accomplishments that person needs in his lifetime. One who rectified the characteristic of love in a past life might have to come back to rectify fear. The simple lesson is how important it is to take advantage of where one is at any given moment and use it to the fullest (Reb Peretz Auerbach).

Let us now break down these four elements and see how they manifest themselves in this world.

Fire

The Midrash states, "Fire conceived and gave birth to light." (Shemos Rabbah 15:22) Fire comes from the *Sefirah* of *Binah*, understanding. As you know, Heaven was created from fire. It is the electromagnetic force through which all matter interacts; fire is energy. It is dry and hot, and its corresponding humor (bile) is red. Fire is represented by the letter *Shin. Shin* is the dominant letter in the word *esh,* meaning fire. It is joined with the *Alef,* representing air, because a fire cannot exist without air. (Raziel 11b) The three heads of the *Shin* also suggest the flames of the fire. The hissing sound of this letter furthermore is like the hiss of a flame. (Sefer Yetzirah by Rabbi Aryeh Kaplan)

Fire rises; the flames reach up and out to consume and conquer everything around it. The positive aspect of this element is the desire to strive and accomplish, to reach great heights, to lead and take responsibility. Many people who possess this dominant element are leaders and visionaries. They see the big picture and the long-term ramifications of their actions. They are ambitious and goal-oriented.

However, there are common character flaws generated from the element of fire. These could be arrogance, anger, criticism and condescension toward others, and the tendency to crave power and control.

Once ignited by anger and pride, a man (like fire) soars aloft. Pride is the state of considering oneself superior to others. Anger, too, is an offshoot of pride. Would a person not be proud, he would not be angered when someone defied his will. (Tanya)

As you probably can tell, I really enjoy the idea of fire. My first name, Moshe, only bears within it the element of fire. This is generally not a healthy thing; if a person has an uncontrolled fire, he can simply burn up. In life, he can dream and dream and end up accomplishing nothing. But, should he channel the fire and direct it positively, it truly becomes a valuable element. This is because the element of fire gives the ability to accomplish things quickly and energetically. Fire is a very spiritual element.

Tradition has it that, when certain *tzaddikim* left this world, those closest to them were able to see a ray of fire ascend from their bodies. Angels are often referred to in terms of fire. *Sefiros* are sometimes seen as lights flashing round about. It could be that some see them behaving as fire does. Of course, there is nothing physical about the spiritual realms. We can only refer to them in terms we understand.

Earth

Earth is characterized by heaviness and lowliness. (Tanya) It remains in one place, continuously stepped on and caught in gravity's domain. It is dry and cold; its corresponding humor is black. People who have additional strength in this element tend toward laziness, sadness, and despair, their main weaknesses to overcome. Such people tend toward heaviness, craving comfort, and lack of effort. The main work in overcoming this flaw is pushing toward accomplishment and growth. Some may constantly battle sloth, melancholy, and sense a heaviness of the limbs. (Tanya)

On the positive side, these people don't tend to get into power struggles. They are compliant, humble, and willing to cooperate. They often forgo and give in. They are good team players and can be reliable and trustworthy, loyal and steadfast in their preferences and relationships. These people are often referred to as being "grounded", which ironically is exactly what their element is.

Water

Water can represent solids (ice), liquids (water) and gasses (water vapors). Water spreads and tends to go everywhere. It takes on the contours of whatever vessel attempts to contain it. It goes with the flow, literally, naturally unbound and unlimited, feeling unrestricted. It is damp and hot; its corresponding humor is green. The ability of water to make pleasurable things grow indicates that concealed within it is the element of pleasure. Water promotes the growth of all kinds of pleasure-giving things. (Tanya)

People with a "water" nature have an easy time giving, connecting with others, and spreading themselves to acquiesce to the needs of others. They have a nurturing trait, just as their element. They tend to be friendly, flexible, outgoing and generous (even to a fault).

Their main weakness lies in a lack of self-restraint and pursuit of physical pleasures. They may at times veer toward immorality, thinking that normal restrictions in human behavior don't apply to them, and materialism.

In the Talmud, there is a suggestion that the firmament is composed of water and fire. (Chagigah 12a)

Air

Air is the most complicated of the elements because it is ephemeral, seemingly non-existent. It blows one way and another, never fixed permanently in one place, never taking a stand. It is invisible and could be in one habitation when you think it is in another. Those with this dominant element tend to lack concern about the physical world. They may be more spiritual, idealistic, living in the world of ideas that are difficult to bring to reality. They may have a yearning to transcend this world and bond with energies and non-tangible aspects of existence. It is damp and hot; its corresponding humor is white.

I find people with airy names to be very friendly, outgoing, and social. They don't seem grounded and seem to be huge dreamers. They can have a fun and playful nature.

An airy person's weakness could involve the power of speech, which also depends on the air for its life-source. They tend toward meaningless chatter, gossip, flattery, and deceit. They are able to manipulate the truth for their own gains (Tanya). The person may experience a challenging time sticking to routine and order, as they subconsciously assume they can be everywhere at the same time.

If you were to look at things scientifically, you would see how the elements play out in nature. Thus, oxygen is the most vital component of air for human beings. Hydrogen, our subject of interest (combined with oxygen, which we have already mentioned with air) makes up water.

Lesson 11: How to Read a Person's Name

Have you ever wondered how the big *rebbes* are able to look at your name on a paper and understand the secrets of your soul?

Well, there are many methods which enable them to do so. One is to have such purity that you simply see what you need to know about the person, in order to assist them. *Hashem* does not give a gift like this to those who judge others unfavorably. Through purity and only seeing others with a good eye, can you then attain the ability to see into another's soul.

Another method used is to look at the shine reflected on a person's forehead and face. This tells a lot about a person and can even reveal his true nature.

The Zohar explains how to look at the shape of the head, the color of eyes and hair, the nose, beard, ears, etc. Through this, Rabbi Shimon explains, you can know the complete makeup of the person. You can know his good traits and his bad traits. You can know if he will be successful in *Torah* study, business, relationships, and life.

There are a few methods of looking at a person's Hebrew name that also helps you understand their nature. If you notice, the *gabbayim* of *rebbes* always write a person's name on a white sheet of paper with no lines, before giving it to the *rebbe*. I was told by one *gabbai* that they don't use lined paper because it interferes with the *rebbes* seeing of the name. For a great *tzaddik*, when he sees a person's name, he sees the *gematria* of the letters. He sees the four elements of the person's makeup and without thinking, if he is on a high level, he sees the complete root of the soul. He is sometimes able to even see previous incarnations of the person's soul.

I will explain to you how to look at the four elements inside a person's name. Through testing, I have found this way to be quite accurate. Other things such as the year, month, date, day of the week and time you are born, plays a role in shaping you as a person.

This is a basic chart showing which letters match a corresponding element.

Now that you know the basic classifications of the letters, let us explain how much power each letter has in its corresponding element. *Sefer* Midrash Talfeos tells us that the power of the letters A*lef, Gimel, Daled,* and *Beis* have twenty-eight strengths. The lowest one out of twenty-eight of these letters is higher than the highest power of the next letter, and so on. So, bearing this in mind, we gave each letter a certain number corresponding to its strength, in order to weigh all the letters in a name. See the chart.

FIRE	1ן 2ש 3פ 4מ 5ט 6ה 7א
AIR	1ף 2ך 3ק 4כ 5ס 6ז 7ג
WATER	1ם 2ר 3ע 4ל 5ח 6ד
EARTH	1ץ 2ת 3נ 4צ 5י 6ו 7ב

So, let us take the name Rivka רבקה as an example to learn from.

WATER	2 Total
EARTH	7 Total
AIR	3 Total
FIRE	6 Total

Rivka is a very balanced name as you can see, bearing all the elements. Its strongest elements are earth and fire. It is a bit weak in the element of water. We will learn soon what that could mean in Rivka's life. Usually, a person doesn't have

64

too much air in his name and it is normal to have a lower number.

Now we will take the name Moshe Simcha משה שמחה. As you can see, this name is very off balance. It has a tremendous amount of fire but very little earth. It is good that it has earth, as it helps to stabilize the strong fire, but it is not nearly enough to balance it. Lacking both the other elements will give this person certain challenges to face in the world. It will affect his life and personality.

Having never met Moshe Simcha, I would assume the following about him. He is a very spiritual person and has a lot of trouble grounding himself in worldly affairs. The things he starts, he has trouble finishing and he has many dreams, not knowing how to make them a reality. His personal life is an interesting one since he prefers to keep to himself. He doesn't really pursue a materialistic life.

WATER			0 Total
EARTH	ה	5	5 Total
AIR			0 Total
FIRE	משהשמחה	4,2,6,2,4,6	24 Total

So how do we help Moshe Simcha? Well, if Moshe asked me where to live, I would recommend not to live in Jerusalem because it is the city that bears the element of fire.

WATER	Tiberias
EARTH	Chevron
AIR	Tzfat
FIRE	Jerusalem

I would also recommend that Moshe pays special attention to caring for his materialistic needs, for example make an effort to stay organized and physically presentable. He should push himself to attend social events and finish the projects he begins. I would also encourage him to do many acts of *chesed* since he may have a harder time giving and lacks empathy for others. Bearing in mind that he has lots of fire, he should try to direct this in an effective way and use it to learn much Torah and inspire others with it.

As much as I expect Moshe Simcha to fit into this general mold, he might have already overcome some of the negativities his name arouses. It could be that Moshe Simcha knows how to channel the element of fire as it manifests in his life. Therefore, he may be ready to face aspects of these elements head on and use them to his advantage.

Other factors that play a role are his upbringing and the merit of his ancestors. How much he has worked on himself, his age and his marriage partner also play important roles. If he is a gilgul, then the level he reached in his former life, also effect his natural level he was born with.

Another secret of the letters is that the first letter of each name has a very powerful effect on the person. So, even though the name Rivka (which we used above) doesn't have so much water, since it starts with the letter *Raish*, water has a strong hold on Rivka.

WATER	MAKES GROW ALL KINDS OF ENJOYMENT	APPETITE FOR PLEASURES FRIENDLY, FLEXIBLE, OUTGOING AND GENEROUS (EVEN TO A FAULT).	VEGETABLE LIFE FORM	EVIL PASSIONS
EARTH	HEAVINESS & LOWNESS. SLOTH & MELANCHOLY	LAZINESS & LOOKING FOR SUPPORT	MINERAL LIFE FORM, DRY, COLD, INANIMATE	SADNESS & DESPAIR, HUMBLE TRUSTWORTHY RELIABLE
AIR		FRIVOLITY & SCOFFING, BOASTING & IDLE TALK		FLATTERY AND DECEIT
FIRE	NATURE TO RISE UPWARDS ANGER, PRIDE,	ARROGANCE, CRITICISM & CONDESCENSION TOWARDS OTHERS, CRAVE POWER & CONTROLENERGY, DRY & HOT		

Above, in their root, the elements correspond to the four letters of *Hashem's* name, YKVK. But below (in our world), they are a mixture of both good and bad. Rebbe Nachman explains the *possuk*, "*Mashpil resha'im ah'dey eretz* - He casts the wicked down to the ground." (Tehillim 147:6) The initial letters correspond to the initial letters of the four elements: *Esh, Ruach, Mayim,* and *Afar* (fire, air, water, and earth). They encompass all qualities and traits. A person has to completely purify these traits, so that none of the bad found in any trait of the four elements has any hold on him. (Likutey Maharan 8)

This is the basic *tikkun* of man, to understand his inborn nature and to be balanced. That which is most challenging for him is usually the most important aspect to fix. The more a person perfects his character, the greater vessel he becomes for light and holiness.

Many people cast aside their biggest fears and difficulties, but we learn from a person's name that everyone has inborn challenges to overcome. Each element also has great blessings and powers that can be used for good.

Without an understanding of yourself, you really can't create a plan to perfect your nature. Once you use these methods, and make a true commitment to change, the world becomes more open to you.

Most *rabbis* are there to remind us what we already know. None of these ideas for reading your name should be anything new to you. You already know what your true nature is by the difficulties you face in your life. The light it does shed is enabling you to look from outside yourself for a moment, to see that your name shows your life's challenges, and that you are going to become what you make of your efforts.

You can also now look at others as not just people who may have failed or succeeded in life, but also as souls that have just been given a different challenge in life. Everything in the world has a name, a job, and a task to complete. It really isn't always a person's fault that he has pride, anger, melancholy, etc. You too have your challenges.

Lesson 12: Five Souls of Light

The human soul consists of three parts: *Nefesh, Ruach,* and *Neshamah,* according to Kabbalistic thought. The first component of the soul is the *Nefesh.* It is present in each person from birth. The *Nefesh* is the wellspring of physical and psychological aspects of human nature. The *Ruach* and *Neshamah* are not inborn and can only be attained through the intentions and activities of the individual. Kabbalistic thought shows that these two elements of the soul come to full fruition only in people who have spiritual enlightenment. Here is a brief explanation of the three levels that comprise the human soul:

*Nefesh- This part of the soul is the lowest level. It is the life-giving force for all life on Earth. The *Nefesh* concerns itself with physical desires and instincts. The word *Nefesh* comes from the root word of *Nafash,* meaning to rest, as in the verse, "And on the seventh day, He ceased work and rested (*nafash*)." (Shemos 31:17)

*Ruach- This is the intermediate level of the soul and translates as "spirit". The *Ruach* is the portion of the soul that can distinguish between good and evil. The word Ruach is often translated as "spirit," but it is also found with the connotations of wind, air or direction. This aspect of the soul is specific to man and elevates him beyond other forms of life.

*Neshamah- Through the *Neshamah,* we recognize our intellect and attain awareness of God. The *Neshamah* lives on after death. The word *Neshamah* stems from *Neshimah* meaning "breath". On the level of *Neshamah,* you not only become aware of spirituality, but also of its source. It is here that a person gets to the level of a very close intimacy with *Hashem.*

Neshamah and *Nefesh* represent, respectively, the two opposite concepts of giving and receiving. They are spiritually opposite and therefore distant from each other. In our context, they can be defined as the thesis and antithesis. Thus, *Ruach,* which represents the transmission of spiritual energy, is the synthesis which links the two.

Two More

The Zohar expands on the fourth and fifth parts of the human soul (Zohar,

Chassidus, Kabbalah and Meditation

Raava Mahemna). However, the first mention of these parts of the soul, the *Chaya* and the *Yechida*, is contained in the Midrash Rabbah. These aspects of the soul represent the highest level of intuitive understanding; only special individuals might attain these elements after much toil in purifying themselves in *tikkun habris* and overall holiness. These two parts of the soul remain external to the body and can sometimes manifest themselves for brief moments after much toil in *Torah*, in a *mitzvah* done scrupulously, and connection to *Hashem* through holy names.

Chaya- This is the aspect of the soul that gives one consciousness of the Divine life force.

Yechida- This is the highest level the soul can reach. The soul achieves full union with G-d.

Nefesh	נפש	Earthly soul, receives spiritual sustenance
Ruach	רוּח	Wind, spirit in breathing; animal/human, *Ruach Hakodesh*
Neshamah	נשמה	Soul; Intimacy with *Hashem* as if *Hashem* were breathing on you
Chaya	חיה	Life force
Yechida	יחידה	The universal Oneness- G-d

Three More

Other states of the soul are revealed in both the rabbinic and Kabbalistic literature. These states are not considered to be perpetual states but are developed according to need. They have no need to play roles in the afterlife as do the other soul roots. Here is some clarification of these special circumstantial elements of the human soul:

Ruach Hakodesh (spirit of holiness) - This state of the soul is where it attains some forms of prophecy. While we have no prophets in our current age, there are some minor forms of *ruach hakodesh* that are attained through holiness.

Neshamah Yeteira (extra soul) - Jews attain a supplemental soul on *Shabbos*. This soul enhances the spiritual enjoyment of the day, and only visits those who observe the *Shabbos* according to the letter of the law.

Neshamah Kedosha- This soul is attained by Jews reaching the age of maturity - thirteen years for boys, twelve years for girls - and is linked to the observance of the commandments and study of the Torah. One can gain or lose this aspect of the soul, relative to the level of observance and time spent in study.

Man, in this world, includes all of the worlds. In the beginning, man merits to *Nefesh* of *Asiyah* (also called *Asiyah* of *Asiyah*). If this man has blemished his soul and through his deeds has fallen into the *klipos*, or evil forces, he does not merit *Ruach* (the next level up). If the man does not sin, then the *Nefesh* of *Asiyah* is called "the secret of the *Ophanim*" (lower angels). Sometimes a man who has only a *Nefesh* of *Asiyah* can be more important and greater than a man who has a soul on the level of *Ruach*. The reason for this is that each and every world includes in it the four worlds. The *Nefesh* of *Asiyah* includes in it *Nefesh* of *Nefesh* of *Asiyah*, *Ruach* of *Nefesh* of *Asiyah*, *Neshamah* of *Nefesh* of *Asiyah* and *Neshamah* of *Neshamah* of *Nefesh* of *Asiyah*, called in short language *Naran* of *Nefesh* of *Asiyah*. These four divisions of the world of *Asiyah* are called the general *Nefesh*. Sometimes a man who is on the level of *Neshamah* of *Asiyah* (*Neshamah* of *Nefesh*), because he already has begun to radiate and somewhat correct his *Nefesh*, immediately radiates the *Neshamah* of the *Ruach* of *Yetzirah*, even if it has not yet become completely enclothed in his *Nefesh*. The general rule applies that, until the *Nefesh* is corrected and complete, it is impossible for the *Ruach* of *Yetzirah* to become enclothed in him. However, the reflection of *Neshamah* of *Yetzirah* (*Neshamah* of *Ruach*) can radiate below into the *Neshamah* of *Asiyah* (*Neshamah* of *Nefesh*). Then there is another man on the level of *Nefesh* of *Yetzirah* (*Nefesh* of *Ruach*) who is from the higher source (*Ruach*). However, the man of *Neshamah* of *Nefesh* (*Neshamah* of *Asiyah*) is a higher category because he is receiving this radiation from above, from the level of *Neshamah* of *Ruach*. (Shaar Hagilgulim p. 98) Rav Chaim Vital further teaches us that a man who occupies himself with the doing of a *mitzvah* only merits to *Nefesh* called *Asiyah* and no more. When the man will have only *Nefesh*, he receives radiance only from the name of *Hashem*, *ADNA*. When he occupies himself in learning Torah *lishmah*, he will merit to *Ruach* that comes from the name *YKVK*. When he further occupies himself in the secrets of *Torah* and merits to *Neshamah* of *Beriyah*, strength, and life is being drawn upon his soul from the name *EKYEH*.

Lesson 13: Fear of Hashem / Seeing Black Fire on White Fire

In order to begin connecting yourself to the spiritual, you must work on the aspect of fear of *Hashem*. One must know and have a true realization that he stands before *Hashem* at all times. This is why the Code of Jewish Law begins by speaking about the importance of picturing *YKVK* before one constantly. To your surprise, this is also how I shall begin teaching you the ways of Kabbalah. You see, for those *rabbis* who entered the great halls of Kabbalistic study, this was a basic principle. In truth, it wasn't even a principle; it was a given that they had trained themselves to always see the four-letter Name before them. For without it, how can one even begin to think about the spiritual realms, since all the worlds are sustained through this holy Name? Below I will systematically teach you how to do this, but first, let me tell you some stories about *tzaddikim* who saw the Holy Name of *Hashem*.

In our generation, there is a holy *rebbe* who sees the holy fire in his natural eye, not by force, but due to his holiness alone. I will refrain from mentioning his name for the sake of his privacy. The story goes like this: Some years ago, I called to let him know I was in town and wanted to say *Tehillim* at the holy *Kotel* with him. When we finished *Tehillim*, he suggested, "Let us say the *Ketores*." So together we went to the large *Ketores*, written on *klaf* near the entrance to the *Kotel* cave. After a few moments reciting it, I noticed that he saw not only the letters on fire but the klaf as well (which is the proper way). I picked up on this as I noticed his eyes and fingers were flickering. I mentioned to him that this is very hard for me and doesn't come naturally. Surprised, he responded, "I don't understand why you don't just look and see it." He implied that, for him, it comes so naturally that he assumed everyone could simply see it like this. This is the way the *Torah* was given to us on *Har Sinai*, in flashing fire, black fire on white fire. We should cry in *teshuvah* that we have to be taught this technique, and have not simply seen it on our own, due to our fallen level.

Here is an excerpt from my *sefer* Kavanos Halev:

Once, while riding on the highway, Rabbi Avigdor Miller shouted to the driver to stop. Thinking a tire had blown, the driver pulled to the side of the road immediately. The *rabbi* got out of the car and stood towards the corner of the road. Realizing that there were no problems with the car, the driver patiently awaited his passenger's return to the vehicle. Upon his return, the bewildered driver asked what was wrong. Rabbi Miller responded, "I forgot about *Hashem* for a brief moment."

The pious Rabbi Yitzchok of Drobitch traveled from town to town, giving over Torah. One ice-cold winter, he was traveling on the road by foot, when some fellow Jews passed by in a carriage. Having compassion, they took him into the carriage. During the journey, they came upon a river. Without warning, Rabbi Yitzchok leaped off the carriage, removed his garments and went into the freezing river. The others looked on in astonishment. After a few minutes, Rabbi Yitzchok emerged, dressed, and returned to the carriage. His fellow travelers asked Rabbi Yitzchok to explain his actions. He answered, "My practice is to always have the name *YKVK* before my eyes, in black fire on a background of white fire. While we were traveling, at that moment, it disappeared from before me. So, I went into the river and pleaded, 'Master of the World, if You return to me, good; but if not, why should I live any longer?' And it was returned to me." (Missions Chassidim - pg.415, #7)

Rabbi Isaac ben Solomon of Acco once remarked, "I proclaim this, both to individuals and the masses, who wish to know the mystery of binding one's soul on high. One can attach his thoughts to *Hashem*, and when one does so consistently, there is no question that he will be worthy of the world to come, and *Hashem's* name will be with him constantly, both in this world and in the next. You should constantly keep the letters of the Unique Name in your mind as if they were in front of you, written in a book with Torah *ashuris* script. Each letter should appear infinitely large. When you depict the letters of the Unique Name in this manner, your mind's eye should gaze on them, and at the same time, your heart should be directed toward the *Ain Sof* (Unique Being). Your gazing and thought should be as one. This is the mystery of true attachment, regarding which the Torah says, 'To Him, you shall attach yourself.' (Devarim 10:20) If you are able to do this, no evil will befall you. You will not be subject to errors caused by logic nor emotion, and you will not be the victim of accidents. As long as you are attached to *Hashem*, you are above all accidents, and are in control of events." (Meir Eynayim, Ekev)

Here are some words spoken directly by the Rabbi:

"I, the young Isaac of Acre, have been reading the portion of Genesis in the secrets of the Torah by our master Nahmanides, blessed be his memory. While reading that the Torah preceded the creation of the world by two thousand years, and that a black fire was written on a white fire, I understood the secret of the matter, and I thirsted to placate the wrath of the difficult questions of the philosophers who said that the number of the days and years depends upon time, and time depends upon the motions of the sun and moon and stars, as it is said: 'Let them be for signs and for seasons, for days and for years.' (Genesis 1:14) Because upon their motions and revolutions the 'measures of time' depends, so how can we mention years before the existence of the Sphere [earth]?"

Due to this problem, R. Isaac of Acre proceeds to give a non-literal Kabbalistic/symbolic interpretation of the rabbinic dictum:

"And those two thousand years by which it had been mentioned that the Torah preceded the world, hint at *Chesed* and *Binah,* and this world is *Tiferes,* as it is said that immediately with the emanation of *Chochmah* the Torah was emanated. That is because *Chochmah* is the Torah, and the Torah is *Chochmah,* and it was written by black fire on white fire. It was not by a down-to-earth fire as believed by those of little faith who speak about the righteous in a boastful manner, thinking that the sayings of the sages, blessed be their memory, all concern the down-to-earth fire and the [two thousand] years that they depend on the motions of the Spheres of the firmament and of the planets. However, this is a fire that is not a fire, as is said by the sages, of blessed memory. So too, is the matter of this fire; the black fire hints at the attribute of judgment, which is *Binah,* and the white fire hints at the attribute of mercy, which is *Chochmah...*"

In other words, since "world" (*olam*) does not denote the created world, and "two thousand years" does not refer to time that is measured, there is no longer a contradiction between this statement and the philosophic notions of time and causality. R. Isaac interprets the statement in terms of the ten *Sefiros* (aspects/attributes/powers of *Hashem*). Since "world" and "two thousand years" refer to *Sefirosic* powers, the philosophic problem (how could there be a Torah before the creation of the universe?) is solved. The preexistence of the Torah to the world is ontic, not a temporal priority. The 'white fire' means *Chochmah,* the second *Sefirah.* This is the white substratum upon which the black letters are written. The black letters (black fire) means *Binah,* the third *Sefirah,* and this material world is expressed with the *Sefirah* of *Tiferes. Binah* and *Chochmah* are indeed prior to *Tiferes,* in R. Isaac of Acre's striking explanation. (The translation of the passage by R. Isaac of Acre is taken from a manuscript of his work Otzar Hayyim)

According to him, the white fire is the written Torah and the black fire is the oral Torah. The image of black fire over white fire conveys the interrelation of the oral and written Toros. What we have today, in which we think of as the written Torah, is not exactly the same as the written Torah of white fire. The Torah we read, of black ink handwritten on parchment, is perceived through the prism of the oral Torah of black fire. Only someone who has attained the level of *ruach hakodesh* can still perceive the written Torah of white fire.

There is a Talmudic teaching of Rabbi Shimon Ben Lakish that says the Torah is written with "black fire on white fire". Nachmanides quotes this within the introduction to his commentary on the *Chumash.* He further mentions that the writing was continuous, without a break between words, and a reading was possible according to the "way of the Names of *Hashem*", meaning that the entire Torah comprises Names of *Hashem* and you could read it according to our [conventional] reading concerning the Torah and the *mitzvah.* (Shemos 24:12) The Torah was given to Moshe according to the division of the reading of the *mitzvah* and was transmitted orally to him according to the reading of the Names.

This holy name of YKVK is very serious and should not be taken lightly, but it must also be placed before your mind's eye on a regular basis. Please study the *halachos* explaining the use of Holy Names if you are currently unfamiliar. One should not take this Name by force and usher it into his thoughts. Rather, one should provoke it gently and with training, and it is forbidden to be said.

I will attempt to bring this technique down to you in more practical ways. First, I would like you to think about the fear you have of *Hashem*, and then the love you have for Him. Dwell on this concept a few minutes, as this is really the first step towards opening the spiritual channels of Holy Names. Then slowly bring the letters before your eyes in a natural way, appearing in black letters. The actual way it should be seen is as flashing black fire on white fire; this was how the Torah was originally given to us. We all saw it with our own eyes when we were on *Har Sinai*, so, therefore, it is already engraved into our minds. It is simply a matter of retraining our holy souls, which have been lowered by the physical worlds, to recall seeing the Hebrew alphabet in flashing fire. The more one seeks to purify his mind, going to the *mikvah* and drawing holy thoughts, the greater this revelation will be. It may formulate itself differently for every person, as no two souls are completely alike.

Let me try to explain to you in more practical ways how to see these images. First, I must tell you that it takes a lot of patience. It may even take many years, but if you persevere you will be successful. At first, your main goal should simply be to see the letters of *YKVK* in black color, or preferably black or orange/red fire. Start by taking it one letter at a time. For an entire day, keep putting before your eyes the letter *Yud*. Draw it out as if you were writing it like a *sofer stam*. The next day, take the letter, *Hay*, alone and picture it. Slowly build yourself up and learn to see all the letters of the Hebrew alphabet individually. Then begin to build your mind's strength by picturing two letters at a time. From there, build on a third letter and so on. For those who have been reading Hebrew letters for years, it's a bit easier. I found it very helpful being that I am a *sofer*, to meditate on the holy letters, having written them often. The holiest scribes are able to write the letters placing them on fire as they are written. However, these scribes are few in our generation. You can also add the *tagin* of the letters as a chimney for the smoke rising from the letters.

The way the mind works is that it constantly seeks information. In order to keep the letters in your view, you need to give them movement. Some try this with surrounding triangles flipping back and forth, while others might try to continually draw the letters over and over again in their minds. It might help to carefully create a small fire or to look upon the light of a candle. With time, the practice becomes more natural. The most proper way would be to see everything in black-and-white fire.

Let us attempt to go through this process together. Begin by closing your eyes and picturing a burning bush. It is very large, and its blaze is very bright. Orange and red lights sparkle from it and you can even feel its heat radiating upon your face... It is flashing brighter and brighter, almost blinding. You must squint your eyes to protect yourself from its bright rays. Imagine orange, then red, orange and then red. Back and forth the colors are flashing before you. Their heat is making your forehead begin to sweat. Out from this blaze comes the letter *Yud*, becoming larger and larger. It is totally aflame, burning and flashing. Out from the top of it comes forth a bit of black smoke and the letter appears surrounded by a white burnt smoke cloud. The *Yud* begins to flash even faster and faster until it's so bright you have squint just to see. Then forthcoming is the letter *Hay* appearing next to it, ablaze. They both become larger and the heat intensifies. Then the letter *Vav* appears in your mind, and you place it next to the *Hay*. Now you join the letter *Hay* and together all the letters appear flashing, totally surrounded by fire.

My father *zt"l,* was once sitting with a man studying Torah. He told me that he saw the Hebrew letters flying off the page and ascending to the heavens. He and the man just glanced at each other without saying a word as they both had this spiritual experience.

You have now learned the secret of "*Shivisi Hashem, lenegdi samid.*" (Tehillim 16:8) The other names can also be seen in this way, as well as their *miluim*, written out forms. When you pray, you can see all the letters of your prayer in sparkling fire, and you might even see the essence of the letters as they leave your lips, elevating to the worlds above.

As you teach yourself this technique, you must also work on your purity. It is important to go to the *mikvah* regularly and to recite the *Tikkun Haklali*, daily. There were many great sages who said that a person should not even learn one word of Kabbalah unless they immersed in the *mikvah* that day. The Baal Shem Tov said that all his spiritual attainments were accomplished through immersion in the *mikvah*. He said to never go three days without immersing. It goes without saying the importance of regular study in *halachos* and *Gemara*, wearing clean clothes, and watching the words that come out of one's mouth.

If you are feeling the necessity to push ahead with *Kabbalah* study before you're properly prepared, at the very least you must simultaneously fill in the gaps in your learning. You must study all the Mishna and Talmud in order, completing both.

Lesson 14: Holy Names Handed Down

There are many holy names which have been handed down through tradition. Some of these were used by Moshe Rabbenu, Aharon Hakohein, Rabbi Akiva, and others. We know this by tradition and they are written in certain holy books. The author of one of these books, knowing the greatness of what he was putting into writing, asked, "Please, if you deal in selling *seforim*, only sell this book to those you know worthy of learning it." I personally will not tell its name for a few reasons. First, the book is full of mistakes due to printing errors, mistakes that could cost people their lives, *chas v'shalom*. Second, it must be taught through a teacher with much understanding. Third, within this book are some of the greatest secrets in the world. One risks his very life by its study, and its study must have a serious purpose. The person who taught me these secrets suffered greatly for months from having done so, but *baruch Hashem*, he has recovered. I will share with you excerpts of my choosing, which I feel will increase your *Yiras Shamayim* and love of the Torah.

Before I do so, I must tell you it has become clear to me, through this learning, the insignificance of witchcraft, magic and idol worship. For instance, the Chinese have a tradition that the true form of Kung Fu involved the artist's being able to suspend himself in the air and jump large leaps. This took the artist years of isolation, fasting, meditation and torturous discipline. The holy *tzaddikim*, even a few hundred years ago, needed no such foolish ways. By using a combination of letters from the Torah, they could move mountains, travel to cities and even countries in a fleeting time with *kefitzas haderech*. Dovid Hamelech was suspended in the air through holy names when his colleague tried to keep him from harm's way. (Shmuel) The Talmudists were able to reincarnate, bringing people back to life, and this was said to be a small thing for them. Most of these techniques were done through understanding the use of Holy Names.

So, do we still have great people within our generation who have this secret knowledge? Many people say things haphazardly like, "If only I had the holy Chozeh of Lublin, Chazon Ish or other great rabbis that I could ask my questions to. They too knew these secrets, but now I have nobody to ask." This statement is far from the truth, as Toras Moshe is complete in each generation.

The Torah has not been forgotten! Especially its secrets! Who would let such knowledge be forgotten? Even if it somehow was, would not *Hashem* send a holy *malach* down to the *tzaddik* of the generation, to teach it to him?

For instance, in each generation, there is a special *kavanah* for washing the hands that only one holy *tzaddik* is blessed to know. It is higher than all the Arizal's known *kavanah* teachings on the matter. This information has been passed on to someone in our generation. As soon as the *tzaddik* who was blessed with this knowledge passes on *chas v'shalom*, *Hashem* through an intermediary will have taught it a new *tzaddik*.

It should go without saying, to pray to *Hashem* for worthiness of meeting such *tzaddikim* in our generation, whom He has entrusted with knowledge such as what I have mentioned. I cannot share with you most of my firsthand experiences with *tzaddikim*, and those of *chassidim* who stood and watched their *rabbis* perform miracles (like that of the Baal Shem Tov), in order to protect their privacy.

These are some of the holy names I will now share with you. These are for meditation, they are not for pronunciation nor to be written in vain.

THIS NAME WAS THE FIRE OF MOSHE RABBENU	ה-ה-י ה-י-ה י-ה-ה
THIS IS ONE OF THE 72 HOLY NAMES. ONE OF ITS GREAT QUALITIES IS TO BRING HEALING; ALSO, TO ELEVATE SPARKS FROM THE *KLIPAH*	י-ל-י
THIS NAME IS ON *HASHEM'S* ROD.	יְ-הָ-אָ הָ-נַ-דָ וַ-הְ-נָ הָ-רֵ-יֲ

By meditating on the first combination, one connects himself to the fire of Moshe Rabbenu. This can help a person to have more *kavanah* and strength in Torah learning and prayer.

Through meditating on the second name, one can draw down healing to others and also rid himself and others from *klipah*, thereby elevating sparks back up to their source. It is one of the 72 holy Names of *Hashem*.

The third one Moshe Rabbenu had on his staff. Eliyahu Hanavi also gave it to Elisha, who then gave it to Pinchas. Please don't be overly wise; meditation is fine and sometimes better for many *kavanos*.

Just to clarify, we do not pray to these names; rather they are used as a tool to open gates in the heavens.

א-ד-ט-ד   One   Letter   א-ה-י-ה
Backwards

א-ז-ב-ו-ג-ה   Name of 8, *Segulah Tefilah* Answered

א-ו-י	י-ה-ו-ה in the future will be *Kohen Hagadol* says on *Yom Kippur*
א-ה-ב-ה	Name of *Hashem's* Clothes for *Shabbos*; good to meditate while getting dressed for *Shabbos*
א-ה-ר-ר-י-א-ל or ז-ה-ר-ר-י-א-ל	
ב-י-ס-ק *Atbash*	שמחה
ב-מ-ס-ב ש-צ-ב ס-ב-מ-ו	א-ל נ-א ר-פ-א נ-א ל-ה one letter forward (good for any sickness)
א - ט ב ה	Power of *Chein*; Gematria ו-ה
ל-ט-ב ל-א-ן נ-ח-ב	לֵב טָהוֹר בְּרָא לִי אֱלֹהִים וְרוּחַ נָכוֹן חַדֵּשׁ בְּקִרְבִּי To purify one's mind
נ-ל-ך	Power to see wonders; no pain while walking large distances; often used as a *Kamaya*
י-ה-ו-ה א-ל-ה-י-נ-ו ב-מ-ו-כ-ס-ז כ-ו-ז-ו	כ-ו-ז-ו ב-מ-ו-כ-ס-ז כ-ו-ז-ו י-ה-ו-ה א-ל-ה-י-נ-ו י-ה-ו-ה
א-ה-צ-צ-י-צ-ר-ו-ן	צ-י-ץ א-ה-ר-ן Meditate to feel wonders
א-י-ה א-י-ר-ו-ן א-י-א-ל	
ה-ר-ח-מ-ן	א-ב-ר-ק *Gematria*
ר-א-ה	Lost in road; Meditate to see the right way to go.
א-י-ט-מ-ו-ן	י-ה-ו-ה מלך *Gematria* *Shefa* comes to all *Klal Yisrael*
ג-ב-י-ל-ו-ן ן	Good prayer in time of trouble (from posuk in Shemos 16:2)
ע-ז-ו-ז-י	הַו-א יְ-שׁ-ל-ח מַ-ל-ל-א-כ-ו
ה-י-מ-ל	לַ-פ-נ-י-ך *Hatzlacha*
ז-ג-נ-ז-ג-א-ל	מ-י-כ-א-ל + תגין 21=א-ה-י-ה =
ז-כ-ר-י-א-ל	*Malach* of Memory
ח-ת-ך	פותֵחַ אֶת יָדֶ
א-ל-ו-ה	The Dressing of the Soul
א-ר-ט-י-מ-ו-ס	Makes *tumah* run away
י-א-י-א	יָ-ה-ו-ה אֵ-ל-ה-י-נ-ו יְ-ה-ו-ה אֶחָד
י-ו-ח-צ-צ-ב-י-ר-ו-ן + שמע ישראל	Combine and Meditate to bring

someone back to *teshuvah*

יא-ץ יב-ץ יג-ץ יד-ץ י-ה-ץ י-ו-ץ יז-ץ יח-	ה' אֲהבצַדיקים Great Name
ץ יט-ץ יי-ץ יכ-ץ יל-ץ ימ-ץ ינ-ץ יס-ץ יע-	
ץ יפ-ץ יצ-ץ יק-ץ יר-ץ יש-ץ ית-	
א-ץ ב-ץ ג-ץ ד-ץ ה-ץ ו-ץ ז-ץ ח-ץ ט-ץ	Great Name
י-ץ כ-ץ ל-ץ מ-ץ נ-ץ ס-ץ ע-ץ פ-ץ צ-ץ	
ק-ץ ר-ץ ש-ץ ת-ץ	

There are known holy Names that are used for guarding and protecting a person. Written in different combinations or meditations, these names are extremely powerful if someone understands how to use them.

Guarding Names

ב-ק-י	Guarding
ב-ר-ז-ל	בלהה רחל זלפה לאה
ט-פ-ט-פ-י-ה	Guarding can use colors to direct the desired need.
י-ו-ב-ב	יִקראני וַאעננהו בַצרה ואכבדהו
	(תהלים צא,טו)
צ-ד-נ-ל-ב-ש	Guarding
צ-מ-ר-כ-ד	Guarding
ר-ה-א ת-מ-פ א-ד-ם ת-מ-י-א	Meditate to save from any trouble

I have limited how many holy Names I have shared, as it is more than plenty for most souls. There are endless numbers of holy Names handed down to us through tradition. Many as you can see are initials of the first or last letter of every word in a *possuk*. It is best to also think about the source *possuk* when you can. The holy Names mentioned have more specific uses than the more general meditations of *Hashem's* names. For those who properly understand *Hashem's* names, they too can be very specific and open many gates in the Heavens. The most common name of *Hashem* to meditate on is *YKVK*.

Lesson 15: Secrets of YKVK

We are now going to explore the secret combinations of the vowels of *YKVK*. The vowels are the souls of the letters. With each combination of *YKVK* and vowels, certain effects are able to be drawn. Don't think for a moment that this knowledge gives you powers. They are meditative names used in prayer to draw down light from *Hashem*.

You MUST be clean physically/spiritually, and your intentions should be pure. Do not practice with these names for selfish purposes, but only to bring pleasure to *Hashem* and to draw you close to Him. The letters shown are in regular Hebrew calligraphy; when you picture them, it is preferable to do so in *ashurit* script, as how it would appear in a *sefer* Torah.

It goes without saying that it is forbidden to view holy Names [as a man] without a *kippah* on, for a married woman who has her head uncovered, or body parts uncovered. Please do not write these letters yourself (one should add dashes between the letters). There are many *halachos*, Jewish laws you must be familiar with before use of these. Please see the Shulchan Aruch, Code of Jewish Law, for details.

OPENS A PERSON'S HEART	הּ-וּ-הּ-יָ
REVEALS HIGH SECRETS, HIGHEST COMBINATION	הּ-וָ-הָ-יָ
BIG IN SOCIETY, FOR *HATZLACHA*	הֶ-וֹ-הֵ-יֵ
TO BRING HEALING	הּ-וּ-הָ-יּ
ELEVATE YOUR *TEFILLAH*	ה-וּ-הּ-יָ
HAPPINESS, HEALING, GRACE, REMOVE WORRIES	הּ-וָ-הָ-יּ
FOR WEALTH; SAFE AND EASY TRAVEL,	הּ-וֶ-הָ-יָ
TRAVEL SAFELY & EASILY, *HATZLACHA*	הָ-וָ-הֵ-יֵ
OPEN HEART TO UNDERSTAND TORAH LEARNING	הּ-וֹ-הָ-יָ
TO DRAW DOWN *CHESED*, KINDNESS	הָ-וָ-הָ-יָ
FROM THIS COMBINATION, ISRAEL WILL BE RELEASED FROM *GALLUS*/GOOD FOR ANSWER IN DREAM	הּ-וּ-הּ-יֶ
FOR FRIENDSHIP/LOVE	הּ-וּ-הּ-יָ

There are many more combinations and secrets beyond this. Some of these combinations were handed down, and are well known, while some I intertwined on my own based on the strength of the *nekudos* and letters. Please note that the dashes between the letters are there because it is forbidden to write the Name of *Hashem* without reason.

Now we will teach you the combinations of letters with *nekudos* in the way of the *Sefiros*. We have combined two methods in one in this diagram. You can, therefore, view the *Sefiros* by *nikud* and through their color. The color method is handed down to us from the Ramak.

In order to connect to a specific *Sefirah*, you simply meditate on the corresponding color and/or *nikud* of YKVK that corresponds to the desired effect.

INVISABLE WHITE	KETER	CROWN	יְ-הָ-וָ-הָ
A COLOR THAT INCLUDES ALL COLORS	CHOCHMAH	WISDOM	יַ-הָ-וָ-הָ
YELLOW & GREEN	BINAH	UNDERSTANDING	יֶ-הֶ-וֶ-הֶ
WHITE & SILVER	CHESED	LOVE	יַ-הָ-וָ-הָ
RED & GOLD	GEVURAH	STRENGTH	יִ-הִ-וֹ-הִ
YELLOW & PURPLE	TIFERES	BEAUTY	יֹ-הֹ-וֹ-הֹ
LIGHT PINK	NETZACH	VICTORY	יֻ-הֻ-וֻ-הֻ
DARK PINK	HOD	SPLENDOR	יֻ-הֻ-וֻ-הֻ
ORANGE	YESOD	FOUNDATION	יְ-הֹ-וֹ-הֹ-וֹ-הֹ-וֹ
BLUE	MALCHUS	KINGSHIP	יְ-הֹ-וֹ-הֹ

You can also take the colors and combine them with the secret *nikudos* we spoke about before. For instance, in order to strengthen this combination

יִ-הַ-וַ-הַ

, (used for happiness, healing, grace, remove worries) you can meditate on it in white letters in order to draw down light from *Chesed*. You can

81

add *Binah* to it by thinking of it in green/yellow.

So, in what situations would you use these color combinations? Well when living in Tzfat during the war with Hezballah, I would meditate and imagine the name *YKVK* in white letters in the sky above the city. I thought to do this in order to draw down compassion from *Hashem*. To strengthen this meditation more, I added the *nikudo*s of *segol* to my meditation. If you want to take these methods further, you can imagine the light of *Chesed* being elevated to the *Sefirah* of *Binah* and further. You can also think about how Avraham had the *middah* of *Chesed* always in his heart and how he represents this concept of *Chesed*, thereby binding yourself to him.

When you want to connect yourself to a higher level in *kedusha* and *bris milah*, you can think about the *Sefirah* of *Yesod* in orange colors, or its *YKVK* combination, with *Vav*s as shown above. You could also think about Yosef Hatzaddik and how he exemplified this *middah*.

The *Sefiros*, their colors and their *nikud* can be used as a meditative ladder going up or down. You could start your meditation in *Asiyah*, and climb your way to the next world, then continue further. There is no end to the climb from our perspective really, so you can just keep climbing them drawing closer to *Hashem* and the *Tzimtzum*, should you be pure enough.

You can also combine meditations. I always like to imagine the *Tzimtzum* being an endless rope that I can climb further and further by repetition of the climbing method I used, or through imagining other holy Names, drawing light from above to below. For instance, the name ג-ב-ר-ל-ו-ן, which draws down *shefa* to all of *Klal Yisrael*. I also think about this name many times during my *kiddush* Friday night.

There is a teaching from the Ramchal. It is a wonderful and awesome *chiddush*. You can take any four-letter word (3 or 5 will not work) in Hebrew, and meditate on it in *YKVK*, with the *nikud* of that word. You would do this in order to meditate and pray to *Hashem*, for that effect to take place. Be careful to always use the correct *nikud* without a mistake. Again, all these teachings can only be used for the sake of bringing pleasure to our Creator. Selfish motives will only prove to block the light of *Hashem* from you. It can also lead to increased *klipah* and opposing forces attaching your soul.

Here is an example of the Ramchal's Method.

I used the example with the word, *shalom*, which means peace. If you want to bring peace into a certain relationship, which is having marriage problems, meditate on *YKVK* with the combination of *nekudos* from *shalom*. Also, always have in mind the word itself, and let these both fill your mind back and forth.

These are the 12 different ways you can spell the letters of *Hashem's* name YKVK. It is very holy to meditate on.

Lesson 16: Art of kamayas

Tzaddikim have been writing *kamayas* for hundreds of years. The secrets behind *kamayas* were handed down from teacher to student, and many are printed in various *sefarim*.

While some *kamayas* entail the writing of *malachim*, angels, the majority of them do not. Others use combinations of the seventy-two letter names of *Hashem*, though this too is a minority. Most *kamayas* are simply combinations of *possukim* from the Torah, thereby taking either the first letter of each word or the last letter of each word.

For instance, a common *kamaya* for healing is one that uses a combination from a *possuk* in Bamidbar 12:13.

"O *Hashem*, please heal her!"

Alone, this *kamaya* can bring healing but those who know the art of *kamayas* know that there are special seals or additional combinations to strengthen any type of *kamaya*. for healing or one of another specific purpose. This is why sometimes you will see a word written out in a *kamaya* with a box of letters or other words placed beside it.

Today, many write *kamayas* as a business and they never really studied the *halachos* and necessary *kavanos* needed for such a holy act. On the streets of Israel, you can find names carved on silver, lead, *klaf* and other surfaces. They are more like art pieces than actual real *kamayas* which are supposed to be written by someone *Yiras Shamayim*, someone who fears heaven. It should be written by someone who understands the combinations of the letters and their source. Maybe it would even be better to avoid many of them not knowing the intentions of their author.

Do *kamayas* work? Well, there are a few important factors involved:

1. *Kavanah*, the intention of the writer.

Chassidus, Kabbalah and Meditation

2. The correct combinations of letters.

3. That the writer learned the laws of *soferous*, and he knows how to make *kosher* letters and erase them, as needed.

4. The worthiness of the writer, that *Hashem* blessed him through this, to help others. There is a teaching that once the sofer helped three people through three different *kamayas*, then we know he is legitimate in this art and can be trustworthy.

5. The person wearing the *kamaya* has to be worthy of it working. If a person is not following the Torah, the *kamaya* can actually hurt them, instead of helping. It may possess too much *kedusha* for their vessel to handle.

6. It MUST be *Hashem's* will that blessing should come in this form to help this person.

7. One has to believe the power of the *possukim*, the writer and *Hashem's* ability to send down blessing through all things.

It is known that many who write *kamayas*, suffer many hardships by doing so. You MUST be learned in *soferous* and keep the commandments of the Torah with fear.

As *Moshiach* nears, the Kabbalah of *kamayas* is sure to begin to re-surface. The powers of *kamayas* have not been as strong as they once were, but this too will change during the messianic times.

Being a *sofer*, I stumbled upon the wisdom of writing *kamayas*. I have been able to help many through them. I personally do not seek to write them unless there is a situation which calls for it, or the person would benefit greatly from it. There are some rather harmless *kamayas* as well. For instance, most anyone could write the full name of a *tzaddik* and carry it with them for extra protection.

There is one very important *kamaya* that anyone seeking to draw close to *Hashem* should have. It was taught to me, by the Biala Rebbe of New York, and is a teaching from the Arizal. A person should have written for them, their name intertwined with the word *neshamah*. If they have two names, then both should be written first starting with the letter of their name. Then starting with the *Nun* from the word *neshamah*, followed by a person's second letter of their name, and so on. If you have two names, then you are to write both names this same way. One should look at this a few times a day, as its power is to strengthen a person's connection with their *neshamah*. It helps a person to see themselves in a clearer light and the purpose of their existence. Through this, with working on *middos* and purity, one could even attain some aspects of *ruach hakodesh*. When I recite in the morning the prayer for the *neshamah*, *Elokai neshama*, I usually glance upon my name with *neshamah* written out on *klaf*.

Here is a *kamaya* with my name Moshe Eliezer intertwined with *neshamah*.

85

מנששהלמה
אנלשיימעהזר
למששמהה ־ץ
צאשלמידהעזר

"It is good, immediately upon arising from one's bed, to meditate upon the Divine Name '*Alef-Lamed-Vav-Hey*' *(Eloh-ah - Hashem)*, for it is the Divine Name which is the garment for the soul, as it is taught in the name of the righteous *tzaddikim*." (Kuntress Seder HaYom, Rabbi Yechiel Rabinowitz, *zt"l*, Biala Rebbe)

Some things *kamayas* can be written for:
-To find one's *bashert*
-Peace between friends and partners
-To have children
-For healing
-To remember and understand one's learning
-To get rid of evil thoughts
-To be liked by others
-*Parnasa*, business success
-To have holier dreams
-For a pregnant woman to have an easy delivery
-To protect from miscarriage
-Against, *Ayin Hara*, evil eye
-Baby crying
-To guard a person against thieves, dangers, the difficulties of traveling
-Tooth ache

There are even some *kamayas* and combinations of letters which allow someone to have *kefizas haderch* (travel long distances in a shorter time). Some secret *kamayas* can be used to even split a sea, in order to pass, as was used by Moshe Rabbenu. There are some which can save lives and even some which can take away the breath of life. *Baruch Hashem*, most of the more powerful *kamayas* have been kept a secret, and they are held quietly among masters.

Some *kamayas* also involve saying combinations of letters and *possukim*. There are some that are very complicated, involving horns of goats, teeth of certain animals, drawing circles in the sand and many other such symbolisms. Many can only be written during specific days of the year, or hours when the constellations are in alignment.

There are some great *rabbis* who discouraged their use, while there were also many great *rabbis* who encouraged it. Both sources are correct. I am in no way encouraging either stance, but I am here to share with you the wisdom of the sages. With wisdom comes understanding the creation.

If a person doesn't know that the Torah has all of their desires, they will turn to *avodah zara* to find answers. The only place to search is in the *Torah Shebal Peh* and *Torah Shebecasav*. All the answers are waiting for anyone thirsty for *Hashem*.

Kabbalistic *rabbis* have always been faced with the dilemma, how much mysticism to reveal to the world. Sometimes it takes a simple thing, like wearing a *kamaya*, to open a person's mind up to *Hashem's* strength. For others, not relying upon *Hashem* with absolute emunah, can hamper their spiritual connection. While for some the *kamaya* is like medicine, for others it can be a poison. That is why it is so important that someone who has studied the works of the Talmud and attained a real *yishuv-hadaas* be the one to guide you in this art.

There is no reason to needlessly fear this holy art. In fact, it is something handed down through tradition, but it is important to note that many great sages didn't feel they needed to rely upon any *segulos* at all when prayer and faith alone is enough.

Lesson 17: The Prayer of the Baal Shem Tov & Hidden Secrets I have found

I have often wondered if chassidim today truly understand the method of prayer used by the Baal Shem Tov and our holy *rebbes*. You see, the Baal Shem Tov understood the hidden meaning and secrets behind the essence of prayer itself. He saw that the root of prayer is the Hebrew letters themselves and how we connect to them.

From the twenty-two letters, *Hashem* created the entire world. Everything in the world has a particular name and *malach*, the angel that controls it. One of the students of the Ramchal actually explains how to know the name of each of these *malachim*, but it's not my place to discuss this openly. The Baal Shem Tov teaches that each letter is a world, and each word is a combination of many worlds. I'd rather explain it as follows; each letter is a light, and each word is a combination of these lights. Henceforth, every sentence is an abundance of light flowing through the spiritual realms. Now the greatest secret of prayer is connecting to these flowing lights, then utilizing these lights to better one's *kavanah*, thereby creating a neatly wrapped gift package (containing praises, thanksgiving, and requests) to our Creator. I would now like the privilege of explaining to you how to do this.

Before delving into this topic more deeply, I would like to emphasize the greatness of simple prayer said to *Hashem*. Nothing truly can compare to someone who speaks to *Hashem* in their own words, very simply from their heart. There are no *kavanos* of the Arizal, or anything, as great as true simplicity. If you find that what I am teaching here complicates things and deviates your attention from the simple prayer said with proper intention and understanding, please desist from it.

When one prays, they should think of themselves as a poor person. As a child beseeching his father for help. They should believe this with great humility and selflessness. Wanting their prayers heard to only help others and be able to give back to *Hashem* in great humility as a servant. In this way, they will be praying for the lack of the *Shechinah's* presence, and on behalf of the Jewish people, rather than selfishly for themselves. Rebbe Nachman teaches that the words of the prayer should be said concentrating on their simple meaning. Then with time, naturally the *kavanah* will come of itself.

The Baal Shem Tov looked at prayer as a mantra, meditation. This is why our daily prayers follow the same patterns. Most religious Jews, after saying the same prayers for most of their lives, have them memorized, or at least are very familiar with them. This allows for the mind to use this pattern and repetition in order to form a meditative state. Through thinking about the letters, and drawing oneself to them, one is able to elevate their thoughts. The Baal Shem Tov teaches that the letters yearn for a person to hold onto them and not let them go. One should also not want to let go of each letter, trying to hold it in their heart, with great longing and pleasure. If you take an opera singer, you will see they don't want to let go of the sound, as they draw themselves to it. This same idea can be applied to listening to music. If you take someone with a genuine appreciation for musical arrangement and accompaniment, the music is an entire meditation, mantra and their appreciation for it is beyond our understanding. We can learn from this how much respect we should have for speech, thereby valuing every word we say. Also, do we truly appreciate the artistic nature of music and the gift *Hashem* gave us?

I am now going to share with you some of my own *chiddushim*, findings which I have never shared previously. Sefer Yetzirah explains that *Alef-Chet-Hey-Ayin* in the throat (Gutturals), *Gimel-Yud-Kaf Kuf* in the palate (Palatals), *Dalet-Tet-Lamed-Nun-Tav* in the tongue (Lingual), *Zayin-Samech-Shin-Resh-Tzaddi* in the teeth (Dentals), *Bet-Vav-Mem-Peh* in the lips (Labials). This is considered the secret of (מנצפך).

There are five parts of the mouth used to articulate speech. They are represented by the letters מנצפך.

It says in Sefer Yetzirah, "Engrave them with voice, carve them with breath, and set them in the mouth in five places." The instruction is to carefully pronounce each letter of these five families. This is "engrave them with voice." Then one must "carve them with breath", contemplating each letter carefully, and concentrating on the breath that is exhaled while it is pronounced. Finally, one must "set them in the mouth", mediating on the place in the mouth with which the letter is pronounced.

Actual	English Name	Hebrew	Ari Method
Throat	Gutturals	אחהע	Hod
Palate	Palatals	גיכק	Netzach
Tongue	Lingual	דטלנת	Tiferes
Teeth	Dentals	זסשרצ	Gevurah
Lips	Labials	בומף	Chesed

I found that during prayer, one can meditate on each letter as it goes forth from the specific area in the mouth. You can meditate on the breath, its feeling as it leaves your mouth, and its sound. Through this one can bind themselves to the letters very strongly. This is not something to do all the time but once in a while in order to rejuvenate one's connection to the letters. It is a very great meditation. The following are other things I have learned during my most trying moments throughout my life.

Many times, a person tries very hard to have *Kavanah*, so much so that they wear themselves out, and have little energy left to pray the *Shema* and *Shemoneh Esray* with concentration. Therefore, one should bear this in mind, and make sure to leave the greatest of their strength for the important parts, after all, is not everything else preliminary prayers to ready oneself for the highest prayers in *Beriyah* and *Atzulos*? This is the secret of the preliminary prayers. To utilize them with the intention to build oneself, so to speak, and become nullified before *Hashem*. *Shemoneh Esray* is the prayer of *Atzulos*, the highest *Sefirah*. In the first three and last three paragraphs of the *Shemoneh Esray*, one can entirely change their day and their life. So deep is this part that it should take a person longer to say these parts than all the larger middle passages. To invoke the merit of our forefathers, to speak about the greatness of *Hashem*, to thank Him, this is everything.

I never quite understood why people wait until right before the *Shemoneh Esray* to daven loudly and strongly. This should be done during the first prayers with the eventual goal of praying softly to *Hashem*, during *Shemoneh Esray*. If one desires to light a piece of wood, at first, they rub two sticks together to create friction. Eventually, when the stick is light, one holds them still and then the flame itself is what moves. Therefore, when one sways back and forth, to draw concentration, this is similar to starting a fire. Once started, when a person has real *Kavanah* and has attained humility, one should remain still allowing the flame, their *neshamah* alone to move.

During prayer, one can also meditate that they are standing next to any *tzaddik* of their choice. One in which they wish to draw a connection to, in order to draw strength from them. By connecting to sages that are close to *Hashem*, with access to the inner gates, can be beneficial. This is of course not to be confused with praying to the *rabbi, Chas v'Shalom*. Listening to the advice and instruction of *rabbis* binds you to their soul root, you thereby become included in them. The Talmud explains that the lips of the sages can move within their grave. *Chazal* teach that when we recite the Psalms, King David himself is accompanying us and reciting them as well.

Another great meditation is to picture oneself standing in the heavens in all simplify before *Hashem*, our Creator, praying in absolute humility. The Baal Shem Tov taught, wherever a person places their thought, that is where all of them is. We truly don't make the most of this concept. It may be the biggest disappointment in all of Judaism, that we don't place this teaching as the forefront in our entire *avodah*, service. It teaches a person to value their thoughts, to constantly strive for attachment to *Hashem* and spirituality. As spoken through this *sefer*, this is the entire point of our existence.

Having explored both avenues, prayer through Kabbalah and prayer through totally simple means, I have learned that both arrive at the same destination. This means that through total simplicity, one can reach the same levels as one who meditates on the Kabbalistic *yichudim*. This is why, when someone tells me they want to learn Kabbalah before they are truly ready, inside of me is a little tear. It is not that I don't respect their longing, or think nothing will come out of it, but should they apply themselves where they are truly holding in life, they would be far more successful.

I envy those who have attained what they have through total simplicity. I've noticed in my own life that certain things I attained through Kabbalah were natural for me in my youth. However, I passed them off as not real or an unrealistic vision when in fact it was a totally pure image at the time. We all too often underestimate ourselves and what we see. What we feel we pass off as nothing. This is because of our lack of *emunah* in *HaShem*. If we have emunah, we would never pass off anything as coincidence, even a simple thought that comes to us. Even when you look at the time on your clock, you should not pass off the numbers as mere coincidence. Everything is totally from *HaShem*.

Rabbi Nachman Horodenker told the following story

I was once traveling on a ship. We ran out of provisions and were without food for many days. Finally, we reached an Arab city where no Jews lived.

An Arab took me in and offered me some food. I had not eaten for several days, and quickly washed my hands and recited the blessing for bread. I was just about to take a bite when a thought entered my mind: "Do not eat the bread of one with a mean eye." (Proverbs 23:6)

A random thought is not without meaning, and therefore, I did not know what to do. I had already said the blessing, but I realized the significance of this thought and was determined not to eat anything of this Arab. Just then another thought entered my mind. "I have commanded the Arabs to feed you." (1 Malachim 17:4)

Rebbe Nachman continued by explaining how proper it was that his grandfather paid attention to thoughts that came to him. He taught every thought entering the mind must contain some element of truth. (Rebbe Nachman's Wisdom 113)

Pulling the Letters

Every letter of the Hebrew alphabet can be *Meloy*, have a pulled meaning. It can be expanded and through this expansion, one can connect to the letter's root. For instance, *Alef* is spelled *Alef Lamed Pey* and so on. Here are three examples of this in Hebrew:

Regular	Expanded
א	אלף
ל	למד
מ	מם

ד	דלת=4	ג	גימל=3	ב	בית=2	א	אלף=1
ח	חית=8	ז	זין=7	ו	וו=6	ה	הא=5
ל	למד=30	כ	כף=20	י	יוד=10	ט	טית=9
ע	עין=70	ס	סמך=60	נ	נון=50	מ	מם=40
ר	ריש=200	ק	קוף=100	צ	צדיק=90	פ	פה=80
				ת	תו=400	ש	שין=300

So, say you are meditating or praying with the word ברור, *Boruch* which means to bless. You can meditate on the expanded forms for each letter as you are saying them. Through this, you draw yourself to the letter and the light of its root form. There is truly no end to this, as even the expanded form can then be expanded once again, and so on. For example:

Regular	Expanded
א	אלף
אלף	אלף, למד, פא
אלף, למד, פא	אלף, למד, פא, למד, מם, דלת, פא, אלף

On *Parshas Tetzave*, the Baal Shem Tov taught the following:

"And Aaron shall bear the names of the children of Israel on the breastplate of judgment upon his heart, when he goes into the holy place, for a memorial before *Hashem* continually. And you shall put in the breastplate of judgment the *Urim* and the *Tummim*, and they shall be upon Aaron's heart when he goes in before the L-rd..." (Shemos 28:29-30)

It is known that the breastplate barely contained all twenty-two letters of the Hebrew alphabet, as our Sages have said. Therefore, when they had to ask a question that used several of the same letters, so how were they answered through this?

There is a very great mystery in this. The Baal Shem Tov explains that each of the twenty-two letters [of the Hebrew alphabet] contains within it all the other letters of the alphabet (except for the letter *Mem*). Since G-d commanded that all twenty-two letters be inscribed on the breastplate, when the priest would be enwrapped in Divine inspiration, the letters would shine in their expanded forms This enabled them to receive everything they needed to know. Understand this! (Translation and Commentary on the Baal Shem Tov by Rabbi Eliezer Shore).

There is also another important secret to prayer, and that is to know and understand the sources of the Holy Names in prayer. For instance, when the great sages wanted a certain effect to be drawn from above, they used a certain Divine Name which would draw from this aspect. It is not for nothing that they used names like *ADNA* in one place, *Eloh-im* in another, and combined many in a row in some instances. Each Divine Name is connected to a certain *Sefirah* and certain attributes of *Hashem*, so to speak. This mystery is taught in *Sefer Sha'are Orah* and other very holy books. We will also explore this concept more in the next chapter. Without knowing the light behind the name being said, one is clueless as to what light they are drawing down. Then again, most of us are barely even concentrating on the simple meaning of our prayers.

Helpful practices for before and during prayers:

1. It is good to give charity before and after praying, even if only a quarter.
2. One should say, "I bind myself to the *tzaddik* of the generation," before praying.
3. One should wear a *gartle*, with a hat and jacket to show respect during prayers.
4. It is important not to look around too much during davening, but to try to read in the siddur or to close one's eyes.
5. One should try to draw the light from the tefillin into one's mind.
6. "All my bones should say, 'who is like unto You?'" (Tehillim 35:10) It is good to try to get all one's limbs involved in the prayer. Think about this and find your own method.
7. It is good to meditate on YKVK at times during prayer, especially when saying it.
8. When you daven with ten men, your prayer immediately goes through to the heavens, for the *Shechinah* rests with ten men.
9. One's prayer should be made beautiful for *Hashem*, with a soft, sweet tone.
10. Bring yourself to humility before praying.
11. Slow down when you come to *Hashem's* Name, in order to concentrate on it.
12. It is important to daven in the same place, daily.
13. It is good to go to the *mikvah* daily, before prayer.
14. There is a special *segulah* to pray from *Ashrus* script (it is good to have one such siddur in your home to use once in a while).
15. There are special *kavanah* siddurim available that add more Kabbalistic meditations to your prayers. Many of the Baal Shem Tov's followers used to pray from Siddur Rebbe Shabti. Other masters would use different versions of the Siddur Rashash.

Lesson 18: Understanding the Names

Often the name for an object, person or places also its definition or description. So, *Hashem*, Who is infinite and undefinable, cannot truly be named. Thus, G-d has no name, only names which are descriptions of the various behavior patterns that can be ascribed to His influence on our lives.

Hashem said to Moshe, "Tell the children of Israel, that My name is *Eh-he-yeh*. Where was I all these years and where can I be found? With you. I am being, I am existence, I am reality."

In the words of the Midrash, "G-d said to Moses: You want to know My name? I am called by My deeds. I might be called *E-l Sha-dai*, or *Tzeva-os*, or *Elohim*, or *HavaY-ah*. When I judge My creatures, I am called *Eloh-im*. When I wage war on the wicked, I am called *Tzeva-os*. When I tolerate the sins of man, I am called *E-l Sha-dai*. When I have compassion on My world, I am called *Hava-Y-ah*..." (Shemos Rabbah 3:6)

So, if we want to understand how to direct our prayers through the correct channels, it helps to understand the holy Names of *Hashem*.

"One should be aware that all the names revealed in the Torah are the keys for anything a person needs in the world. When one contemplates these Names, they will understand that all of the Torah and the commandments are dependent upon them. At that point when he knows the purpose of every Name he will realize the greatness of 'He who spoke and thus the world came into being.' He will be fearful of Him and he will desire to cleave to Him through His Blessed Names. Then he will be near to *Hashem* and his petitions will be accepted, as it is written: 'I will keep him safe, for he knows My Name. When he calls on Me I will answer him.' The passage does not promise safety by merely mentioning His Name but by knowing His Name. It is the knowing, that is the most significant. Only after the knowledge does the passage present the petition, 'when he calls on Me I will answer.'

This means that when the time arrives he should know the Name that is intrinsically tied to what he needs; then when he calls, 'I will answer.' An example of this is when Jacob in time of trouble calls out to *E-l Shad-day* saying, 'And may *E-l Shad-day* dispose the man to mercy toward you.'" (Genesis 43:15) (Introduction to Sha'are Orah)

"Then will you understand the fear of *YKVK* and attain knowledge of

Hashem." (Proverbs 2:5) It is a shame that people who are beginning scholars of Kabbalah abuse these names, writing and saying them freely with no true fear of *Hashem.* "Before His fury who can stand, who will rise when He is angry?" (Nahum 1:6)

ADO-NOI / א-ד-נ-י

The holy name as we refer to it when teaching, *ADNA* represents the *Adon hakol* - the Master of all. This is the simple definition as recorded in the Code of Jewish Law. *Ado-noi* is sensed and experienced in the Divine majesty and royalty within the universe. Today *Hashem's* name, while in prayer, is pronounced as *Ado-noi.* So, in a way, *Ado-noi* is the garb, the vessel through which the Name bestows itself within creation.

As the Name that is most connected with the *Sefirah* of *Malchus, ADNA* is the most far-reaching name we can draw to, when beginning to come close to *Hashem.* When we start the prayer of *Shemoneh Esray,* we begin by saying, "*Hashem,* (*Ado-noi*) open my lips, that my mouth may declare Your praise." When I want to meditate on holy Names, and I know that I am currently so far from *Hashem,* I usually start thinking of this Name. Slowly I allow it into my mind, not by force, but gradually. When it is ready, I begin to purify my heart with this Name that begins to open the gates of Heaven.

Ekyeh / א-ה-י-ה

Ekyeh is the Name of *Hashem* associated with the highest Sphere *(Sefirah).* In Hebrew, this word literally means, "I shall be." It implies new birth or revelation of self. As in, "I shall be *[Ekyeh],* what I shall be *[Ekyeh].* So, shall you say to the children of Israel: *'Ekyeh* sent me to you.'" [Shemos 3:14] The Name *Ekyeh,* along with the two Names *Y-ah* and *Havay-a,* are considered essential Names of *Hashem* because they are all composed exclusively of the letters *Alef* (א), *Hey* (ה), *Vav* (ו), and *Yud* (י), the four letters considered the essential origins of the holy language.

Hashem's own becoming, as it were, reflects the power of the *Sefirah* of *Keter,* for which reason the Name *Ekyeh* is associated with the crown. In *Atbash,* the letters of *Ekyeh* transforms to תצמת, whose value is 620, the *gematria* of crown (כֶּתֶר).

Ekyeh appears exactly 3 times in the entire Torah (as seen above in one verse). These three instances correspond to the sum of three possible fillings of the Name, which is 455.

- אלף הא א יוד הא = 143
- אלף הה יוד הה = 151
- אלף הי יוד הי = 161

455 is the value of the verse, "The whole earth is full of His glory." (Isaiah 6:3) מְלֹא כָל הָאָרֶץ כְּבוֹדוֹ

Name	Sefirah	Attribute
Ekyeh	Keser	Desire
Y-ah	Chochmah	Wisdom
YHVH punctuated as Eloh-im	Binah	Understanding
E-l	Chesed	Kindness
Eloh-im	Gevurah	Might / Strength
YHVH punct. Tziva-os	Tiferes	Compassion
YHVH Tziva-os	Netzach	Victory
Eloh-im Tziva-os	Hod	Glory
Sha-dai	Yesod	Foundation
Ado-noi	Malchus	Royalty

ELOH-IM / אֱ-ל-הֵ-י-ם

The Code of Jewish Law describes the name *Eloh-im* as the Mighty, the Ruler and Sovereign of the Heavens and Earth. He is the Master of all-natural forces, the Force of all forces. We get a foretaste of this ruling name as we meditate on the corporeal laws of nature and the apparent deep symmetrical order of creation. It appears to us as the storyline of created reality.

Eloh-im is connected to the *Sefirah* of *Gevurah* and bears the notion of *din*, strict judgment, which sets limitations and apparent constrictions in creation. Its position is toward the left in the *Sefiros*.

The creation of the physical stems from *Eloh-im*. The first words of the Torah are: "In the beginning, *Eloh-im* created the heaven and the earth." (Genesis 1)

Physical reality, both time and space, echoes of this Divine force—so much so that the word for nature in Hebrew, *Ha'tevah*, has the same *gematria* as the word *Eloh-im*. Both *Eloh-im* and *Ha'tevah* are numerically equivalent to eighty-six. *Eloh-im* is the finite vessel which contains, albeit in a concealed manner, the Infinite Light of *Havay-a*, the *Yud-Hey-Vav-Hey*. Therefore *Eloh-im*, which is eighty-six, equals the Name *Havay-a* - twenty-six with the word *kli* - vessel - sixty; 26 + 60 = 86.

Eloh-im itself embodies both its finite revealed self and its infinite concealed self. Therefore, the Name *Eloh-im* can also be divided into *mi* (Who) and *eile* (these). The aspect of "Who" is the hidden, the Infinite *Hashem*, and yet this hidden mystery has become revealed in *eile* "these", the physical, the multiplicity, the creation.

Eloh-im is essentially the revelation that can be grasped by human logic. *YKVK*, on the other hand, is a revelation transcending human logic. *YKVK* is above time. Instead of operating in a temporal sequence, which is the way our minds work, on the level of *YKVK*, *Hashem* operates in a non-temporal sequence. *YKVK* also alludes to the hidden *Sefirah* of *Keser*, the level of *Hashem's* will that completely transcends the logic of the universe.

When the Torah describes the creation of man's body, it uses the name *Eloh-im* because, ultimately, man can use his intellect and logic to understand his body, and the physical world of which it is a part. When the Torah wishes to describe man's soul, however, the name *YKVK* is used. This is because man cannot understand his soul. It is on a level that completely transcends logic.

The Torah says, "*YKVK*, *Eloh-im* formed man out of the dust of the ground and breathed into his nostrils a soul-breath (*Neshamah*) of life; man, thus became a living creature." (Genesis 1:27) This means that a number of significant aspects of man's existence, namely his logic, his mental processes, and his physical nature, derived from the Name *Eloh-im*. (Inner Space, Rabbi Aryeh Kaplan p. 147)

YKVK / י-ה-ו-ה

YUD-HEY-VAV-HEY
Hashem—The Name

This name is referred to as the *Shem ha'mefurash* - the explicit name, or the *shem ha'etzem* - essential name. In English, it is called the Tetragrammaton. We do not pronounce it. The precise pronunciation and articulation of the four letters

Yud-Hey-Vav-Hey has been lost over time and will return with the *Bais Hamikdosh*. When this name is vocalized, as done throughout the *siddur*, it is pronounced as *Ado-noi*.

This is the highest and deepest name. The Kabbalists often refer to it as the actual tree, with all the other names being mere branches. A way to refer to this name is as the name *Havay-a*, which means *havi-ya* (being), the Ultimate Being which is the source of all beginnings.

When the Torah wishes to describe man's soul, the name *YKVK* is used. This is because man cannot understand his soul. It is on a level that completely transcends logic.

E-l / א-ל

E-l represents the *Sefirah* of *Chesed*, and the position toward the right. It is known to show Divine supernal boundless kindness. The verse in Psalm 52:3 says, "The *Chesed* of *E-l* endures for all the days." We sense this characteristic and expression of the Divine in the kindness within our life and within all the goodness of creation. It balances out the strength of the name *Eloh-im*.

During the course of prayers, the name *E-l* often comes with an epithet attached to it, as in *E-l Elyon* (most high *E-l*), or *E-l Gadol* (Great *E-l*).

The first of the thirteen attributes of mercy is the name *E-l*. When trying to draw down kindness from the heavens and to confront *din*, one can imagine this name. In our prayer book, it is used in this way.

The primordial desire to create an otherness comes from *E-l*, Divine Kindness, a benevolence which desires to create an apparently separate existence upon whom He can bestow kindness. Once there is this desire, there can then begin the actual process of creation, which occurs through Divine Speech.

Other Names connected with *E-l* are, *Eloh-ei* (the *Eloh-ei*) and *Eloh-ienu* (our *Eloh-ie*), where the name is more personal, our G-d.

ELO-HA / א-ל-ו-ה

Elo-ha represents an aspect of Divine kindness and a kindness that extends and infuses all dimensions of creation. The name is comprised of four letters: the first two are *Alef Lamed*, spelling the name *E-l*; the next two letters are *Vav-Hey*, and the final two are in the name *Yud-Hey-Vav-Hey*.

E'in Sof (without end), the Kabbalistic name of G-d.

Y-AH / י-ה

Y-ah embodies the *Sefirah* of *Chochmah*, wisdom. The name *Y-ah* is created from the first two letters of the Tetragrammaton, the *Yud* and the upper *Hey*. *Yud* reflects *Chochmah*, Divine wisdom and intuition. While *Hey* represents *Binah*, Divine reason and understanding. This name manifests itself in the inner Divine wisdom and intelligence which permeates all of creation.

When a person realizes that nothing is empty of meaning and wisdom, he is sensing the name *Y-ah*. The perception of suffering, that in it is *Hashem's* will and only good, stems from this *Y-ah* wisdom and meaning.

When praising *Hashem*, we often use this expression *hallelu Y-ah*, which is comprised of two Hebrew words: *Hallelu* (praise You) and *Y-ah*. We also say, "*kol ha'Neshamah tehallel Y-ah*," (let all living beings, with every breath we take, praise *Ya-h*). Through praising *Hashem*, we divulge and draw down into the world and our consciousness the *Y-ah*. We draw Divine wisdom, its goodness, purpose, and meaning—within all aspects of our life, even into the placings which otherwise seemed purposeless, meaningless and trivial.

SHAD-DAI / ש-ד-י

Shad-dai embodies the *Sefirah* of *Yesod*, foundation, and the position is in the bottom middle. From *Shad-dai*/*Yesod* is the distribution of *shefa* to the world. When *Hashem* blessed Yaakov that he would be fruitful and multiply, He used this Holy Name. Therefore, we see that *Shad-dai* and *bris* are interrelated. When a person guards the covenant, he allows the *shefa* to flow freely. However, if he is impure in the covenant, he hampers the flow of blessing from *Yesod* to *Malchus*.

The name *Shad-dai* conjures up various images and interpretations, but mostly it secures boundaries which express one fundamental idea—the notion of Divine protection and nurture. *Shad-dai* reflects the flow of creation. Nature is continually being created and self-destroying, building and pulling down, in one continuous rhythmical motion.

The word *Shad-dai* literal translation is "when it is enough", since *Hashem* is the one Who gives out our tests and decides when it is enough for our *tikkun*. It can denote both a "destroyer" (*Shad-dai* from the word *shoded*-to break and destroy) and a "nurturer" (from the word *shadayim*-that which nourishes a young suckling).

When the name *Shad-dai* is combined with the prefix *E-l*, which is *Chesed*, this signifies the Divine flow of blessings into Creation, to the extent where the receiver of the blessings says, "enough. We are fulfilled." "*Hashem* said to the world, *Shad-dai* – Enough" (Bereshis 17:1).

TZEVA-OS / צב-אות

The literal translation of *Tzeva-os* is "L-rd of Hosts." Though this name does not appear in the five books of the *Torah*, it is chronicled in the book of Prophets. This name is connected with the orchestrating element of the Creator that cares about the details of all legions. We sense this name in the place where the Infinite collapses upon the space of the finite.

The name *Tzeva-os* is related to the *Sefirah* of *Netzach*- victory and ambition, and *Hod*- Splendor, devotion; and *temimus*, sincerity. When the name is written with a prefix of *Hashem*, as in "*Hashem Tzeva-os*," it is connected with the right column and expansive *Sefirah*, the *Sefirah* of *Netzach*. It is thereby able to draw from the *Sefiros* above it on the right. When it is written as "*Eloh-im Tzeva-os*," it relates to the left restrictive column *Sefirah*, the *Sefirah* of *Hod*, and thereby is easily able to draw from *Sefiros* relating to the left.

Netzach and *Hod* are referred to in the Zohar as, "the scales of justice." *Netzach* merits while *Hod* concedes, "acknowledges" or "confesses". As the two hips of the body, they are responsible for the general state of equilibrium of the body.

There is so much more to learn about the Names of *Hashem* in order to become closer to Him. I have provided only a brief summary of Holy Names in order to excite you about what is still out there to learn. Rabbi Gikatilla in his important work, Sha'are Orah goes into depth on the concept of directing one's prayers through the channels. I think it is important to be aware of these channels when directing your prayers. If you use this understanding for ill intentions, your prayer certainly will be rejected. This truly is a pathway to becoming close to *Hashem*. "For what great nation is there that has *Hashem* so close at hand as is *Hashem* whenever we call upon Him?" (Devarim 4:8)

Lesson 19: The 42-Letter Name

The mystical and lofty prayer of *Ana B'Koach* is attributed to the first-century sage Rabbi Nechunyah Ben HaKana. It is a prayer that consists of seven passages, each corresponding to the seven expressive *Sefiros* through which the Divine energy sustains and nourishes our universe. This *koach* itself was created in a seven-day cycle and is recited in prayers wherever there is a symbolic ascent of Divine energy from a lower sphere to a higher one, or whenever there is any movement from one reality to the next. The forty-two letter Name (*Ana B'Koach*) is the aspect of the "head", which is a male form of energy (Giver/conduit of light), and it is the power force and source of everything in the whole Creation. Nothing moves in this world without the power of the forty-two letter Name.

It is interesting to note that if you take the names of the *Sefiros* from *Crown* to *Kingdom* [including Knowledge (דעת, *Da'as*)]

כתר חכמה בינה דעת חסד גבורה תפארת נצח הוד יסוד מלכות they contain 42 letters (Torah Science Foundation): Thereby, our Sages tell us that the Name with which the universe was created was the 42-letter Name, of which it is said (Zohar II 234a; III 256b):

"This is the gate to G-d, the righteous will come through it." (Tehillim 118:20) - it is the name of 42 letters, with which the higher and the lower were created.

Ana B'Koach is also known as the forty-two Names of *Hashem*, being that there are forty-two words in this prayer. The initials of these words create the forty-two lettered name of *Hashem*. Seven six-letter names are found in each line, using the first letter of each of the six words in that line. This can be used as a form of meditation while reciting the prayer.

There are six words in each of the seven lines that correspond to the six surfaces of a directional cube: up, down, right, left, front, and back. These six directions are parallel with the verse from the vision of Yechezkel that says, "With two they covered their faces, with two they covered their feet, and with two they flew." *(Isaiah 6:2)*

The holy name of *Mab* י-ו-ד ה-א ו-א-ו ה-א also has the numerical value of forty-two. When recited with proper intentions, the *Ana B'Koach* prayer brings blessing and connects one to *Hashem's* name YKVK.

101

אָנָּא, בְּכֹחַ גְּדֻלַּת יְמִינְךָ, תַּתִּיר צְרוּרָה.   אב״ג ית״ץ

קַבֵּל רִנַּת עַמְּךָ, שַׂגְּבֵנוּ, טַהֲרֵנוּ, נוֹרָא.   קר״ע שט״ן

נָא גִבּוֹר, דּוֹרְשֵׁי יִחוּדְךָ, כְּבָבַת שָׁמְרֵם.   נג״ד יכ״ש

בָּרְכֵם, טַהֲרֵם, רַחֲמֵי צִדְקָתְךָ, תָּמִיד גָּמְלֵם.   בט״ר צת״ג

חֲסִין קָדוֹשׁ, בְּרוֹב טוּבְךָ, נַהֵל עֲדָתֶךָ.   חק״ב טנ״ע

יָחִיד, גֵּאֶה, לְעַמְּךָ פְּנֵה, זוֹכְרֵי קְדֻשָּׁתֶךָ.   יג״ל פז״ק

שַׁוְעָתֵנוּ קַבֵּל, וּשְׁמַע צַעֲקָתֵנוּ, יוֹדֵעַ תַּעֲלֻמוֹת.   שק״ו צי״ת

בָּרוּךְ שֵׁם כְּבוֹד מַלְכוּתוֹ לְעוֹלָם וָעֶד.

Rav Hai Haga'on (cited by the Tur) argues with major *meforshim* saying that the *Kohen Hagadol* used the forty-two letter Name of *Hashem* and not the four-letter Name of *Yud* and *Hey* on *Yom Kippur*. (Yoma 39b)

This name is also related to Moshe and the burning bush. When G-d first appeared to Moshe, he humbly asked what name he should use to call to the Infinite. *Hashem* replied, "*E'heye Asher E'heye*," which has been translated to "I will be as I will be."

The numerical value of the name *E'heye* is twenty-one:

Alef = 1
Hey = 5
Yud = 10
Hey = 5

The name *E'heye* is repeated twice for a total *gematria* of forty-two. We see from this how the combination of forty-two is no simple matter, but rather a way to connect to *Hashem* on very high levels.

Forty-two is also connected with the forty-two letters in the Name of *Hashem*, the *Yud-Hey-Vav-Hey*. This name has four letters which, when spelled out, develop into ten letters. When these ten letters are permuted, there are twenty-eight letters.

Yud – Hey – Vav – Hey = 4

Spelled out:

Yud: Yud – Vav – Daled + *Hey*: Hey – Yud + *Vav*: Vav – Yud – Vav + *Hey*: Hey – Yud = *10*

Spelled out:

Yud: Yud – Vav – Daled | *Vav*: Vav – Yud – Vav | *Daled*: Daled – Lamed – Tof | *Hey*: Hey – Yud | *Yud*: Yud – Vav – Daled | *Vav*: Vav – Yud – Vav

Yud: Yud – Vav – Daled | *Vav*: Vav – Yud – Vav | *Hey*: Hey – Yud | *Yud*: Yud – Vav – Daled = *28*

4 + 10 + 28 = 42

The name Mab (Mem + Bais = 42)

There are different opinions on how these names should be meditated upon. One view sees each line as one whole name; another holds that there are three letters per name and two names per line. Thus, the names should be said as two words together, as in the first line, "*Ana b'koach, gedulas yemincha, tatir tzrurah.*" There is also a method to connect the name to each day of the week, in the teachings of Rav Chai Hagaon.

The Talmud says that Rav Yehudah said in the name of the *rav*, the forty-two-letter name, is entrusted only to him who is unassuming, humble, middle-aged, free from anger, never gets drunk and is not demanding on his rights. He who knows it is heedful thereof and observes it in purity is treasured Above and popular below, feared by man, and inherits two worlds: this world and the future world. (Avodah Zara 17b-18a)

So how else does this name manifest itself and pertain to our life? When we entered the Promised Land, the Jewish people engaged in forty-two journeys. (Parshas Maasei). According to the Baal Shem Tov, these are known as the forty-two journeys which represent the forty-two stages a person goes through in life. The forty-two-letter name represents the idea of going from one reality to the next, the ultimate movement of elevation and expansion. Thus, contemplating it puts one in touch with the very "genetic code" of the universe. Through it, all things ascend. One could have in mind the elevation of *Asiyah* to *Yetzirah* and similar thoughts while saying the *Ana b'koach* prayer.

In Kabbalistic prayer books, you will notice letters above the first passage of the *Shema*, representing the *Ana b'koach* prayer. The first paragraph of *Shema* has forty-two words in it and has a connecting power to the forty-two lettered Name. When you think of the forty-two name and letters while reciting the *Shema*, it can bring you to a high meditative state.

Following this, you have the Name of seventy-two.

Some menorah charts written on *klaf* or in prayer books, display the *Ana b'koach*. Tremendous *shefa*, blessing, flows from utilizing the forty-two lettered Name, in holy ways. It is far from simple, and it helps your soul to bind itself on High.

Here is one meditation from the Arizal using the name of 42. It has the power to elevate your *Nefesh* from *Asiyah* to *Yetzirah*.

Contemplate on the mystery of wings. Through wings, man can fly and ascend on high. A bird cannot fly except with its wings, paralleling the wings of a bird are the arms of man.

There are five loves (*Chassidim*). These permeate the six directions of the body [which parallel] the six *Sefiros, Chesed, Gevurah, Tiferes, Netzach, Hod,* and *Yesod*.

In the arms and upper third of the torso, these Loves are concealed. In the lower part of the body, they are revealed.

It is for this reason that man flies with his arms, which are his wings, and not with his legs or other limbs.

The Loves in the arms are concealed and cannot expand or escape. They therefore exert pressure and oscillate in their effort to escape. This causes the arms to vibrate.

The upper Root of these Loves is *Daas*, and this is their source. The Loves that permeate the body therefore attempt to fly upward. Since they cannot escape, however, they elevate the man along with them. It is for this reason that the wings parallel the arms more than any other limbs.

This is the *Kavanah* upon which you should meditate. Every ascent is through this Name of Fourty-Two.

Meditate on your right arm (*Chesed*). Contemplate that this is the name *ABG YThTz* (אבג יתצ).

Then meditate on our left arm (*Gevurah*). Contemplate that this is the name *KRE ShTN* (קרע שטן).

Finally, mediate on the upper third of your torso, where [the Loves are] hidden. Contemplate that this is the *NGD YKhSh* (נגד יכש).

Through these three names, the Loves [that are in the arms and upper torso] fly upwards to their root, which is *Daas*. When they ascend they also take along the man and elevate him to the Universe of *Yetzirah*. You will then be like a bird, flying in the air.

If you wish to strengthen your power of light, meditate to bring down new Loves from the *Daas* of the *Parzuf* of *Zer Anpin* for the purpose of union. Through this, you will add strength to the Loves. This will bring you to fly with greater strength, and you will be able to ascend from *Asiyah* to *Yetzirah*. (Shaar Ruach HaKodesh)

Drawing down *Daas* is important because it enables the meditator to understand his spiritual experience. Having an experience that doesn't inspire someone with a new understanding of Hashem and the Torah is not as beneficial. With the drawing of *Daas*, the meditation takes on an all new meaning.

Lesson 20: The 72-Letter Name

(Verse 19) ויסע מלאך האלהים ההלך לפני מחנה ישראל וילך מאחריהם ויסע עמוד הענן מפניהם ויעמד מאחריהם

(Verse 20) ויבא בין מחנה מצרים ובין מחנה ישראל ויהי הענן והחשך ויאר את הלילה ולא קרב זה אל זה כל הלילה

(Verse 21) ויט משה את ידו על הים ויולך יהוה את הים ברוח קדים עזה כל הלילה וישם את הים לחרבה ויבקעו המים

The three consecutive verses from Shemos 14:19-21 each contain seventy-two letters, an obviously rare and holy phenomenon. The seventy-two triplets become seventy-two "Names" of *Hashem*. The three verses of seventy-two letters each refer in sequence to the Divine attributes of *Chesed, Gevurah,* and *Tiferes.*

The letters of these three verses can be arranged as seventy-two triplets of letters. But we are taught in Kabbalah that if we reverse the order of the letters in the middle set, the seventy-two triplets become seventy-two "Names" of G-d. According to the Bahir, one takes the letters of the first verse in direct order, those of the second in reverse order, and those of the third verse in direct order once again.

The Zohar similarly teaches: The first verse is to be written in its proper order since it represents G-d's loving-kindness or a direct revelation of G-d's goodness. The second verse is to be completed in reverse order, from the last letter to the first, since it represents G-d's severity, which is an indirect revelation of His goodness. Although *Tiferes* is a blend of both *Chesed* and *Gevurah,* the third verse should not be written half in the proper order and half in reverse order, as one might expect. This is because in *Tiferes*, *Chesed* dominates over *Gevurah* and, as the ideal blend of *Chesed* and *Gevurah*, *Tiferes* is a direct revelation of *Hashem's* goodness and glory rather than an indirect one.

You begin with the first letter of the first verse, which is a *Vav*. Then you take the last letter of the middle verse, which is a *Hey*. Following this, you take the first letter of the third verse, which is a *Vav*. When you combine these, you obtain the first triplet, *VHV*.

In order to contract the second triplet, you proceed as in the first combination. You take the second letter, *Yud*, of the first verse, the second letter from the end of the middle verse, *Lamed*, and then the second letter of the last verse, *Yud*. This creates the second triplet, *Y-L-Y*. You continue in this way until you complete the seventy-two triplets.

כהת	אכא	ללה	מהש	עלם	סיט	ילי	והו
הקם	הרי	מבה	יזל	ההע	לאו	אלד	הזי
והו	מלה	ייי	נלך	פהל	לוו	כלי	לאו
ועד	לכב	אום	ריי	שאה	ירת	האא	נתה
ייז	רהע	ועם	אני	מנד	כוק	להח	יוז
מיה	עשל	ערי	סאל	ילה	וול	מיכ	ההה
פוי	מבה	נית	ננא	עמם	הוזש	דני	והו
מוזי	ענו	יהה	ומב	מצר	הרוז	ייל	נמם
מום	היי	יבמ	ראה	וזבו	איע	מנק	דמב

If you're going to first say the *Ana b'koach* prayer, do not recite the line of "*Baruch Shem*", and continue to scan the seventy-two names afterward. Then when you are finished, recite the "*Baruch Shem*".

Having learned how to form the words, we now need to give them vowels. Rav Abulafia explains that each consonant has a "natural vowel" that is associated with it. (See Shaar HaKavanos, Adam Yashar p. 5b, Shmirot U'Segulos Niflaos 4b, Shemirah LeChaim, Seder Pitum HaKetores, Shnei Luchos HaBris vol 2, page

141b.)

For example, the first vowel in the name of the letter *Bet* is *Tzer'e*. Similarly, the first vowel in *Gimel* is *Chirek*, as it is the natural vowel for *Gimel.* The same is true of all the other letters. There are holy meditations that can be done with the vowels of the letters, especially in their relation to the seventy-two Names.

There are many *kavanos* that have to do with the names of seventy-two. Each set of 3 letters has its own strength and meditations. Some are known to have powers in *Kamaya*. This is beside their meditations as a whole. One can also meditate on their source *possukim*.

A common meditation of the seventy-two letters is in the recitation of the *Shema*, as seen in Kabbalistic prayer books. The first paragraph of the *Shema* uses the forty-two letters from *Ana b'koach* as spoken before. The second paragraph of *Shema*, *Vhaya Im Shemoa*, uses the seventy-two names in various orders. The final paragraph, *Vayomair*, then uses the seventy-two names, but in the regular order.

A person can also scan the Holy Names with the intention of strengthening your connection to *Hashem*, which will give pleasure or *nachas* to *Hashem*. You can also have the *Kavanah* to receive more power and energy, which you will use to help and share with others.

As with all things in the Kabbalah, the more one learns about these Names the stronger will be your connection. For most of us, the learning itself is enough, as with knowledge comes understanding. One should evaluate his current spiritual level to decide if he is worthy of meditating on the Names.

The light that comes from each name should not be limited to one form of energy unless you're doing specific meditations. Rather, scan the whole seventy-two Names as one. As a whole, the seventy-two names have the strength that bears all spiritual and worldly needs.

Should you decide to also view them separately, here are a few samples that show how the three letter combinations have individual strength. (Please view the chart.)

ה-א-ו	Lost on road, meditate to see the right way to go.
י-ל-י	Elevate sparks from the *Klipah*, power to heal
נ-ל-ך	Power to see wonders, no pain while walking large distances

Let us explore an interesting *gematria* of *Gevurah*, which equals 216. This is three times seventy-two, where *chesed* is *gematria* seventy-two. Each of *Hashem's* seventy-two hidden Names possesses three letters, in total - 216 letters. Meaning inheres to both words and names. The vital "meaning" of every one of *Hashem's* Names is His expression of love *(chesed)* for His creation. Every Name expresses His love in individual ways. The components of each word and name, their letters, and combinations are the "building blocks" of creation. The letters, "hewn" from the "raw material" of "procreation", which is the secret of the *reshimu*, the "impression" of *Hashem's* Infinite Light which remains after the initial act of *tzimtzum*, "contraction", reflecting from *Hashem's Gevurah*.

ה-י ו-י-ו ה-י י-ו-ד

If one adds up the letter *Yud*, plus *'Yud Vav Daled'*, plus the letter *'Hey'*, plus *'Hey Yud'*, plus the letter *'Vav'*, plus *'Vav Vav'*, plus the letter *'Hey'*, plus *'Hey Yud'*, one arrives at seventy-one, which together with the Holy Name itself, equals seventy-two.

The Rambam tells over that the secrets to the *Merkava* are occurring in the book of Ezekiel. He states, "It contains the Names which are the keys to the supernal Chambers." (Toras Hashem Temimah (in Kisvay Ramban, p.168) In the original Hebrew, these three verses each contain 72 letters similar to the holy name of 72. In the writings of Rabbi Abraham Abulafia, similar verses of 72 are discussed as being used like a mantra device. Therefore, if you were to repeat these verses over and over, eventually, they have the ability to open the gates of Heaven.

וַיְהִי בִּשְׁלֹשִׁים שָׁנָה בָּרְבִיעִי בַּחֲמִשָּׁה לַחֹדֶשׁ וַאֲנִי בְתוֹךְ-הַגּוֹלָה
עַל-נְהַר כְּבָר נִפְתְּחוּ הַשָּׁמַיִם וָאֶרְאֶה מַרְאוֹת אֱלֹהִים

And it was in the thirtieth year, in the fourth month, on the fifth day of the month, as I was among the captive by the river Chabar, the heavens were opened, and I saw the visions of Hashem. (1:1)

וָאֵרֶא וְהִנֵּה רוּחַ סְעָרָה בָּאָה מִן-הַצָּפוֹן עָנָן גָּדוֹל וְאֵשׁ מִתְלַקַּחַת
וְנֹגַהּ לוֹ סָבִיב וּמִתּוֹכָהּ כְּעֵין הַחַשְׁמַל מִתּוֹךְ הָאֵשׁ

And I looked, and behold, a stormy wind coming from the north, a great cloud and flashing fire, and a glow round about it, and from the midst, the vision of the Chashmal, in the midst of the fire. (1:4)

וּמִמַּעַל לָרָקִיעַ אֲשֶׁר עַל-רֹאשָׁם כְּמַרְאֵה אֶבֶן-סַפִּיר דְּמוּת כִּסֵּא
וְעַל דְּמוּת הַכִּסֵּא דְּמוּת כְּמַרְאֵה אָדָם עָלָיו מִלְמָעְלָה

And above the firmament that was over their heads, like a vision of sapphire, there was the form of a Throne, and above the form of the Throne, was a form like the vision of a man on it from above. (1:26)

In a torah video filmed at the Idra Rabbah, I attempted a live meditation on these verses. Personally, I have found them to be quite a tool in spiritual meditations. However, the information we have on them being used in this method is lacking. When it comes to any holy verses from Ezikiel, they contain many hidden gems and their study is endless.

Lesson 21: Understanding the Worlds

The earlier kabbalists spoke of four Universes: *Atzilus, Beriyah, Yetzirah* and *Asiyah*, paralleling the four letters of the Tetragrammaton. There were also hints of a universe above these four, corresponding to the apex of the *Yud* in the Tetragrammaton. The Ramak speaks of this fifth universe and calls it the Universe of the *Tzachtzachim* (Splendors, but one is hard pressed to find any reference to it in the Zohar).

The Ari, however, identified this fifth Universe as the realm of another mysterious *Partzuf* mentioned in the Zohar - *Adam Kadmon* (First Man) - the primary *Partzuf*. Within this fifth Universe, there are another four levels, again paralleling the four letters of the Tetragrammaton. These are the four expansions of the Tetragrammaton, usually referred to by their numerical value: *AB*=72, *Sag* 63, *Mah* 45 and *Ben* 52.

These worlds are very important in the meditative experience. They represent the structure of Creation and the flow of light. Without a continuous flow from below to above and above to below, there could be no existence.

Hashem originally created a perfect world, but it was designed nonetheless to fail. Who builds a beautiful house only in order to break it down? It was because *Hashem* wanted us to be a part of Creation. How do we do this? We rebuild and repair his foundational structures. Basically, we are here to elevate the sparks that fell during Adam and Eve's sin of the *Etz Hadas*.

When we do *mitzvos* and serve *Hashem*, we are similar to construction workers. Those with a greater understanding of how things work, *tzaddikim*, are like engineers and architects telling us workers how to repair our souls and the world.

You know what happens when a construction worker tries to build a structure without a proper plan? It falls down and becomes unstable. That is what we are like when we don't have rabbinical guidance in our life.

How do you get a promotion and become an engineer? You study about foundations and how all the parts of a building come together. That is what we are doing when we study the worlds. We are learning how to be much more than a simple worker. Still, without the simple worker, the person fulfilling commandments, the worlds could not be completed. We must not only understand the design, we must be simple workers as well.

The *rebbeim* teach us that nothing can flow from above unless there is action below in some form of *mitzvos* or deeds. The upper and lower worlds are therefore intertwined. The more we study about the worlds, the more we realize how little we understand.

In our day and age when someone creates a product, no matter what it is, scientists can dissect the product, analyze it, and in most cases, create an identical item. But when it comes to the worlds, nobody can make a perfect replica of *Hashem's* creations. He is too great, too powerful, and even the greatest man cannot understand His ways. However, the study of His *middos* and His Torah, the blueprint of Creation, allows us an insight into our Creator, Blessed Be He, and from there, we can begin to know how to serve Him.

Rabbi Chaim Vital teaches that included in each of the four worlds are the other four worlds. Therefore, there can be *Atzilus* of *Atzilus*, *Beriyah* of *Atzilus* and further. So, what do we know about these individual worlds that are so important to the structure of *Hashem's* creations?

Atzilus

The highest and most perfected level of *Tikkun* is called the world of *Atzilus*. In English, we refer to it as the world of Emanation. The word *Atzilus* in Hebrew stems from the word *etzel*, meaning "close to" or "near". The world of *Atzilus* is "close to" the Infinite Light, although it is not united and identified with it to the same degree as the world of *Adam Kadmon*. The Ramchal calls *Atzilus* the radiance of the face of *Adam Kadmon*.

The word *Atzilus* also can also mean "to set aside", "take from", or "draw down", for the light of the world of *Atzilus* is the idea of "taken from" and "drawn down" from the world above it, the world of *Adam Kadmon*.

At every stage of the revelation of the Infinite Light, an additional factor of limitation must be added. The dimension and limitation that increases in the world of *Atzilus* is the aspect of inner structure, *Adam Kadmon* being unstructured and so tightly bound together that it is not possible to distinguish its dimensions. The top and bottom, inside and outside, beginning and end are endless and unknowable. In *Atzilus*, however, the dimension of the internal structure is added. In fact, the entire concept of internalization, of immanence - as opposed to transcendence - is first evident in the world of *Atzilus*. However, it is far from most souls' ability to experience.

In the world of *Atzilus*, there is a distinction between "lights" and "vessels" --called *orot* and *kelim*. However, there is not a true separation between them, since the lights and vessels of *Atzilus* are integrally bound up with each other. Nevertheless, there is some distinction between them. One aspect is recognizable as light, while the other is recognizable as vessels which contain and limit the light.

The world of *Atzilus* corresponds to the structuring of an idea and the process of understanding it. However, since its presence is sensed suddenly and without full understanding, it may be perceived as fast bursts of light. It is inspirational, however, far from our minds' ability to comprehend and interpret. The amount of light revealed solely depends on the capability of the vessels to receive.

In the world of *Atzilus,* the correspondence between lights and vessels is about as perfect as it can be without the vessels actually disappearing, as they do in *Adam Kadmon.* This is why the world of *Atzilus* is entitled the world of *Tikkun,* which can be defined as rectification and order. This is because in *Atzilus* the light becomes ordered and structured, according to the capability of the vessels to receive it. The vessels of *Atzilus* are as capable of receiving light as vessels can be, before disappearing into oblivion. From this, you can understand that structure in the world of *Atzilus* does not hinder nor obscure the light, as it does in the lower worlds. Rather, it is a still world of non-being, a world of thought, since the vessels are nullified to the light.

The ten *Sefiros* of the world of *Atzilus,* in relation to the three lower worlds, are as the ten essential powers of the soul in relation to its three garments: thought, speech, and action. Though all forms of self-expression derive ultimately from the *Malchus* of *Atzilus,* the Divine "World of Speech", the actual "garments" of the soul (separate, as it were, from the soul itself), relate to the three lower worlds of *Beriyah, Yetzirah* and *Asiyah.*

Beriyah

The next world is called the world of *Beriyah* (Creation). The word creation always implies creating something (*yesh*), from nothing (*ayin*). It is here that the initial concept of *Atzilus* has been broadened, both in length and depth.

The world of *Beriyah* takes the initial manifestation of the *Sefiros* in *Atzilus* and creates with them some form of existence. The world of *Beriyah* is also referred to as the world of the "Divine Throne" (*Kisei Hakavod*). In essence, a throne is a chair upon which man lowers his posture. So too, the Divine Throne is the idea of the Divine lowering itself to come into contact with the worlds. This lowering of posture takes place in the world of *Beriyah.*

The angels in the world of *Beriyah* are called *Serafim,* from the Hebrew word *Seraifah* (a fire). The world of *Beriyah* is also the place of the upper Garden of Eden, which is a dwelling place for the holiest souls that have merited great rewards for their efforts in this world.

Yetzirah

In the next world of *Yetzirah* (Formation), finite plans are drawn up for actual creation. The principal *Sefiros* in this world are the six emotional *Sefiros* from *Chesed* to *Yesod.*

111

It is here that creation goes beyond a mere concept, and concrete steps are taken to actualize the idea. Here exists the lower Garden of Eden, the abode for souls who merit basking in its Divine Light.

In this realm, the angels are called *Chayos Hakodesh* (lit. holy beings). The angels here take on names corresponding to the *Sefiros*. For example, the angel Michael corresponds to the *Sefirah* of *Chesed*, Gabriel to *Gevurah*, and Raphael to *Tiferes*, etc. It was here that Ezekiel's prophecy was experienced through meditative techniques. He described the angels there in the form of creatures. Below him were the *Ofanim*, the angels of the world of *Asiyah*. Above him was the Throne of the world of *Beriyah*. Sitting on the Throne was the form of a man describing the *Sefiroistic* array in the world of *Atzilus*. Isaiah's prophecy entered an even deeper state of the world of *Beriyah*, and subsequently, his description is much less detailed. Most of his prophecy took place in the lower worlds. The spiritual distance from *Asiyah* to *Yetzirah* is already ever so great for a human being, though further travel is possible at the right time and place.

Asiyah

Lastly, the fourth world is *Asiyah* (the world of Action), where the creation is actualized. The Divine creative flow from the world of *Yetzirah* flows down into the creation of the four kingdoms: Mineral, Vegetable, Animal, and Human. The predominant *Sefirah* in the world of *Asiyah* is *Malchus*. *Malchus* suggests sovereignty - the idea of a distant king ruling over willing subjects. *Asiyah* is the world in which the creation takes on a form of total independence, yet the place where the subjects accept *Hashem* as King.

The world of *Asiyah* can be seen as somewhat contrary. On the one hand, the Master Creator, who is a supreme artist, has created a most beautiful and diverse creation; yet He has hidden Himself therein to such a degree that some may be unaware of an Ultimate Creator. This concealment allows this world to be a realm of free choice, where a person can choose to serve or ignore, as well as a realm of a challenge, where the hand of *Hashem* is sometimes overt and at other times covert. This world is the ultimate purpose of Creation. It is here that G-d wishes His creatures to make an abode for Him through adherence to Torah and *mitzvos*. In Torah, *Hashem* has communicated the truth of Creation and provided a path where people can navigate the turbulence of life. This is done by attaching themselves to Him through *mitzvos*.

In the higher worlds what is manifest is the Divine Light; however here are rays shining forth, similar to rays of sunlight peeking through the clouds. In this world, we perceive ourselves as separate and distinct from the flow of G-dliness. This, in turn, causes our souls to crave reunification with holiness, and this permits us to behold the essence of *Hashem* to a greater degree.

In the higher worlds, one is blinded somewhat by rays of "Divine Light" (*Giluyim*). The higher one goes, either in the lower or higher Garden of Eden, the more sublime the revelation and the more a person is blinded. Yet, from Earth, we can appreciate the sun in a far greater manner. It is specifically in this realm, where the Divine Light is eclipsed, that the observer can actually come into contact with *Atzmus*, Himself. Though He stands far beyond comprehension, one can observe Creation and realize that this can only be the work of G-d Himself. (Rabbi Nissan Dovid Dubov)

To sum up the upper worlds, in laymen's terms, you could say that *Atzilus* is the world of Initial Inspiration, *Chochmah* (Wisdom). *Beriyah* is the idea of broadening concepts and preparing the ideas of Creation with both understanding and vision. *Yetzirah* is the idea of being emotionally involved in a plan and going through all the spiritual stages of planning. *Asiyah* becomes the idea of Kingship, action and the building of projects.

After a person has learned *Ma'aseh Bereshis*, the *Ma'aseh Merkavah* teaches him to go from level to level in advanced meditation, what Names to recite, and how to engage this persona in a dialogue.

Lesson: 22 Understanding the Sefiros

The *Sefiros* are channels of Divine energy and are life-forces. They are part of the fundamental structure in a process of creation as finite reality. These channels are called the ten *Sefiros*, Ten Divine Emanations, which are the basic terms and concepts of the inner wisdom of the Torah.

The interaction between the various *Sefiros* is depicted through a network of channels which illustrate the flow of Divine energy throughout Creation. These connections suggest various subgroupings of the *Sefiros*.

Each *Sefirah* is associated with the particular limb or organ which corresponds to its position in the anatomical *Sefirosic* structure, since man was fashioned "in the image of G-d." The configuration of the *Sefiros* is graphically depicted in Kabbalistic texts by a vertical array along three parallel axes, each representing a mode of Divine influence within Creation.

The *Sefiros* are distributed into three triplets of three. There is the right side, left and middle which are at three different levels. The first triplet of right, left, middle, is the triplet of the mind: *Da'as* (or alternatively, *Keter, Chochmah,* and *Binah*). The second triplet is the inner emotive powers of the heart before one begins to do things: *Chesed, Gevurah,* and *Tiferes.* The third, final triplet is of action, which refers to behavioristic characteristics: *Netzach, Hod,* and *Yesod.* These are also emotions, but emotions that merely become manifest in behavior. The concluding point, *Malchus,* can be observed as either an appendage of this last subgrouping or as an independent entity receiving those energies which precede it. *Malchus* is the final product of all the experiences of the soul.

A common metaphor used in Kabbalah is the idea of a stream. From the great depth of waters, called in Hebrew the *tehom rabba* (signifying *Keter*), a spring of water spurts out. The spring is attached by hidden channels to the great depth of waters. The spring represents *Chochmah* as the first revelation coming forth. The bubbling spring forms into a trickle and the trickle becomes a stream and the stream becomes a mighty river; the river represents *Binah*. The birthplace or depth of the river is the spring of *Chochmah* and corresponds to the power of the flow descending from *Chochmah*. The breadth of the river is the quantity of the river's expanse over a wide area. The length of the river is the distance from its original source, via many levels and stages (signifying the other *Sefiros*), until the river ultimately flows into the sea, which represents *Malchus*.

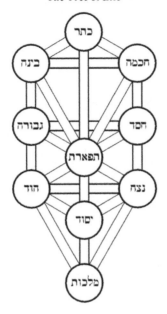

Most often the *Sefiros* are enumerated as being ten levels. However, there are altogether eleven *Sefiros* spoken of in Kabbalistic literature. This is because the *Sefirah* of *Keter* and *Da'as* are in reality one, representing differing dimensions of a single force. When *Keter*, which is the super-consciousness of the soul, exhibits itself in consciousness, it transforms into the *Sefirah* of *Da'as*. *Keter* and *Da'as* can be seen as two sides of the same coin, a conscious side, and an unconscious side. Typically, when referring to the ten *Sefiros*, one will either count *Keter*, in which case one does not count *Da'as*, or one counts *Da'as*, in which case one does not count *Keter*. As you can see, there are actually only ten *Sefiros* but there are altogether eleven names. Still, many times in various models all eleven *Sefiros* are used at once.

Keter

Keter, or Crown, is the first of the ten *Sefiros*. The image of a crown suggests an aura surrounding one's consciousness, and it appears at the top of the middle axis. The Zohar relates, "The supernal crown [*Keter elyon*] is the crown of the kingdom [*Keser Malchus*]." The first, highest of the Divine emanations – *Keter* – is thus linked to the last–*Malchus* (kingdom). As with all the *Sefiros* and everything in creation, there is usually a corresponding pair. When two things unite, they create a flow of ideas, peace, and a flow of blessing.

The *Sefirah* of *Keter* cultivates into two *partzufim* (personas). A *partzuf* is a level in which the *Sefiros* are recognizable as distinct qualities, but nonetheless, unite and connect to work in conjunction with a unified system. The external *partzuf* of *Keter* is referred to as *Arich Anpin* (the Elongated Face), corresponding to the super-conscious power of *ratzon* (will) in the soul. It is *ratzon*, willpower, that creates all things, and it is the beginning of all flow. When we pray for something, it is our wish to change *Hashem's ratzon* so that Divine Energy should flow through all the lower *Sefiros* and bestow on us blessing.

The inner *partzuf* of *Keter* is referred to as *Atik Yomin* (the Ancient of Days), corresponding to the power of *ta'anug* (pleasure) in the soul. The Ramchal teaches that *Atik Yomin* is clothed in *Arich Anpin* in order to strengthen *Arich* in all its *Sefiros* through the balance that is rooted in the Head that is unknown. In this respect, *Arich Anpin* stands under the rule of *Adam Kadmon*. *Atik Yomin* thus serves as the link between the World of Work - *Atzilus*- and the World of Reward - *Adam Kadmon*. (Ramchal 138 Openings of Wisdom, number 96)

Chochmah

Chochmah is the first power of conscious intellect within Creation itself. It is configured at the top of the right axis and corresponds to the *Tzelem Elokim* in the right hemisphere of the brain. *Chochmah* possesses two *partzufim*: the higher of these is referred to as *Abba Ila'ah* (the higher father), whereas the lower is referred to as *Yisrael Saba* (Israel, the Elder). These two *partzufim* are referred to jointly as *Abba* (the father).

Chochmah is connected in the soul with the power of intuitive insight, flashing lightning-like across consciousness. The *Partzuf* of *Abba Ila'ah* is linked with the power to instinctively extract such insight from the superconscious realm, whereas the *Partzuf* of *Yisrael Saba* is associated with the power to subsequently direct it into consciousness. So basically, in *Chochmah* lies the subconscious and unconscious mind in how it processes information. *Chochmah* is consisting of two Hebrew words: *koach mah*, meaning potential. For *Chochmah* is pure potential. It is an idea waiting to be developed. *Chochmah* is thereby referred to as wisdom. This wisdom is the ability to look at something and search for its inner truth. After uncovering the wisdom, one then seeks to further clarify the underlying truth of matter and life through analysis, development in the *Sefirah* of *Binah*.

The spiritual state identified in *Chassidus* as corresponding to the *Sefirah* of *Chochmah* is that of *bitul* (selflessness). The verse in Job 28:12 relates: "*V'chochmah me'ayin timatze?*" One way to translate this verse is a rhetorical question: "And wisdom. From where, can it be found?" Meaning, that wisdom is difficult to come by. The Kabbalists read this verse: "And wisdom is nowhere found." This is because the word *me'ayin* can be appropriately translated as "from where" or "nowhere." This shows us that it is not possible to intellectually inquire above the level of *Chochmah*. *Hashem's* activities may be researched, inquired, thought about and analyzed up to a certain point. Beyond this point, intellectual understanding is impossible because higher aspects of *Hashem's* providence simply do not come through intellectual channels.

Torah is an example of *Chochmah*. It is an outside injection of *Hashem's* wisdom into the world. Superficially man views wisdom as making him strong and powerful. While this may be true, it is he who thinks of himself as wise. He thinks, "I study Mishna... I think I know something. Talmud... I think I know even more... Then, I study Kabbalah and realize I know nothing and have to start all over again from the Chumash." This is how you can see the wise words of King Solomon come to fruition; that the ultimate goal of knowledge is to realize that we know nothing at all. This is a good indication if your study is Torah *lishmah*, if your ego grows as your study, it's not truthful. If you are more embarrassed by your lack of knowledge even though you have attained more, then you know the study is pure.

The Targum Yonatan ben Uziel interprets the words "In the beginning, *Hashem* created the world" as "with *Chochmah*, *Hashem* created the world". He interprets beginning as meaning *Chochmah*. For *Chochmah* is a beginning process. First, comes *Ratzon*, willpower to be creative, which stems from *Keter*. Then comes *Chochmah*, which is that distinct moment of inspiration that comes out of nowhere, and only then does it become logically fleshed out into full *Binah*, understanding, and action.

Binah

The next *Sefirah* is that of *Binah*, or "processed wisdom", also known as deductive reasoning. A person has an idea, first generated by *Chochmah*, but he has no way to articulate it and make it useful. It is raw and must be analyzed, processed and made into something practical.

The metaphor for this in Kabbalistic literature is that of a "father" and a "mother". This is why *Chochmah* is referred to as *Aba* and *Binah* are referred to as the *Partzuf* of *Ema*. Just as a father sows a seed, so *Chochmah* is a mere seed. The father's seed is a small drop infinitesimally tiny, containing an undeveloped code that has the only potential. It is in the mother's womb that the potential begins to develop into reality. Every line of DNA code begins to become a human cell, a budding tissue, or a specific organ.

The "breadth" of *Binah* signifies the idea of expansion, which is the definitive characteristic of *Binah*. The sages of the Talmud describe *Binah* as *"hameivin davar mi toch davar"*– "understanding one thing from another." (Chagigah 14a) It configured at the top of the left axis of the *Sefiros* and corresponds in the *Tzelem Elokim* to the left hemisphere of the brain.

The word *Binah* stems from the root *bein* which means "between." The power of *Binah* is to distinguish and differentiate between ideas. *Binah* itself is the second "brain", between *Chochmah* and *Da'as*. *Chochmah* and *Binah* together are referred to as "the two beloved friends who never part", for where there is

Chochmah, Binah invariably follows. The Zohar, therefore, calls the relationship of *Chochmah* and *Binah* as, "the supernal point (*Chochmah*) within its palace (*Binah*)."

This union is necessary for the continual recreation of the world (beginning with the birth of the seven attributes of the heart, corresponding to the seven days of Creation, from the womb of "mother", *Binah*). The birth of seven *middos* of the heart, the seven lower *Sefiros*.

In *Chassidus, Binah's* spiritual state is identified as *simcha*, joy. This is because when a person starts to understand wisdom, the heart is joyous. Wisdom alone is not enough; its value is nothingness, and only with *Binah* is it complete. Tomer Devorah teaches that who ever lives all his days in thoughts of repentance causes *Binah* to shine upon all his days. Repentance contains within itself the roots of all being; just as intelligence tempers judgments and destroys their bitterness, so must man return in true penitence and correct every imperfection.

The letter *Hey*, the second letter of the Tetragrammaton, is a symbol of the Divine Presence, more precisely of *Binah* or the Supernal *Shechinah*, for the last *Hey* of the Divine Name symbolizes *Malchus*, the Lower *Shechinah*.

The Seven Sefiros

"The secret things belong to *YKVK* our *Elokim*." (Devarim 29:29) The two Spheres *Chochmah* and *Binah* are called 'secret things' because they never become manifest by themselves, but only by means of further emanations through lower Spheres. The seven-lower emotional *Sefiros* of pleasure (*Atik Yomin*) are clothed in the *Sefiros* of desire (*Arich Anpin*) and enliven them.

The remaining seven *Sefiros* are called 'the seven *middos*' (singular: *middah*). The word '*middah*' in Hebrew translates as a measurement or an amount. This is the functioning of these seven *Sefiros,* to measure out a distribution of life force on a particular plane of reality or a particular world. They are often related to the seven days of creation, for it is essentially through them that the constitution of each plane of reality is built. If *Binah* is analogous to the builder or the process of building, as explained previously, then the seven *middos* are analogous to the structure itself.

The acronym for the intellectual *Sefiros* is *chabad* (חָכְמָה בִּינָה דָעַת); how is the *chabad* reflected in its children?

Our matriarch Leah had six sons and one daughter. She is a perfect model for the relationship between the intellectual and emotive *Sefiros*. As such, Leah is the archetypal soul of understanding or the mother principle.

Her six sons relate to the *Sefiros* from Loving-kindness to Foundation; the daughter is Kingdom. Each of the *Sefiros* is associated with an inner experience and motivating force.

A quick summary of the Seven Lower *Sefiros* corresponding to the emotions are *Chesed* (Kindness), *Gevurah* (Might), *Tiferes* (Beauty), *Netzach* (Conquest), *Hod* (Majesty), *Yesod* (Foundation) and *Malchus* (Kingdom).

These *Sefiros* are called *igullim* (Circles). From this, it is apparent that in the *Sefiros* of *igullim* (Circles), which are primal desires, the original primal desire is the outermost circle, while the desire for the action is the innermost circle.

The *Sefiros* of *tikkun* are distributed into three lines of expression. These are Kindness, Judgment, and Mercy (*Chesed, Din,* and *Rachamim*). The quality of Kindness is represented as a line to the right, and the quality of Judgment as a line to the left. In the center, between the other two lines, is the quality of Mercy.

The three *Sefiros Chochmah, Chesed,* and *Netzach* make up the right side, the *Sefiros* of *Binah, Gevurah* and *Hod* make up the left side, and the *Sefiros* of *Da'as, Tiferes,* and *Yesod* make up the middle line. It should be understood that on the level of *Keter* of *Keter,* the inner aspect of *Keter,* there is no separation into three lines. This is because *Keter* of *Keter* is a simple, essential desire, indivisible into parts. Instead, the three lines begin to separate as distinct modes of expression beginning with the external aspect of *Keter.* This external aspect starts with *Chochmah* of *Keter* onward. The inclusion and connection of the right and left lines with each other manifests specifically through the middle line, which represents the quality of the connection.

Chesed appears in the setup of the *Sefiros* along the right axis, directly beneath *Chochmah,* and corresponds in the *tzelem Elokim* to the "right arm". The biblical personality associated with *Chesed* is Abraham.

Chesed (Kindness), the quality of loving, giving and revealing to others, is when something spreads forth in great abundance. It represents abundant pleasure in something, giving unconditionally and endlessly in order to give pleasure.

If nothing in life brought pain, there would be no need for specific desires that it should be one way and not the other. Further, it would make little difference at all what we did, because the pleasure for everything would be equal. It is specifically *Chochmah* (Insight) that determines what is or isn't desirable. For this purpose, *Chochmah* of *Arich* (Insight of Desire) is the source for the *mitzvos* (commandments) of the Torah.

Without an opposing force of *Gevurah,* there would be nothing to counteract against kindness. *Chesed* would be unending and therefore not appreciated. It would be abused and taken for granted. Kindness would not be weighed or understood. *Tiferes* comes between these two aspects in order to make them all work harmoniously.

Gevurah (Might), appears in the configuration of the *Sefiros* along the left axis, directly beneath *Binah,* and corresponds in the *tzelem Elokim* to the "left arm". The biblical personality associated with *Gevurah* is Isaac.

Gevurah is the diametric opposite of *Chesed.* This is the quality of withholding and concealing from others. It is the aspect of judgment and *din,* referred to in *Kabbalah* as *midas hadin.* It is the primal desire for might. It is the restraining might of *Gevurah* that allows one to overcome his enemies, be they from without or from within (his evil inclination).

Chesed and *Gevurah* act together to create an inner balance in the soul's approach to the outside world. While the "right arm" of *chesed* functions to draw others near, the "left arm" of *Gevurah* reserves the option of repelling those deemed undeserving.

In the Shir HaShirim, it says "His left hand is under my head, and the right one embraces me." Similarly, in the *Mishkan* (a portable temple in the desert), gold corresponding to *Gevurah* is mentioned first before silver, which corresponds to *Chesed*. So, why is *Gevurah* mentioned first? It is because, ultimately, the might of *Gevurah* becomes the power and forcefulness to implement one's innate desire for *Chesed*. Only through the power of *Gevurah* is *Chesed* able to penetrate the course, opposing the surface of reality. The main purpose of *Hashem's* deeds is kindness. Thus, *Chesed* is the stronger and more dominant of the two *Sefiros*. And it is performing the act that *Hashem* really had in mind.

The two hands which act together to form all reality, *Chesed* (72) plus *Gevurah* (216), equal 288 (which is 2 times 12 squared). The number 288 is the sum of *nitzotzos* "fallen sparks" (from the primordial cataclysm of "the breaking of the vessels") which clutter all of the created reality. Through the "combined effort" of *Chesed* and *Gevurah*, not only to form reality, but also to rectify reality (through "the left arm repels while the right draws near"), these fallen sparks are redeemed and uplifted to unite with their ultimate source, bringing a *Tikkun* to the world according to the secret of *Mashiach's* arrival and the resurrection of the dead.

The spiritual state identified in *Chassidus* as corresponding to the *Sefirah* of *Gevurah* is that of *yirah* (fear). It is fear of *Hashem* that allows us to grow and come closer to our Creator through repentance.

Tiferes (Beauty) represents the merging of *Chesed* and *Gevurah*, thereby bringing harmony and mercy. *Tiferes* brings harmony, truth, compassion, and beauty. It's the balance of the powers of attraction and repulsion.

The *Sefirah* of *Tiferes* represents the harmonious blending of varying colors and forms, producing a world of great beauty. The word *Tiferes* is derived from the Hebrew word *pe'er*, meaning "beauty". The attribute of *Tiferes* balances *Chesed* and *Gevurah* so that a proper mixture of the two can bring a bearable exposure of *Chesed* to finite created beings. It is *Tiferes* that merges the benevolent flow of *Chesed* and the restrictive severity of *Gevurah* so that each creature will receive its proper measure of Divine Light and life-force.

Tiferes is sometimes called *rachamim* (Mercy) and other times *mishpat* (fair and proper Judgment). *Tiferes* is, therefore, merciful judgment; judgment tempered with mercy. However, mercy is only applicable after the eminence of judgment has concluded that the person is guilty. Through *Tiferes*, even though there was a guilty verdict, mercy discharges him. The role of a judge in a dispute is to adjudicate between contending parties and help them arrive at a peaceful settlement.

Just as *Chesed* is the feature of Avraham and *Gevurah* is the quality of Yitzchak, so is the mercy and beauty of *Tiferes* the quality of Yaakov.

Tiferes appears in the configuration of *Sefiros* along the middle axis, directly beneath *Da'as* (or beneath *Keser,* when *Da'as* is excluded), and corresponds in the *Tzelem Elokim* to the upper torso (in particular, the heart). We see that *Tiferes* is branching out to the right and left sides, receiving from the upper *Sefiros* and transferring their bounty into the lower levels. This blending is the true beauty of *Tiferes,* which is able to unite and harmonize different energies and channel them in a manner that brings beneficence to all.

Tiferes manifests the peace that results from unity despite divergent approaches. *Tiferes* also corresponds to Torah study. Similar to *Tiferes,* the Torah has many "branches". Like *Tiferes,* the Torah is bringing a person to know how to live life with balance and harmony.

Whereas *Chesed* is unrestrained loving-kindness and *Gevurah* is its constriction, allowing finite creatures to receive according to their abilities, *Netzach* and *Hod* are the two *Sefiros* which delineate capability of the recipient to receive. They also work together as the "joint distribution committee", which decides how, and in what measure, each recipient will collect its sustenance.

So, similar to *Chesed* and *Gevurah,* we have *Netzach* and *Hod* laboring together. The quality of *Yesod,* on the next level of the middle line, also acts as a mediator and combines the two opposing gut emotions of *Netzach* and *Hod.* These gut emotions are no longer heartfelt, but rather relate to action.

Netzach refers to actions of *Hashem* that are *Chesed* in essence but are presented with an overtone of harshness. *Hod* refers specifically to events where the wicked prosper. It is retribution - *Gevurah,* strength/restraint, in essence, but presented with an overtone of pleasantness.

These *Sefiros* mark a turning point in the structure of the order. Whereas the first two groups of *Sefiros* deal with *Hashem's* inherent will, and what it is that He desires to bestow upon man, these *Sefiros* are fixed on man: What is the most appropriate way for man to receive *Hashem's* message? How can *Hashem's* will be implemented in the best conceivable way?

Yesod represents the levers that tip the scales and resolves how *Netzach* and *Hod* will be put into action and in what proportion the action will take place. Each time a decision is made, it comes about by tilting the balance of the scales to one side or the other.

Netzach is opposite *Hod* in the configuration of the *Sefiros* along the right axis, directly beneath *Chesed,* and corresponds in the *tzelem Elokim* to the right leg. The biblical personality associated with *Netzach* is Moses.

Netzach is the *Sefirah* of victory, or of overcoming all obstacles. It is the primal desire to triumph and succeed. It is an extension of *Chesed,* and *Netzach* is the will to do something about the feeling from *Chesed* to move. It is able to now expand. This *Sefirah* is called Victory; when we embrace this determination to do something about our feeling to move forward, we are victorious. We are able to overcome whatever might block the way of our movement.

The spiritual state identified in *Chassidus* as corresponding to the *Sefirah* of *Netzach* is *bitachon* (confidence). With this confidence, we are actually able to do what is needed to move a new feeling forward.

Reb Moshe Steinerman

Hod (Majesty), is the quality of grandeur and splendor. *Hod* is persistence or holding on. It's the power to overcome obstacles and persevere; it's also the source of humility. The biblical personality associated with *Hod* is Aaron.

The function and meaning of *Netzach* and *Hod* is obscure. While *Netzach* may mean either eternity or victory, *Hod* means splendor or glory. The commentators are very chary on the functions of these two. See, Or Zakh, where it is held that these Spheres represent the source of all movement, i.e. the opposites heat and cold, rest and motion, etc. (Rabbi Aryeh Kaplan).

Hod is the *Sefirah* of glory and the extension of *Gevurah*. In *Gevurah* there is only the sense of moving away or limiting but, as in *Chesed*, there is no determination to manifest this sensation of moving away or limiting. *Hod* is the will or intent to do something about this emotion of moving away. The *Sefirah* is called glory because when we embrace our determination to do something about the urge to move away, to appropriately limit our own tendency toward expansiveness; it becomes possible for others to willingly receive what we might be giving. *Hod* functions on the pillar of contraction. In *Hod*, we are, in spirit, giving up our desire to fill up our world, leaving some of it accessible to others. This is the glory. *Hod* entails a sense of subservience to another's expansiveness.

Hod performs in the configuration of *Sefiros* along the left axis, directly beneath *Gevurah*, and corresponds in the *tzelem Elokim* to the left leg.

The spiritual state recognized in *Chassidus* as corresponding to the *Sefirah* of *Hod* is that of *temimus* (sincerity). A person can perform many actions and *mitzvos* without proper intention for the commandment itself. With *Hod*, a person performs tasks with honesty and heartfelt emotion.

The quality of *Yesod*, the next level of the middle line, acts as a mediator and combines the two opposite gut emotions of *Netzach* and *Hod*. The gut emotions are no longer heartfelt, but rather relate to action.

Yesod (Foundation), is the desire and ability to influence others. It is related to purity and foundational aspects of life. *Yesod* is the carrier from one thing or situation to another. It's the influence of joining and the capacity or will to build bridges, to make connections, and relate to others. The biblical personality associated with *Yesod* is Joseph Hatzaddik.

The male genital organ is called Foundation because just as the world is continuous by procreative activity, so do the Spheres give birth to *Malchus*, the Spheres, by the erotic mystery of male and female. Rebbe Nachman teaches that the *bris* and the mouth are connected. When a person sins with the *bris*, his speech is slurred or without contemplation. In reverse, when a person talks foolishly or improperly, this affects his guarding of the *bris*. "Suffer not thy mouth to bring thy flesh into guilt." (Eccl. 5:5)

When a person stands in the synagogue, the mouth is a wellspring from which prayer flows. By identification with *Yesod*, the source of the Fountain, the Fountain which is the synagogue is opened, and he corrects or repairs the *Shechinah* by the *Kavanos* which he puts into his prayer.

Yesod is the *Sefirah* of Foundation. It is the extension of *Netzach* and *Hod*. In

122

Netzach and *Hod*, there is the resolve to do something, but there is no binding of this willpower to an action by means of a plan. *Yesod* brings determination into an action. It is the connecting of resolving to an actual plan of action that brings balance. It is the determination to manifest balance of moving toward and moving away that forms a foundation to all of life's tasks.

Malchus (Kingdom), which corresponds to speech and action, is called *Malchus* because, for a king, speech is regarded as an action. What a king decrees with his mouth, must take place. *Malchus* represents the desire to rule over others. The biblical personality associated with *Malchus* is King David.

Malchus is the extension of *Yesod*. Having already figured out a clear plan of action, in *Malchus* the action is carried out. It is here in *Malchus* that the feelings of *Chesed* and *Gevurah* are finally manifested in physical reality by action and deed. It functions on the pillar of balance as similar to *Yesod* and is also represented in the middle line.

This *Sefirah* is considered passive - it shows our readiness to accept *Hashem's* rule and His blessings. We finally realize that we too must accept the reality of life and give back. Nothing will happen without our taking action ourselves, so therefore we no longer put off important tasks but rather do them.

There is a rule in Kabbalah that the lowest level of the upper realm becomes the highest level of the lower realm. This means that the *Malchus* of the upper world becomes the *Keter* of the lower world. For instance, the *Sefirah* of *Keter* is desire, and the *Sefirah* of *Malchus* is speech. We understand from this that the speech of the king becomes the inner motivating desire of the servant or that the speech of the teacher becomes the inner motivating desire of the student etc. Everything is a give and take. The world is systematically created to work in pairs, except the one Deity, *Hashem*. Likewise, the last level of *Adam Kadmon* (Primal Man) becomes the source of *Atzilus* (The World of Emanation). This is to say that *Malchus* of *Adam Kadmon* becomes the *Keter* of Atzilus.

Malchus is compared to the moon. Its light is only a reflected light of the sun just as our nation receives everything only from the Creator. Sometimes we see the moon's shiny surface, and sometimes none of its light reaches us. So, is the readiness of our nation to accept the light of the Creator varies throughout time. When *Mashiach* comes, *Chazal* teach us that the moon will be like the light of the sun. So too, the union between *Keter* and *Malchus* and all the *Sefiros* will be complete. Blessings will flow up and down without any intervention or blockage. *Malchus* is the concluding revelation of the Divine Light for which the entire process began; it was for the purpose of *Malchus* that all the *Sefiros* were emanated. Thus, *Malchus* is mutually the receiver and the consummation of giving.

Malchus is seen as a feminine principle. Our holy mother Rochel is very much attached to this aspect and she is bound up with the idea of the *Shechinah* and exile. "A voice is heard in Ramah, lamentation, bitter weeping, Rachel is weeping for her children; she will not be comforted for her children for they are absent." (Yermeyah 31:15) She is so firmly bound to the idea of *Malchus* and the *Shechinah*, the moon, that she takes to heart all of the sufferings of the Jewish nation and the broken sparks from the *Sefiros.*

When we look at the six days of the week, these are from the masculine side. These days have six directions which point outward. The *Shabbos,* on the other hand, is the feminine aspect similar to *Malchus* and this is the center point. This teaches us that when we look at ourselves in terms of our external relationships, we are looking at our masculine identity. When we look at our self, our inner core, we are looking at a feminine entity.

All week long in our struggle to gain spirituality, we are on a male level. On the *Shabbos,* we are on a female level because we can absorb the fruits of all we have done during the week. Thus, a person could work very hard spiritually all week long, but without the *Shabbos,* he would have no way of receiving it. This is because the *Shabbos* is like the final Heh of the *Tetragrammaton.* It is the hand that receives. Without the *Shabbos,* therefore, it is like cutting off a person's hand, preventing him from receiving spirituality. It is like working for something but never receiving it. This is why the *Shabbos* is of such importance in Judaism. (Inner Space, Chapter 9)

Shabbos is a time when the Worlds meet in unity. Blessing begins to flow from *Keter* to *Malchus* without as much hindrance as during the week. Sins are placed aside and there is no judgment on this day. Low souls are elevated and peace reigns in Heaven and Earth. It is this unity that we must strive to accomplish during the weekdays striving to encourage a perfect unity during the *Shabbos.* So, how do we do this; how do we elevate the weekdays into the aspect of harmony? We must bring the feminine influence inside the weekdays. This is done by connecting to the *Shechinah* and *Malchus* through *Shabbos* preparation. It is done through appreciating the *Shabbos* and utilizing every moment of this day for righteous acts and study, thereby causing the *Shabbos,* the center point, into all the other six directions and giving light to these days.

Malchus, being the lowest sphere, is the bringing of Heaven down to Earth. *Malchus* is the idea of *Hashem's* actions and attributes not expressed by *Hashem* Himself but rather by us human beings. It is *Hashem* who is watching how we fulfill his commandments at this point. It is as if *Hashem's* actions have struck a resonant chord in us, and we act in a similar manner, and this is the real beauty of *Malchus.* It is that we, *Hashem's* creatures attempt to emulate his ways, having learned from them.

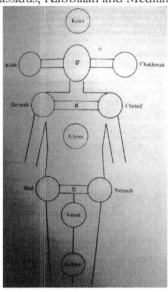

The archetypal man - *Adam Kadmon* - is described here. The Spheres are symbolized by the organs of man because of their abstruseness, the three highest Spheres are mentioned last. The right and left arms mingle to form the torso; Lovingkindness and Power mingle to form Beauty. From the torso extend the two thighs - Eternity and Splendor. The torso ends in the male genital organ, which is Foundation, for circumcision, the covenant between *Hashem* and man is the mystery upon which the existence of the world depends. The kingdom is the lowest of the Spheres, and the most manifest, and hence it is termed the Mount, which reveals the inner thought. It is also called the Oral Law, which expounds the hidden meanings of the Written Law. Crown is the first of all Spheres, and yet the last, for the Spheres are also conceived as the circle in which the first and last points merge. Furthermore, Kingdom in one world merges imperceptibly with Crown in the world below it, which is, as it were, its garment. (Aryeh Kaplan notes to Maamar Patah Eliyahu*)*

When a person sins, it is like throwing stones in a walkway; one must walk around them. Many stones or sins can eventually gather up to completely block the pathway for anything to get by. This is what has happened to us through sin; we have allowed only a narrow pathway in which light can shine and blessings can flow.

The connecting lines from *Yesod* to *Malchus* are thereby messed up and the finalizing of actuality can't take place. The *bris* becomes the main stumbling block of a person and, having no real foundation in life, there is no ability for *shefa*, blessings to be complete.

Can you imagine how many events must transpire for blessings to flow from all the *Sefiros,* only to be stuck between the last two ladders *(Yesod & Malchus)* because of sexual desires, which truly hold little fulfillment but are rather the final stumbling block to all good things ready to reach *Malchus?*

The *Shechinah* is also represented by *Malchus.* She is awaiting her due from Heaven and, for no legitimate reason, someone is piling up sandbags to block the light, and for what? A few hours of meaningless pleasure that has no structure or future?

The wayfarers are *Tiferes* and *Yesod,* for which man should provide a shelter in *Malchus.* These two are called Wayfarers by the Mystery of the Exile, for they are pilgrims seeking the Lost One. Hence, man must accommodate them. As the Zohar says, "'Ye that walks by the way, tell of it' (Judges 5:10); this virtue belongs to those who abandon the comforts of home for the sake of studying the Torah, for they cause the Supernal wayfarers to busy themselves with the needs of *Malchus.*" Further, whoever sets aside times for study of Torah causes *Tiferes* to dwell in *Malchus,* as the Tikuney Zohar makes clear. Now, these wayfarers must be provided food and drink and must be accompanied on their way. Man must, therefore, bring *Tiferes* and *Yesod* into *Malchus* and feed them there. This is symbolically referred to in the verse: "I have come into my garden, my sister my bride; I have gathered my myrrh and my spice; I have eaten my honeycomb with my honey." (Shir HaShirim 5:1) This refers to the Influence guiding the Lower Worlds, which expands from the side of the sweetened *Gevurah.* The wayfarers must also be given drink: "I have drunk my wine with my milk." (Ibid) This refers to the Internal Influence from the Treasured Wine and from the Mystery of the Sweetened Milk, which joins *Tiferes* with *Malchus,* Yaakov with Rochel, *Gevurah* with *Netzach* or *Hod,* as the *Raya Mehemna* explains. Finally, the host owes the wayfarers accompaniment. He should bring his very self and soul there to abide with them and accompany them into the Supernal Image. So, should he endeavor to bring the other *Sefiros* there to accompany them? (Tomer Devorah Chapter 5:58)

The idea of connecting to the *Shechinah* in exile is an important rectification for the *Shechinah* and the *Sefirah* of *Malchus.* Tomer Devorah says, "One should go into voluntary banishment, from place to place, for the sake of the Name of Heaven; and thus, he will become a chariot to the exiled *Shechinah.* Let him imagine: Here am I and my household; here are my instruments, but what shall the Supernal Glory do since the *Shechinah* has been exiled and its instruments are not with it, for they had to be left behind on account of the banishment? So, thinking, man will contract his vanity as much as he can, as it is written, 'Furnish thyself to go into captivity.'" (Jeremiah 46:19) His heart will become submissive in exile, and he will cleave to the *Torah*, and then the *Shechinah* will be with him. Hence one should constantly divorce himself from this house of rest, just as Rebbe Shimon and his associates used to do in order to engage in the study of the Torah. Of highest excellence is the practice of plodding from place to place afoot, without horse or wagon. Concerning those who practice this the Psalmist says, "Happy is he whose help is *Hashem* of Yaakov, whose hope (*sivro*) is *Hashem* his *Hashem*" (Tehillim 146:5); read not *sivro* (his hope) but *shivro* (his breaking), "Who breaks himself for the sake of *Hashem* his *Hashem*"; he breaks his body for the glory of the One on High. (Tomer Devorah, Chapter 9)

In the Zohar, section *Bereshis*, Rabbi Shimon gives a noble piece of advice based on the Torah, how man may attach himself to Supernal Holiness and conduct himself thereby, and thus never be separated from the Spheres. Man's conduct with respect to union with the Spheres is conditioned by time; that is, he ought to know which Sphere governs at a given moment and join himself to it by effecting reparations relative to the ruling Sphere. Let us begin with the night when a man goes to bed. At that time the ruling Force is *Lilah* (night), which is similar to death, and the Tree of Death reigns. What shall man do (to counteract these)? Let him make the proper preparation, allying himself with the Mystery of Holiness; that is, with the Quality of *Malchus* in its holy aspect. To do so, let him upon retiring accept the yoke of the Kingdom of Heaven completely and with full awareness of heart. At midnight let him arise and wash his hands from the Husks which then reign over them, remove the evil from his flesh and recite the appropriate benediction. Then he should repair and perfect the *Shechinah* by occupation with the *Torah*. Concerning such a one it is said, "When you lie down it shall watch over thee" -from the Externals-"and when you awake it shall talk with you." (Proverbs 6:22) She will join herself to him, and he to Her, and the image of his soul will ascend to Paradise together with the *Shechinah*, which enters with the righteous. The quality of *Tiferes* will also arrive to be entertained with him and the other righteous in Her company, for all hearken to his voice. Thus, man actually escapes from death, together with Her, and actually returns her to the Mystery of the Life Above, attached to the Mystery of Paradise! And the light of *Tiferes* which shines over the righteous in Paradise begins to shine over him. The Zohar continues to explain that a person should follow the nighttime Torah study with prayer at sunrise. This completes a great *Tikkun* for the *Shechinah*.

The *Sefiros* are referred to in a few ways. One is a ladder, another is circles, colors, names of *Hashem* and various *nekudos* with the Holy Name of *YKVK* Rav Moshe Cordevoro taught that *Keser* represents the blinding, invisible white color. *Chochmah* is seen as a color that includes all colors. *Binah* is yellow and green. *Chesed* shows in white and silver; *Gevurah* in red and gold. *Tiferes* has the colors of yellow and purple. *Netzach* is light pink, while *Hod* is dark pink. *Yesod* is seen as orange, while *Malchus* is blue.

These color schemes can be used in various meditations of the *Sefiros*.

Depicting the *Sefiros* as a circle or ladder can also help one reach higher levels of spirituality. Combining colors with the Tetragrammaton and their *nikud* is my personal favorite method. Then to add to this, the idea of the letters on fire and flashing as you imagine them, helps all the more.

Lesson: 23 The Incense; The Eleven Incense Spices

"You shall make an altar for bringing incense up in smoke; you shall make it out of acacia wood." (Ex. 30:1)

Chazal teaches us that any person who delves into [the learning about] *karbanos* (ritual sacrifices in the *Bais HaMikdash*) is considered as if he actually brought that sacrifice. Therefore, it is a good custom to recite [and understand the meaning of] the *parsha* of *karbanos* each morning before praying. It is also a good custom to recite the *parshiyos* of the *kiyor* (ritual water basin), *ketores* (ritual incense) and *terumas hadeshen* (ritual *mizbayach* ash shoveling) each day, along with the *parsha* of *karbanos*. (The *sefarim* bring in the name of the RiKanti (one of the *Rishonim*) that saying the above *parshiyos* is a *segulah* for a good memory.)

Ketores קטרת translates to mean incense. The word *Ketores* also means bonding or connecting. We learn about it from the *posuk* in Shemos, "And *Hashem* spoke unto Moses, saying, speak unto the children of Israel, that they bring me an offering: of every man who gives it willingly with his heart you shall take my offering. And this is the offering which you shall take of them: gold, and silver, and brass, And blue, and purple, and scarlet, and fine linen, and goats' hair, And rams' skins dyed red, and badgers' skins, and shittim wood, Oil for the light, spices for anointing oil, and for sweet incense, Onyx stones, and stones to be set in the ephod, and in the breastplate. And let them make me a sanctuary, that I may dwell in them." (Shemos 25:1)

The *ketores*, which was offered up twice daily, symbolized Israel's desire to serve *Hashem* in a pleasing way. It was offered once as part of the *Shacharis* (morning) service and once as part of the *Mincha / Musaf* (afternoon) service. This happened every weekday, including *Shabbos* and *Yom HaKippurim*. The *ketores* weighed five pounds and was burnt daily, half in the morning and half in the afternoon.

"And Aaron shall burn thereon sweet incense every morning: when he dresses the lamps, he shall burn incense upon it. And when Aaron lights the lamps at evening, he shall burn incense upon it, a perpetual incense before HaShem throughout your generations." (Shemos 30:7)

129

In our morning prayers, we read about the specifics of the *ketores*:

"It is You, *Hashem*, our G-d before Whom our forefathers burned the *ketores* in the time when the Holy Temple stood, as You commanded them through Moshe Your prophet, as is written in Your Torah:

"*Hashem* said to Moses: 'Take yourself spices - balsam, onychia, and galbanum spices and pure frankincense; they are all to be of equal weight. You are to make it into *ketores*, a spice compound, the handiwork of an expert spice-compounder, thoroughly mixed, pure and holy. You are to grind some of it finely and place some of it before the Testimony in the Tent of Appointment, where I shall time to meet you; it shall be a holy of holies for you.'" (Shemos 30:34-36, 7-8)

It is also written: "Aaron shall burn upon it the incense spices every morning; when he cleans the lamps, he is to burn it. And when Aaron ignites the lamps in the afternoon, he is to burn it, as continual incense before *Hashem* throughout your generations." (ibid.)

The sages taught: How is the incense mixture formulated? It consisted of three hundred sixty-eight maneh, corresponding to the days of the solar year. A *maneh* for each day, half in the morning and half in the afternoon; and three extra *manehs*, from which the *Kohen Gadol* would bring [into the Holy of Holies] on *Yom Hakippurim*. He would return them to the mortar on the day before *Yom Kippur* and grind them very thoroughly so that it would be exceptionally fine. Eleven kinds of spices were in it. The Torah does not provide the exact recipe for the *ketores*, the incense that was burned daily in the Temple. Only in the oral tradition do we find a detailed list of eleven ingredients:

(1) balsam

(2) onychia

(3) galbanum [chelbena]

(4) frankincense - each weighing seventy maneh

(5) myrrh

(6) cassia

(7) spikenard

(8) saffron - each weighing sixteen manehs

(9) costus - twelve manehs

(10) aromatic bark - three

(11) cinnamon - nine

Why doesn't the Torah explicitly list all of the ingredients of the Temple incense? Rav Kook explains that the *ketores* was a link between the material and spiritual realms. The word *ketores* stems from the root *kesher*, meaning a tie or knot. The incense rose in a straight column upwards. It was like a vertical band, connecting our divided physical world, our *alma d'peruda*, to the unified Divine realm.

From the elevated standpoint of overall holiness, it is difficult to distinguish between the distinct fragrances. Each fragrance signifies a particular quality; but at that elevated level, they are revealed only within the framework of absolute unity. It is only in our divided world that they acquire separate identities.

What is the significance of the various amounts of each ingredient that went into making the *ketores*?

Each of the major four fragrances explicitly mentioned in the Torah contributed seventy measures. Why seventy? The number seven indicates the natural universe, created in seven days. Seven thus corresponds to the framework of the physical universe - especially the boundaries of time, and the seven-day week.

Seventy is the number seven in tens. The number ten represents both plurality and unity, so seventy conveys the idea of unifying the multitude of forces in the natural world. This is the underlying message of the *ketores*. These holy fragrances illuminate and uplift the plurality of natural forces in the world. (Adapted from Olat Re'iyah Vol. I, pp. 136-138.)

Viewing the world from our superficial perspective, we disconnect from the true reality that everything is connected. It is unity that fixes everything. Here you had all types of spices; some make no sense that they would be mixed together, yet when they came together, they arose in a straight line to *shamayim*.

The family of Avtinas would elevate the other spices into a straight line through their *ma'aleh ashan* mixture. So too, the *tzaddik* has the ingredients we are missing to elevate our prayers to the heavens. Yet we too have something special to add to the flavors of elevation.

Hashem gave each of us a talent and something unique about our souls to share with the world. This ingredient and uniqueness that each of us has is similar to the *ma'aleh ashan* used in the Temple. When we do what we need to do and share it with the world, *ma'aleh ashan*, literally "that which causes smoke to rise," we raise up our souls and those around us in a straight line closer to *Hashem*... "But the wise men asked them: 'What is the reason that you do not share secrets of your profession; why won't you teach it to others?'

"They responded: 'Our fathers passed on a tradition to us, that one day the holy Temple will be destroyed. We did not want to teach our secret so that it does not fall into the wrong hands, the hands of idolators; and one day, the holy incense offering which we presented before the holy One would then be used for idolatry.' When the *rabbis* understood that this was the reason for their silence, the Avtinas family was greatly praised." (Yoma 38a)

Just as the family guarded its secret, so you too have something special and secretive about your soul. You too, must know when to share this with others and when to hide it. The Avtinas family understood the gift *Hashem* gave them; they used it at the appropriate times and otherwise guarded it.

Many of us are given a gift from *Hashem* and we put it aside, thinking we have other priorities, but we don't realize that in this gift could come all blessing and *parnasa*. Nothing we have been endowed with should be taken for granted.

Rabbi Akiva said, "Shimon ben Loga related the following to me: 'I was once collecting grasses, and I saw a child from the House of Avtinas. And I saw that he cried, and I saw that he laughed. I said to him, "My son, why did you cry?" He said, "Because of the glory of my Father's house that has decreased." I asked, "And why did you laugh?"

"Because the greatest honor is reserved and established for the righteous in the future world. And in the end result, the Holy One will gladden his descendants, may it be speedy."

"I asked the boy, 'what did you see that reminded of all this?' And he told me, 'As we were gathering, I saw the plant *ma'aleh ashan* in the field.'"

"'Show it to me!' I exclaimed. But he told me, 'We have a tradition never to show it to any man...'" (Shekalim 14a)

You see my friends, just as the child saw that the *maaleh ashan* was next to him, so too you must observe how simple your life has been laid out before your very eyes. I never understood even in my younger years why other teens didn't know what they wanted to do with their life. To me, it was already apparent at a young age. I planned to be in videos, computers, write books and be artistic. These were the things that I loved and obviously, I was going to do my utmost to make them a major part of my life. For some, it took many years before they came to fruition but in the end, looking back, I was able to recognize my personal *maaleh ashan* and talent.

We are told in the Zohar in BeRahamim LeHayyim that "There is a decree from *Hashem* that whoever reads and studies the matters of the incense offered in the Temple shall be protected from all the evils of the world and will in no way be harmed on that day."

When we recite the incense section, we count eleven spices with the fingers of the right hand. (Ben Ish Hai, Miketz 8) This counting denotes the importance that is attached to each of them and is an aid to concentration. These 11 spices counter the negativity of the ten *Sefiros* of the Other Side, plus the negative surrounding energy they might dismay. A hint to this is that the numerical value of the word for incense, *Ketores*, is 715, equal to 11 times that of the Name *A-D-N-Y*.

This holy Name has a judgment aspect, as alluded to in the letters of the word *din - Daled-Yud-Nun* - meaning judgment - embedded in the Name revealed above, *Alef-Daled-Nun-Yud*. Actually, the Aramaic word for law, *dina*, has an *Alef* at the end, giving it the exact same letters as the Name, *A-D-N-Y*.

Whether you accept the influence of incense as a *segula*/remedy or not, know: when the Jewish mystics sought to "clear the air" they read the incense section. This is why the above Zohar suggests reading it before you pray (though not at night when the incense is not offered). Once we remove the stain of negativity, our prayers can soar without faltering.

Chassidic teachings explain that the animal sacrifices offered in the holy Temple represent the person's offering of his own animal soul to *Hashem*--the subjugation of one's natural instincts and desires to the Divine will. This is the deeper significance of the foul odor emitted by the sacrifices, which the *ketores* came to dispel. The animal soul of man, which is the basic drive common to every living creature for self-preservation and self-enhancement, possesses many positive traits which can be directed toward gainful and holy ends; but it is also the source of many negative and destructive traits. When a person brings his animal self to the Temple of *Hashem* and offers what is best and finest in it upon the altar, there is still the foul odor - the selfishness, the brutality and the materiality of the animal in man - that accompanies the process. Hence the burning of the *ketores*, which possessed the unique capability to sublimate the evil odor of the animal soul within its heavenly fragrance.

The sublimation of evil is something that only the *ketores* can achieve, but this is not the sum of its purpose and function. The word *ketores* means "bonding"; the essence of the *ketores* is the pristine yearning of the soul of man to cleave to G-d. This is a yearning that emanates from the innermost sanctum of the soul, and is thus free of all constraints and restraints, of all that inhibits and limits us when we relate to something with the more external elements of our being.

"Its purity and perfection are what give the *ketores* the power to sweeten the foulest of odors, but dealing with evil is not what it is all about. On the contrary, its highest expression is in the utterly evil-free environment of the Holy of Holies on Yom Kippur." (Rabbi M. M. Schneerson; adapted by Yanki Tauber)

The *ketores* is a symbol for atonement, as it says, "And he (Aaron) put on incense [*ketores*]; and made an atonement for the people." (Bamidbar 16:47) It is through the incense and the idea of giving unconditionally back to our Creator that leads us to repentance.

In the days of the Temple, we were able to return to *Hashem* quite simply. If we did something wrong, we would connect to the incense and bring an offering, but the key to all the offerings in the Temple was much more than the simple offering. We see this from the idea mentioned by King David: "My sacrifice, O G-d, is a broken spirit; a broken and contrite heart you, *Hashem*, will not despise." (Tehillim 51:17) What need did *Hashem* have for fragrance and offerings? It wasn't this that was most important but rather our *teshuvah* and wanting to give back to our Father in Heaven that was meaningful.

The *ketores* is a symbol for our prayers, as it says, "Let my prayer be set before You as incense [*ketores*]." (Tehillim 141:2) You can see from this that if a person properly arranges his prayers, it is considered a replacement of the actual *ketores*. Heartfelt prayers are perfume and beautiful to *Hashem*.

I personally would meditate on the incense as if there was a large pot sitting before me, placed on a flame. One by one, I would imagine myself droping the incense into the pot and stir it. All the while, smoke would arise from the incense and go up to Heaven. I would meditate on this during the *ketores* prayer and even during regular prayers... all the while imaging my prayers rising along with the smoke. At times this meditation became so deep that I could even start to smell the beauty of mys own prayers going up to *shamayim*. (See Lesson 37) "Ointment and perfume [*ketores*] make the heart rejoice." (Proverbs 27:9)

The *Parshas Ketores* is often written by scribes on *klaf*, is kept in the *tallis* bag and read during prayers. It isn't required but here is its source: In Seder Hayom it says, "one who fears for himself and for his soul should put great effort into this matter, namely to write the entire text of the *ketores* (the composition of the incense) on *kosher* parchment in *ksav ashuris* (the script in which a *sefer* Torah is written), and he should read from this scroll daily, once in the morning and once in the evening with great concentration, and I guarantee [that this will help]."

The *ketores* is a *segulah* (a remedy) to eliminate epidemics, to save Israel from oppression by the nations, to bring a blessing to a person's work, to save him from the punishment of *Gehinom*, to ward off evil spirits, external forces, and "the other side", i.e. *Satan's* camp.

Reading of the *ketores* also breaks the spell of sorcery, eliminates evil thoughts, enables a person to inherit this world and the world to come, to free him from punishments, to grant him favor in the eyes of all who see him, and to grant him riches. (Ein Ma'avar Yabok)

The Zohar teaches that reciting the *Pitum haKetores* passages brings *berachos* (blessings) for livelihood, health, and peace, as well as atonement for some of the gravest sins and mistakes Jews can make.

The Kaf Hachaim says that the saying of *Pitum haKetores* from *ksav Ashuris*, the script of a Torah scroll, is a *segula* to merit wealth and the reader will be successful in business.

The *korbanos* are a vital component of the *Shacharis* service (O.C. 48:1) and it is only the *korbanos* that the *Shulchan Aruch* twice instructs us to recite. (O.C. 1:7-9) As such, there is no room to suggest that the recitation of *korbanot* is merely a custom or a meritorious practice. At the very least, one should recite the *Tamid*. (Shulchan Aruch Harav O.C. 48:1)

One who properly recites *korbanos* is regarded as one who had actually offered them in the *Beis Hamikdash* and all of one's sins are forgiven. (Ta'anis 27b, Menachos 110a, Aruch Hashulchan 48:1) Furthermore, it is taught that one who recites the entire *korbanos* section, including the accompanying *mishnayos*, assists in destroying the powers of impurity in the world. (Piskei Teshuvos 1: note 4) Hence, the recitation of the *ketores*, the incense component of the *korbanos*, is reputed to serve as a *segulah* for many blessings.

It is a matter of debate whether or not sacrifices will return in the Messianic era. (see Rambam, Moreh Nevuchim 3:46 and Ramban, Vayikra 1:9) It seems that the *halachic* literature supports the notion that *korbanos* will once again return (Rambam Melachim 11:1) while the *Midrashic* texts seem to suggest that there will be no animal sacrifices in the future. (Vayikra Rabba 9:7, Tanchuma Emor 19) Rav Kook was famous for his opinion that only grain sacrifices will be offered in the future. Although the future of *korbanos* is uncertain, what is certain is that a life of prayer and good deeds (Avos D'Rabbi Nosson 4:5, Sukka 49a) have the ability to accomplish everything that *korbanos* were able to and much more.

(Menachos 110a)

"'Of all the sacrifices you offer, there is none dearer to Me than *ketores* [incense],' said the Almighty." (Midrash Tanchuma) I think there is a lot to process in this statement. It would be wise that each person dwells on this thought and find his own personal connection to the *ketores*. Surely you must now have a new perspective of this prayer and its importance. May it bring you to a life of blessing and a better understanding of your existence.

We know that every person has an animalistic part to him [called in Kabbalah the *nefesh habehemis*]. When we bring an animal onto the *mizbeach*, it actually represents ME. I am sacrificing myself to *Hashem*.

It says, "'Master of the World, when the Holy Temple was around, if a person sinned he brought a sacrifice and was forgiven, but now that there is no Temple what will be with the sinners?!' The Holy One answered, 'I have already established for them all of the *Karbanos* prayers; whenever a person says them I consider it as if he brought a sacrifice before me and I forgive them for their sins.'" (Megilla 31b)

When a person recites the *Korbanos* they must imagine the *Beis Hamikdash* right before their eyes, as though it were there in reality. It is there! It was never burned down. It was not destroyed. The *Beis Hamikdash* is right in front of our eyes. The burning of the *Beis Hamikdash* was only an illusion. It was staged purely for the sake of the nations. As it says in Asarah Maamaros, that in the time of the *churban Beis Hamikdash*, *ruchos* and *sheidim* (demons, spirits) came and brought stones with them. "Burnt *avnei sid*," (stones of *sid*, in Hebrew, can be read *Sheid*); they brought burnt stones and planted them in the *Beis Hamikdash*, all for the sake of tricking the *goyim* so they would be satisfied (to think they had succeeded). The Zohar *hakadosh* says (Shemos, Pekudei, 240b) that the stones and foundation of the first and second *Beis Hamikdash* are all still there and shining, though they are hidden away. They have all been hidden. The *Beis Hamikdash* was not harmed in the slightest. Not even one stone was lost. Not one stone from the stones of *Yerushalayim* has been lost; not of *Yerushalayim* of the first *Beis Hamikdash* nor from *Yerushalayim* of the second *Beis Hamikdash*. Everything is in place. "For they will see the return of *Hashem* eye to eye..." (Yeshayahu 52:8-10) When the *Geula* takes place, all will see that the *goyim* never destroyed even one wall. The only thing the *goyim* destroyed was those stones brought by the *ruchos* and *sheidim*. Everyone will see that it was all just an illusion. This is why the Emek Hamelech says about the Gemarah, "I heard that *korbanos* are being offered even though there is no *Beis Mikdash*." (Megilla 10:1) He says, "Know this! The service of the *Korbanos* continues! The *Beis Hamikdash* exists! The *korbanos* exist! The service in the *Beis Hamikdash* continues. Eliyahu Hanavi sacrifices *korbanos* in the *Beis Hamikdash*. The *malach* Gavriel sacrifices *korbanos* in the *Beis Hamikdash*."

It is told about the Baal Shem Tov that he once saw Eliyahu Hanavi buying sheep for *avodas Beis Hamikdash*. When we say *Korbanos* in the morning, we are giving power to Eliyahu Hanavi and the *malach* Michael, who are currently the *kohanim hagedolim*, to continue their service in the *Beis Hamikdash*. By saying the

Korbanos we are literally taking part in the service of the *Beis Hamikdash*. As soon as we begin our *tefilla* in the morning the *kohanim* begin their service of offering *korbanos*. The *kohanim* begin their *avodah*! They light the *chatas* and the *tamid*. When we say *Korbanos* Eliyahu Hanavi and the *malach* Michael get their *koach* to continue their service with the *korbanos*.

When a person sins, he causes *tumah* (impurity) to spread. That *tumah* reaches the *even shtiya*. It goes right up to the *Beis Hamikdash*. Such impurity leads to the destruction of the *Beis Hamikdash*. This is why we say in the *Korbanos*, "And their blood required sprinkling between the staves, upon the veil and the Golden altar." The *tumah* reached all the way "between the staves"! Right up to the *paroches*! Finally, it burned the *Beis Hamikdash*.

"And their blood required sprinkling, upon the veil and the Golden altar." Why is there no *paroches*? Why is there no golden *mizbeach*? This is because we are continuing to defile the *Beis Hamikdash*. No sooner does the person sin than he has already defiled everything. There is no golden *mizbeach*, no *mizbach ha'olah*, and no *azaros*. Therefore, when a man recites the *Korbanos*, he must have the intention that he is saying *korbanos* for his own misdeeds. "Cows that are burning and goats that are burning..." I deserve to burn! I am those burning cows! The whole *inyan* (point) of the *korbanos* is in order to surrender the beastliness within ourselves. We burn the beast and *shecht* it. When we mention, in the *Korbanos*, the part about the *shechita* and the *sreifa*... it is I being burnt; I am being *shechted*.

The Baal Shem Tov explained this with the *pasuk*, "And he slaughtered him '*al yerech hamizbeach*', North, before *Hashem*..." (Vayikra 1:11) When we say, "and he slaughtered him," we must feel that it is we who are being slaughtered. The person is being *shechted* for all of his *aveiros* and he must accept upon himself the four *misos Beis Din* (high court penalties of death): *Skila, sreifa, hereg,* and *chenek*. When he intends this to be for himself, then all of his *aveiros* are forgiven.

Tana Dvei Eliyahu says, "Whether it be a Jew or whether a *goy* - even a *goy* who recites the *passuk*, 'and he slaughtered it on the Northern side of the *mizbeach*,' (with the proper *kavanah*), all of his sins will be forgiven." When you say, "*Hapshat Nituach, klil la'ishim*, skinning and dissecting completely for the fire", you must have in mind that everything is said about yourself! When the *Chatas* is set alight and the *Tamid* is being skinned – this is all happening to me! The *korbanos* of *Asham, Todah, Shelamim*, etc., it is all happening to me. When we say *Korbanos*, all of the *klipos* (shells) crack. The shells surrounding the *olam ha'Asiyah* crack and fall; everything is atoned. You must be sure to recite the *Korbanos* slowly and with a lot of *messirus nefesh* (self-sacrifice). When the person recites *Korbanos*, he is cracking apart the *kelipos* he has created! Just as in the time of the *Beis Hamikdash*, the *Tamid* offering in the morning atoned for the *aveiros* of nighttime and the *Tamid* of *bein ha'arbayim* atoned for the *aveiros* done throughout the day, so it is when a person recites the *Korbanos* of *Tamid* in *Shacharis*, it atones for his sins that he has done at night and then when he recites the part of the *Tamid bein ha'arbayim*, it atones for his sins that he has done in the daytime.

People sin twenty-four hours a day; we have countless sins! We should receive for these *aveiros, hereg, chenek, sreifa,* and *skila*. If a person does not try to recite the *tefilla* with *Kavanah*, he has achieved nothing. *Hashem* says, "What are you coming to Me for?!" You say, "Give me this and give me that," - first, do *teshuvah*! Ask forgiveness for everything you did wrong over the past twenty-four hours. You brought *tumaah* into the world. You had forbidden thoughts, saw forbidden sights... say *Korbanos* with *kavanah*! When you recite "*ba'parim hanisrafim*", (and the burnt cow offerings...) have the intentions of, "I am prepared to be burned, I am prepared to be stoned." The mere fact that you are accepting upon yourself *sreifa, hereg,* and *chenek,* the fact that you admit that you have sinned, makes everything atoned and forgiven and your prayers are accepted.

The morning *tefilla* begins with *Korbanos*. The Zohar says, "You must not skip *Korbanos*. *Korbanos* is the highest thing. The *Korbanos* come from *Atika kadisha,* from *risha dela esyada,* as it says, '*siluka dekorbana ad ein sof.*'" The *tefilla* of *Korbanos* is *ein sof* (endless). You must not skip even one word of *Korbanos;* don't give up on even one word.

Lesson 24: The Holiest of Combinations

When a person meditates through using a *yichud*, the souls of the righteous attach themselves to him and reveal themselves. At times a soul will do this because it comes from the same root as the person who is meditating. Sometimes, it is because the individual does some good deed that pertains particularly to that saint. The saint then appears to him through the mystery of nativity (*ibbur*). One such saint who reveals himself is Benaiah ben Yehoiada. He comes particularly when one meditates with a *yichud* that elevates the Feminine Waters, [involved with spiritual energy that ascends from below].

There were other saints who resembled him in this aspect. They included Moshe, Rabbi Chamnuna the Elder, Rabbi Yebi the Elder, and others like them. These sages were worthy of a very high level during their lifetime. Therefore, even after they passed on, whenever they see sages studying the Torah and meditating on higher *yichudim*, they join them and reveal themselves. Sometimes they are there but remain concealed, not revealing themselves. Such saints can bind themselves to a person even if they do not share the same Soul Root. The reason is that they bind together all universes, and therefore include them all.

These holy rabbis reveal the mysteries of the Torah to certain individuals. This helps you understand how Rabbi Hamnunah the Elder and Benaiah ben Yehoiada revealed themselves to Rabbi Eliezer [son of Rabbi Shimon] and Rabbi Abba, as mentioned in the Zohar. It also explains why the Elder said, "Whenever I find sages, I follow them."

When the soul of a sage reveals himself to an individual who shares the same Soul Root, then this individual achieves very great enlightenment. Even though they can also reveal themselves to one who does not share their Soul Root, the revelation is all the greater when they do share it, since they are then rectified.

If a person starts meditating with a particular *yichud* and then stops, he can cause himself great harm. "If he abandons it for one day, it will abandon him for two." The soul that wished to bind itself to him will then abandon him and repel him instead of drawing him near.

Do not say that the study of Torah is greater, and it is not fitting to neglect it [in order to meditate on *yichudim*.] For some *yichudim* are mentioned as more important than the study of Torah. Through them, one can unify the Supernal

Universes. This is considered to be a combination, including both Torah study and meditation.

Even if souls do not reveal themselves to you, do not be concerned and do not desist from meditating. Your intent should not be to bring souls to yourself, but rather to rectify the Supernal Universes. (Sha'ar Ruach HaKodesh, p.74)

I think one of the reasons people aren't successful in their meditation on holy Names and combinations is because they give up too early. They expect quick results and clear revelations. This could be because their intentions aren't completely pure. There are some combinations which could work instantly, while there are others that could take years of constant repetition before the person receives a revelation. It could also be that a person is making a slight mistake in his understanding of the meditation and therefore it isn't working properly. The other question is, what do you consider to be a working unification?

Is it one that suddenly gives you powers and superhuman abilities? A person has to constantly evaluate his intentions when it comes to the study and use of *kabbalah*. This isn't a game. It isn't supposed to be fun. It is about bringing *Tikunim* and fixing sparks; drawing closer to *Hashem* and purifying one's soul. Most people who enter into Kabbalah do so for the wrong reasons and, sad to say, some are even teaching over Kabbalah for personal benefit. More and more of the holy words of the Ari and Rabbi Shimon Bar Yochai are being distorted. There are so many mistakes being taught in Kabbalah, and its simple grace is being tampered with.

If you look at the Siddur Rashash for example, you will see pages and pages of combinations that at first glance make little sense. An elderly gentleman asked me how I could pray from such a difficult *siddur*, as he had been trying and failing. I explained to him that I too didn't understand much of the Kabbalistic combinations, but the key to grasping them is to see them very often over months and months of time. Eventually, your brain starts to decipher the codes and you slowly understand more and more.

So, when it comes to the Divine Names I am teaching here, they are meant differently for every person depending on their level. For some, knowledge of the existence of such holiness is enough. For others, an occasional meditation during prayers with some of the easier combinations is plenty. For a select few, these names will constantly appear before their eyes as they go about their day and night.

The recitation you are performing, a *mitzvah* in order to bring unity, can be done before prayer, eating, Torah study and other actions. As simple as this action sounds, it is quite a wonderful practice. It provides you with focus and clarity before you perform the commandments. When you occupy yourself in Torah study, even though according to *halacha* you do not have to make the blessing each time, since the morning blessing applies for the whole day, nevertheless, to remember to have *Hashem*-consciousness, say the following blessing each time before you study Torah, and again and again while studying: "For the sake of the unification of the Holy One, blessed be He, and His *Shechinah*. Blessed is the

Merciful One, the King of the Universe, who is *Hashem* of this Torah." (Ohr Ha-Ganuz l'Tzaddikim, p. 45)

It is very appropriate to say this and meditate upon it before performing any commandment.

לשם יחוד קודשא בריך הוא ושכינתה ליחדא שם י-ה בו-ה ביחודא שלים בשם כל ישראל

For the sake of the union of the Holy One, blessed be He, with His *Shechinah*, to unite the Name י-ה with ו-ה in a perfect unity, in the name of all Israel.

Reciting this reminds us that a *mitzvah* is something way beyond just a physical task. It is even far greater then just elevating our soul alone. A *mitzvah* elevates and rectifies the all the Upper Worlds. It brings an elevation to the *Shechinah* and draws the final redemption closer.

Amen

Every time in prayer, when we recite *Amen*, a declaration and affirmation, we are confirming and establishing that the Transcendent Source of all blessings is manifested in our own life, in real time, that there is absolute unity between *Hashem* and *Ado-noi*.

Amen = Gematria 91

The numerical value of the word *amen* is 91. *Alef*-1. *Mem*-40. *Nun*- 50=91. This corresponds to the two Names, *Havayah* and *ADNA*. *Hashem*- Yud-10, Hey-5 *Vav*-6 Hey 5= 26, and *Ado-noi*: Alef-1, Dalet-4. Nun-50. Yud-10= 65. 26+65=91. *amen* signifies the unity between beyond one's grasp, infinite, and the immediate finite; between the hidden and the revealed outer, between reality in a condition of perfection, and reality in a condition of imperfection. The recital of *Amen* forges this gap.

שִׁוִּיתִי יְ-הוָֹ-ה יאהדונהי לְנֶגְדִּי תָמִיד

This passage is good to meditate upon or to recite. If you recite it, you would say, "*Shivisi Hashem lenegdi samid*," in order not to say *Hashem's* Name in vain. What you are saying here is that you have placed *Hashem's* Name and Presence before you. You should have in mind that this should bring you to an increase in fear of *Hashem*.

This is the most common combination to meditate on. The name *ADNA* with *YKVK*. It is commonly seen in many prayer books and is very good to

contemplate during the daily prayer service. Once you're able to memorize this combination, you can begin to think of it naturally whenever you make a blessing or pray. Try to meditate on the meaning of *Ado-noi*, and when this Name is the vocalization of the Name, meditate on the meaning of both names, *Hashem* and *Ado-noi* being unified together.

These combinations of *Ekyeh*, *YKVK*, *ADNA* are commonly seen on the walls near the prayer leader in synagogues. I think it scares many since they only know it is some fearful holy Name without understanding them. These combinations actually reflect our entire purpose in performing *mitzvos*, and they bring rectification to the world. While not simple in the least, they are really not that difficult to meditate on with practice. In the Siddur Rashash, the top two *kavanos* are mediated upon while say the word *boruch*, during blessings.

Kavanos Rashash meditated upon while reciting *Hashem's* name in a blessing and the word *haohlam*. The mediation is drawing light from *Keter* down through all the *Sefiros*.

אֶהְיֶה

יְהֹוָה

אֶהְיֶה	אֶהְיֶה אֶהְיֶה	אֶהְיֶה		אֶהְיֶה
יְהֹוָה	יְהֹוָה יְהֹוָה	יְהֹוָה		יְהֹוָה
אֶהְיֶה	אֶהְיֶה אֶהְיֶה	אֶהְיֶה		אֶהְיֶה
יְהֹוָה	יְהֹוָה יְהֹוָה	יְהֹוָה		יְהֹוָה
אֶהְיֶה	אודהוויודהו אודהוויודהו	אודהוויודהו		אֶהְיֶה
יְהֹוָה	יודהוווהדהו יודהוווהדו			יְהֹוָה

Milui

Each letter of the Hebrew alphabet has a name and the name has a spelling. Many of the letters have two spellings and a few have three different spellings. For example, one spelling of the letter א is אלף. The *milui* (full form) of a word is obtained by writing out the spellings of the letters in that word. For example, one form for the *milui* of the word משה is מם שין הא. The *gematria* value of this *milui* is 446, which equals the numerical value of האמת, the truth. According to these values, Moshe is the truth.

Some of the names of the letters can be spelled several different ways. The following table shows all the various possibilities:

		ל			א
למיד	למד	ל	אליף	אלף	א
	מם	מ	בית	בת	ב
	נון	נ	גימל	גמל	ג
	סמך	ס	דלית	דלת	ד
עיין	עין	ע	הה	הי	הא	ה
פה	פי	פא	פ	ואו	ויו	וו	ו
	צדיק	צדי	צ	זיין	זין	זן	ז
	קוף	ק		חית	חת	ח
ריש	רש	ר		טית	טת	ט
שין	שן	ש		יוד		י
תאו	תיו	תו	ת		כף	כ

Using *miluim* as a form of meditative prayer has great benefits. One of the points of meditation is to draw closer to the root of all matter. Since everything in the world is created by names created from letters, it makes sense that the *Alef Beis* has great meditative powers. But to reach these strengths, you must draw closer to the letters root and purpose.

For me, this means that, while praying and reciting a word, at times I will spell out the word in order to draw closer to it. The Baal Shem Tov says that when you pray, you want to draw out the letters so as not to let them go. While he doesn't specifically mention using *miluim* to do so, I have found this of great benefit even when not meditating on Divine Names as well.

יוד הי ויו הי

יוד הי ואו הי

יוד הא ואו הא

יוד הה וו הה

This is the name *YKVK* permutation written out in the *milui* format. The top line is representing the *Sefirah* of *Atzilus* and is called *AB*, the name of seventy-two. Then the next line you have *Sag* which adds up to sixty-three and represents the *Sefirah* of *Beriyah*. Afterward, you have *Yetzirah* and the value of forty-five being *Mah*. Lastly, you have *Ben* totaling fifty-two and *Asiyah*. It can be thought about as drawing light from above downwards through the four Worlds, or you could think of it in a reverse way, from down to up, thereby climbing the ladder, starting with *Asiyah* as you draw closer and closer to *Hashem's* light. These four can also represent the *Sefiros* from top to bottom: *Chochmah*, then *Binah*, the six, and then the final *Malchus*.

א, אה, אהי, אהיה

א, אד, אדנ, אדני

This is another way of spelling out the letters and meditating on them. It is simple and is commonly used in meditative prayers.

א, אל, אלה, אלהי, אלהים

ש-ד-י   ש   ש-ד ש-ד-י   ש-ד-י
ש-י-ן ד-ל-ת י-ו-ד

מצפץ

This is the gematria of B-Rachamim. It is atbash YKVK.

חיצוניות המרכבה

א	כתר
ל	חב״ד
ה	חגתנה״יה
י	יסוד
ם	מלכות

The name *Elokim* can be seen as drawing blessings through the *Sefiros*. *Alef* being *Keter*, *Lamed*, *Chochmah* and *Binah*; *Hey* representing the five *Sefiros*: *Chesed*, *Gevurah*, *Tiferes*, *Netzach*, and *Hod*; *Yud* representing *Yesod*, and lastly *Mem*, *Malchus*.

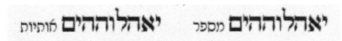

יאהלוההים אותיות יאהלוההים מספר יאהלוההים

This is a combination of *YKVK* and *Elokim*.

אלף הִי יוד הִי

אלף הָא יוד הָא

אלף הֵה יוד הֵה

Expansions of the Holy Name *EHYeH*		
ALEF- HEY- YUD- HEY	161 or "KSA" (i.e. "*Kuf Samech Alef*")	אלף ה-י יוד ה-י
ALEF- HEY- YUD- HEY	143 or "KMG"	אלף ה-א יוד ה-א
ALEF- HEY- YUD- HEY	151 or "KNA"	אלף ה-ה יוד ה-ה

The expansion of the name *Ekyeh* draws down light from the highest levels of *Atzilus / Beriyah* into the world of *Yetzirah* and then *Asiyah*. It reveals the inner mochin of *Zer Anpin*. Through this, you can receive more daas and expansion of the mind. You can draw down light unto the *Shechinah* and to your soul. It is a very holy combination.

Asiyah	א-נ-ד-י
	יה-ו-ה
	א-ה-י-ה
Yetzirah	א-נ-ד-י
	יה-ו-ה
	א-ה-י-ה
Beriyah	א-נ-ד-י
	יה-ו-ה
	א-ה-י-ה
Atzilus	א-נ-ד-י
	יה-ו-ה
	א-ה-י-ה

The lower soul (*Nefesh*) is from the universe of *Asiyah*, which is associated with the name *ADNA*. One should, therefore, meditate on the name *ADNA*, binding it to the name *YKVK* in the universe of *Asiyah*. He should then bind this to the name *Ekyeh* in the Universe of *Asiyah*.

He should then meditate on this, elevating the name *Ekyeh* of *Asiyah*, and bind it to *ADNA* of *Yetzirah*. *ADNA* of *Yetzirah* should then be bound to *YKVK* of *Yetzirah*.

One proceeds in this manner through the Universes of *Yetzirah*, *Beriyah* and *Atzilus*, step by step, until he reaches *Ekyeh* of *Atzilus*. He should then bind *Ekyeh* of *Atzilus* to the very highest level, which is the Infinite Being (*Ain Sof*). (Sha'ar Ruach HaKodesh, p. 29)

א-ל-ו-ה   א-ל-ף ל-מ-ד ו-י-ו ה-י

א-ל-ף ל-מ-ד ו-א-ו ה-י

א-ל-ף ל-מ-ד ו-א-ו ה-א

א-ל-ף ל-מ-ד ו-ו ה-ה

The Biala Rebbe *zt"l* taught that this name is the garment for the soul. It should be meditated on in the morning when one first awakens. I also included it in its expanded form for reference and further meditation.

י-ה-ו-ה א-ל-ה-י-נ-ו י-ה-ו-ה   כ-ו-ז-ו ב-מ-ו-כ-ס-ז כ-ו-ז-ו

The three words at the bottom of the *mezuzah* on the outer side of the parchment are "*Cuzu B'mucsz Cuzu*" - an altered form of the phrase "*Hashem Elokeinu Hashem*." It is actually a form of *gematria* (numerology) where each letter is "raised" to its next letter. Thus, an *Alef* becomes a *Bes*, and a *Bes* becomes *Gimel*, etc. Rav Moshe Isserlis quotes the Hagahos Maimoni as the source for this custom. It is only a custom - a *mezuzah* without these words is still considered valid.

A *Yichud* used by the Baal Shem Tov when he immersed in the *mikvah*:

When you enter the *mikvah* meditate on the name קנה *KNA*. *Kuf Nun Alef*. This is the *gematria* 151 (adding one for the word itself) and is the name *Ekyeh* expanded with *Hey's*. *Alef* - *Hey* - *Yud* – *Hey* אלף ה-ה יוד ה-ה.

This has a numerical value of 151, the same as that of *mikvah*. It is important that you contemplate that the physical *mikvah* in which you are immersing is actually the name *KNA*, through the sequence of spiritual descent. Immerse once and, while you are under water, meditate on the name *KNA*.

Now meditate on the name אגלא *AGLA*. This is the name that is related to strengths. It emanates from [the initial letters of the phrase in the *Amidah*], "You are strong for the world O' Hashem" (*Atah Gibor LeOhlam ADNA*). Immerse a second time and meditate on this name.

Then meditate on the name אלד *ALD* [which is the tenth triplet in the Name of Seventy-Two. This name can be read as *Eled*, meaning, "I will give birth," indicating that one is born anew when he emerges from the *mikvah*.]

Contemplate in the name אגלא *AGLA*: [the *Alef* has a value of one, while the *Gimel* has a value of three. Added together, these two letters have a value of four, the numerical value of *Daled*.] The *Alef* and *Gimel* of *AGLA*, therefore, combine to form the *Daled* of אלד *ALD*.

Immerse a third time and meditate on the name [אלד *ALD*] Then immerse a fourth time and, while you head is under water, meditate on the two names, אלד אלד *ALD*, and the expansion of *Ekyeh*, intertwining the two like this:

אלף-א-הה-ל-יוד-ד-הה *ALF-A-HH-L-YOD-D-HH*

Now, meditate on the subject of your prayer. Contemplate that it is inside this Name and is being attended to as you elevate it. Then immerse a fifth time, and meditate on the two names, *ALD* and the simple Name *Ekyeh*, intertwining the two like this: א-א-ה-ל-י-ד-ה *AA-HL-Y-DH*. Then meditate that you are elevating the subject of your prayer to the highest level of *Binah*-Understanding. Everything is then transformed into pure love and mercy. (Pri HaARetz, Lech Lecha, Keter Shem Tov 2)

A sage didn't need to utilize many *yichudim* to bring flows of *shefa* up and down. Rather, it was most important to choose a few which he would use regularly. With proper intentions, one doesn't need to be a great kabbalist in order to draw down *shefa*. Here is another *Yichud* from the Arizal:

Meditate on the name *Elokim*, with the letters spelled out [and the *Hey* spelled] with a *Yud*.

Alef Lamed Hey-Yod Mem מ-ם   י-ו-ד   ה-א   ל-מ-ד   א-ל-ף.

This has a numerical value of 300. This is the same as the numerical value of *MTz-PTz*, which is *YKVK* transformed by the *Atbash* cipher.

Meditate that *Malchus*-Kingship is called *Elokim* and includes the Thirteen Attributes of Mercy. These parallel the thirteen letters in the expansion of *Elokim*. The Thirteen Attributes are introduced with the Tetragrammaton [*YKVK*], as they are spelled out, "*YKVK, YKVK*, a merciful and loving Hashem..." (Shemos 34:6) The letters *YKVK* are then transformed into *MTz-PTz*. (Shaar Ruach HaKodesh, p. 29)

The prophets would meditate (*hitboded*) on the highest mysteries of the *Sefiros*, as well as on the Supernal Soul, which includes all attributes. They would depict these things in their mind with their imaginative faculty, visualizing them as if they were actually in front of them. When their soul became attached to the Supernal Soul, this vision would be increased and intensified. It would then be revealed automatically through a state where thought is utterly absent.

It was in this manner that the early saints would raise their thoughts, reaching the place from which their souls emanated. This was also the method of attaining prophecy. The prophet would meditate (*hitboded*), directing his heart to attach his mind on high. What the prophet would visualize would depend on the degree and means of his attachment. He would then gaze and know what would happen in the future. This is the meaning of the verse, "To Him shall you cleave." (Devarim 10:20) (Rabbi Menachem Recanati, Minchas Yehudah, on Maarekhes Elokus 10. Shaarey Kedusha part 4, p. 18a)

Rabbi Nachman took a cautionary stance about using Kabbalistic *kavanos* (Sichos ha-Ran 75). Not everyone is capable of engaging in the *kavanos*, nor is everyone meant to do so. Rabbi Nachman taught that the most important *kavanah* is sincerity. Whatever our level of knowledge and spiritual development, we should carry out our devotions with awareness of what we are saying and doing, the binding concentration of the heart to our words and actions. (Likkutei Moharan I, 49; Sichos ha-Ran 66, 75)

Lesson 25: The Angels / Malachim

When a person makes use of Divine Names, he causes great evil for himself. [Through these Names,] he binds angels by an oath, coercing them to do his will. These same angels then come and cause him to sin, destroying him completely. [Since he uses *Hashem's* name incorrectly,] they will cause him to take *Hashem's* Name in vain in other matters, such as blessings, since one sin brings on another.

How much more so, can this be if a person swears angels to do his wishes? Therefore, with trepidation, I reveal these secret names of angels because, unfortunately, people think themselves more prepared than they should be.

However, from another perspective, this too is the learning of Torah *shebal Peh,* the oral Torah. We all know angels exist, but we feel far from the concept of spiritual beings. Even the idea that we have a *neshamah* seems at times unrealistic because we can't see this soul of ours either. So, learning about *malachim* helps us to appreciate the concept of spirituality.

As you will see from the names taught here, and this is only a minute number of them, there are many types of angels and some of the names of them are quite amazing.

There are angels that are in charge of particular categories in creation, while there are smaller angels underneath them controlling a more particular species.

It is my understanding that the permissibility to meditate on angels is far more complicated. There are many who have tried and failed miserably. One requirement would be for a person not to fear angels, even in the slightest. But that would require a person to have complete control of his *Yetzer Hara* at all times. There are very few in our generation like this. In truth, the idea of fearing an angel is a kind of idolatry and thereby forbidden. However, if an angel was to reveal itself to you since you're not used to this type of revelation, you would lose consciousness. Therefore again, it would take tremendous training and preparation to use the names of angels in any way.

(Please be careful with this)

א-ג-ף נ-ג-ף ש-ג-ף   Sleep, prevent *keri*, overcome evil

א-י-ת-י-ל   Sleeping

Hebrew	English
ה-ר-י-א-ל	Animals
ה-ד-ר-נ-י-א-ל	Will of a person for good or bad
פ-ו-ר-ה	Forgetting
ל-ה-ק-י-א-ל	Love
ג-ב-ר-י	Love
ל-י-ל-ה	Pregnancy
מ-ל-ת-י-א-ל	Teacher of Eliyahu Hanavi
מ-י-ש-א-ל	Big angel in charge of animals
מ-ת-נ-י-א-ל	In charge of Knowledge
מ-פ-נ-ה-א-ל	Reptiles & insects
פ-ל-י-א-ל פ-ל-ט-י-א-ל	Teacher of Yaakov Avinu
מ-ק-ט-ו-נ-י-א-ל	Administrator of Rocks
מ-ש-ת-י-א-ל	Brings in Prayers / *Kefitzas ha-derekh* (Jump of the Road)
ס-מ-נ-י-א-ל	Creeping Animals
ס-נ-ר-י-א-ל	Swear *Yetzer Hara* if you understand wisdom
ס-ג-ל-י-א-ל	Administration of *Segulos*
ס-נ-י-י	Swear for enemies to be at peace with you.
פ-ל-פ-י-א-ל	Fruit Trees
פ-ר-ק-י-א-ל	Make someone invisible
צ-ד-ק-י-א-ל	Teacher of Moshe
ק-פ-ר-י-א-ל	In Charge of Love or Locus
ק-מ-ו-א-ל	Hatzlacha
ז-כ-ר-י-א-ל	Memory
ד-ל-ל-י-א-ל	Evil Eye, Fish & Animals
ה-ר-י-א-ל	Large Animals
א-פ-פ-א-ל	Dreams
ג-ב-ר-י-א-ל	Gives power to break through a wall
ג-ז-ד-י-א-ל	Fear & Trembling

151

Two *Malachim* that go with a person

כ-לר י-והך

ס-נ-ד-ד-ל-פ-ו-ן   Asiyah

מ-ט-ט-ר-ו-ן   Yetzirah

א-כ-ת-ר-י-א-ל   Beriyah

The angels were created with a mission to perform. Outside of that mission, they have no other task. Their life is a simple one. They are not bound by a physical body to rectify. Angels neither eat nor sleep. Some are created for but a moment and cease to exist, while others have longer term posts.

Our Sages teach that there are four angels who symbolically accompany man and protect him: Michael on a person's right, Gabriel on his left, Uriel in front of him, and Rafael from behind.

Michael, "*Mi Cael* - who is like the merciful G-d?" is the representative of the attribute of mercy. Gabriel - "my strength is G-d"- represents the attribute of power and judgment; they are therefore on the right and left respectively. Uriel - "my light is G-d," symbolizes the attribute of knowledge by which man wishes to distinguish what lies ahead and how to act accordingly; thus, Uriel "stands before" a man to show him the way. Rafael - "my healer is G-d" - is the attribute by which G-d heals any illness which befalls a person; that is why he "stands behind" man.

The highest type of angels exists in the universe of *Beriyah*. Some Kabbalists refer to them as *kochos*, rather than angels. The prophet consequently said, "I saw *Hashem* sitting on a high and exalted throne... *serafim* stood around Him." (Isaiah 6: 1-2) The prophet Isaiah was visualizing *Beriyah*, the world of the throne, and he saw the *serafim*, the angels of that universe. (See Malbim of Ezekiel 1:1)

When we recite *Kedushah* in the repetition of the *Amidah*, we say *kadosh* (holy) three times. This is a reference to the angels of *Beriyah*, *Yetzirah*, and *Asiyah*, all of whom pay homage to *Hashem* in their different ways.

The word *serafim* comes from the root *saraf* which means to burn. They are called by this name because they are in the world of *Beriyah*, where *Binah*, which is represented by fire, is dominant. (Pardes Rimonim 23:22)

The *chayos* are the angels of *Yetzirah*, and these were the beings envisioned by Ezekiel. He consequently said, "Above the firmament that was over the heads [of the *chayos*] was the likeness of a Throne..." (Ezekiel 1:26) Finally, the *ophanim* are the angels of *Asiyah*. These were therefore seen below the *chayos*, as the prophet said, "There was an *ophan* on the earth near the *chayos*." (Ezekiel 1:15)

In Ezekiel's vision, the *chayos* of *Yetzirah* represent the vehicle - the *Merkavah* - through which *Hashem* reveals Himself in the world. These *chayos*, in turn, are the interface between the higher levels of *Atzilus* and *Beriyah*, on one hand, and the *ophanim* of *Asiyah* on the other. Actually, it is for this reason that some Kabbalistic sources identify the *ophanim* with the astronomical bodies of *Asiyah*, while the *chayos* are placed above these. Ezekiel thus emphasizes a number of times that the *ruach*, spirit, of the *chayos* was in the *ophanim*. What Ezekiel is telling us is that each subsequent level of the spiritual domain is a vehicle for the one above it. This is true all the way up to the highest spiritual levels and beyond. Ultimately, however, it is up to man to reveal *Hashem's* immanence in every universe and the Kabbalistic tradition contained in Ezekiel's vision is a key factor in this. (Inner Space, Rabbi Aryeh Kaplan p. 182)

The Talmud states that "Every word emanating from G-d creates an angel." (Chagigah 14a; see Moreh Nevuchim 2:6) This means that every one of G-d's words is actually an angel. When we speak of "G-d's word", we are actually speaking of His communication with the lower worlds. (Inner Space page 31)

The stars in the sky also form a vital link in G-d's Providence over the physical world. Between G-d and man, there are many stages of interaction, the lowest being those of the angels and the stars. The Midrash and Zohar state, "There is no blade of grass that does not have a constellation, *mazal*, over it, *ha-makeh bo*, telling it to grow." This means that G-d's providence works through the angels, but these angels in turn work through the stars and planets. In a sense, we could tell that the angels are like souls to the stars.

Rabbi Simon said, "There is not a single blade of grass that does not have its *mazal*, a constellation of stars and/or angel, in the heavens that strikes it and says to it 'Grow!' As it is written: 'Do you know the ordinances of Heaven? Can you establish its rule (*mishtaro*) over the earth?'" (Job 38:33). The term for rule, *mishtaro*, is from the root *shoter*, signifying a police officer who gives blows to enforce the law [alluding to the "striking" of the plant by the *mazal*]. The passage continues: "Can you bind the chains of the stars of the Pleiades or loosen the bands of Orion?" (ibid. v.31) The Pleiades ripen the fruits and give them flavor, while Orion lengthens the stalks of the plants to allow the fruits to grow. "Can you lead forth the *mazaros* in their season? Or can you guide the bear with her sons?" (ibid. v.32) This is referring to the constellation that sends winds to blow over the plants and cleanse them of their wastes. (Midrash Rabbah Bereshis 10:6)

According to the Midrash, each plant has its own *mazal* that strikes it and says "Grow!" The term *mazal* alludes to both a constellation of stars and an angel, for the two are interrelated. The physical energy, the light that "strikes" the plant and makes it grow, derives from the physical star, the sun, etc. But this physical energy stems from and is channeled by a spiritual power source, an angel or form (*tzura*) that oversees the physical process through a formula of words, "and says, Grow!"

Everything in the physical world has a counterpart among the transcendental forces. Every entity and process in the physical world is carefully linked to these upper forces as decreed by G-d's wisdom. These forces are therefore the roots of all physical things, and everything in the physical world is a branch and result of these systematic forces created by *Hashem*. The two are thus intertwined, similar to links in a chain. Every physical entity and process is under the charge of some form of an angel. These angels have the responsibility of maintaining each physical entity, as well as bringing about changes within them according to G-d's decree. This could be through shining light upon them or nurturing them in some other way. How great it must be to serve *Hashem* in absolute simplicity. The angels and, in fact, all of the creation are simply servants of *Hashem* to carry out His will.

In fact, the Midrash discusses different opinions as to which day of creation the angels were made. Some say on the second day and others say on the fifth day. Since all opinions seem correct, we must say that they refer to different groups of angels, all of which have diverse functions. Some angels were created on a daily basis and others on a permanent basis, with fixed names, e.g. Michael, Gabriel, etc.

One of the more important factors in astrology is the time and date of a person's birth. The Talmud states that there is a "*mazal* of the hour". The time, day and date when a person is born have a significant influence on his destiny. The Zohar teaches that every star in the universe has a name. The Talmud explains that there is an angel called *Layla* who oversees birth. This angel proclaims if the individual is destined to be strong or weak, wise or foolish, rich or poor.

Every single plant obtains its powers from its own particular planet or star. Every planet and star receive's its power from the stars overhead and the highest stars from the higher powers, until they receive power from the supreme angels, as we are taught. (Tikkuney Zohar #44, #79b) "All the stars borrow one from another: the moon borrows from the sun, etc., for one higher than the high guards, and above them are those who are even higher." (Ecclesiastes 5:7) All of the stars borrow one from the next, until they receive and borrow from the supreme angels, and the angels receive from the influences beyond them, one higher than the other, until they all receive from the root of all things, which is the word of G-d, as it is written, "Through the word of G-d the heavens were prepared and all their hosts by the breath of His mouth." (Tehillim 33:6). (Likutey Moharan II, 1)

Rebbe Nachman told one of his students, as they walked through a grassy meadow early one summer morning: "If only you could hear the song of this grass! Each blade is singing out to G-d for no ulterior motive, not expecting any reward. It is most amazing to hear their song and serve G-d amongst them." (Rabbi Nachman's Wisdom #163)

In the winter all plants "sleep" and appear dead. Their strength is weakened, and they are like the dead. But when the summer comes, they awaken and return to life. As it says: "And Isaac went out to meditate in the field." (Genesis 24:63) The Talmud teaches us that this meditation was none other than a prayer. When summer starts to approach it is very good to meditate in the fields. This is a time when you can pray to G-d with longing and yearning. The Hebrew word for meditation and prayer is *sichah*. The Hebrew word for a bush of the field is *siach*. When every bush (*siach*) of the field begins to return to life and grow, they all yearn to be included in prayer and meditation (*sichah*). (Rabbi Nachman's Wisdom #98)

In the words of Rebbe Nachman: "Go to a grassy field, for the grass will awaken your heart." (Rabbi Nachman's Wisdom #227)

All the grasses and herbs enter into his prayers and assist him, and put strength into his prayers.

Conversely, among the curses is, "The land will not give its produce (*yevul*)." (Devarim 11:17). For all the produce of the earth is supposed to put influence and strength into our prayers to help them. When this power and strength fail to enter our prayers for some reason, this is the negative situation expressed in the curse: the land does not give its produce. Even when a person is not actually praying in a field, the produce of the land still puts power into his prayers and helps them. For all the food and drink and other things a person consumes, all of which are "the produce of the land", also put power into his prayer.

The difference is that when the person is actually on the field, he is very close indeed to the plants, and then all the grasses, herbs and other "produce of the land" put power and strength directly into his prayer. The Hebrew letters of the word *yevul* (produce) are the initial letters of the Hebrew words making up the verse, "And Isaac went out to meditate in the field." (Genesis 24:63) This indicates that all the plants and produce of the field prayed with him.

The angel, then, receives power from the creative word of G-d that brought it into being, and it then hands on this power to the physical entity over which it rules.

Man has a power that goes above that of the angels. For when a man uses his G-d-given faculty of speech in prayer, he manipulates the letters of creation. Then man's own words themselves become the word of G-d, bringing blessing and influence into all creation. (Likutey Moharan II:11)

It is interesting to note that the angels have their own form of writing the *aleph beis*. Some *malachim* write in a different style than others. There is something about their script that makes me uneasy. As a *sofer*, I have written the script before for various reasons, and I only felt regret thereafter. Therefore, I share it with you only as a tool of knowledge, and nothing more, as I fear for your souls.

Lesson 26: Astrology and Mazal

Influence astrologically as we understand it, extends only from the visible members of our solar system. The planets that are set off at a distance, such as Uranus, Neptune, and Pluto, which are invisible to the unaided eye, are not considered to have any significant astrological influence. The influence of the planets in the system does not depend on their position in the sky, but rather on the hour of the day.

In order of their distance from Earth, the planets are Saturn, Jupiter, Mars, Sun, Venus, Mercury, and the moon. Saturn is furthest from the earth while the moon the closest. In Genesis, it says that the stars and the planets were made on the fourth day of creation. Counting from Sunday, this means they were made on Wednesday. The Torah teaches us that night always precedes the day. Therefore, the planets were positioned in their places on the eve of the fourth day, i.e. on Tuesday night. They were placed one by one, an hour apart in order of their distance from the earth. Thus, in the first hour 6 p.m., Saturn was placed in position. During the second hour, 7 p.m., Jupiter was placed in position; Mars 8 p.m., Sun 9 p.m., Venus 10 p.m., Mercury 11 p.m., Moon 12 p.m. Each planet then dominated the hour in which it was positioned and assigned. Following the first seven hours, their dominance began a new cycle, with the planets in the same order. This seven-hour cycle continues through the week, and it is the same every week. One immediately understands following this order that the first hour of each evening is dominated by a different planet. Sunday-Mercury, Monday-Jupiter, Tuesday-Venus, Wednesday-Saturn, Thursday-Sun, Friday-Moon, Saturday-Mars. In the same way, the first hour of each day is dominated by each planet as follows; Sunday-Sun, Monday-Moon, Tuesday-Mars, Wednesday-Mercury, Thursday-Jupiter, Friday-Venus, Saturday-Saturn.

From this, we see that the Divine influence and flow comes from the angels through the stars to earth. We may also now understand why in the days of Enosh they felt they needed to worship the stars. Although the star worshippers knew about *Hashem*, they figured that *Hashem* is far beyond the trivia of this vain world and they would do better by serving the underling stars.

Avraham was a tremendous astrologer and he saw in the stars that he was not destined to have children. *Hashem* seized him "out of the stars", and He told him not to be dependent on astrological calculations. He said that it was true that

Avram and Sarai would not have children but Avraham and Sarah, with the added letters *Hey* in their names, would have children.

Each month of the year is designated by another spelling of the *Tetragrammaton*. There are twelve possible permutations of the *Tetragrammaton*. Each one connects us to the inner purpose of each month of the year and assists us to bring down *Hashem's* transcendental and supernatural light into our lives. When we say the Blessing of the Month (*Birkas Hachodesh*) and the Blessing of the Moon (*Birkas HaLevannah*) we should keep in mind one of these permutations.

נִיסָן	חסד גולגתא דעיק	יְהֹוָה אֱהֹיָה	לשמח השמים ותגל הארץ
אִייָר	גבורה און ימין דעיק	יְהֹיָ אֲהֹיָ	לתהל המתהלל השכל וירוע
סִיוָן	ת"ת און שמאל דעיק	יוֹהָה אֵיָהֹ	לרוחו ורצעו השמן השית
תַמוז	נצח עין ימין דעיק	הֹוֹיָ הֹוִֹא	וה אונך שוה יל
אָב	הוד עין שמאל דעיק	הֹוֹיָ הֹאֹה	הבת ושמע לישראל הלוס
אֱלוּל	יסוד חושמא דעיק	הֹֹיָ הֹֹיָא	וצדקה תהלה מן כל
תִשְרֵי	חסד גולגתא חי"א	וְהֹיָה יְדֹאֹה	ויראל אותה של פרעה
חֶשְוָן	גבורה און ימין חי"א	וְהֹיָ יְהֹדֹא	ודש הים הוה לוה
כִסְלֵו	ת"ת און שמאל דו"א	וָיְהֹד יֹאֹהֹה	וירא ושב הארץ המנעמ
טֵבֵת	נצח עין ימין חי"א	הֹיֹדֹו הֹאֹהֹי	ליהוה אחל ונרוממה שמו
שֵבָט	הוד עין שמאל דו"א	הֹיֹוֹד הֹאֹיֹה	הכר למירנו להוה הלא
אֲדָר	יסוד חושמא דו"א	הֹיֹדֹו הֹאֹיֹ	עירה ולשורקה כל אתונ

It must also be noted that, although Divine flow comes through the angels and the stars, one must in no way worship the stars or depend on their horoscopes. The Torah tells us, "There shall not be found among you one who calculates times." (Devarim 18:10) Rabbi Akiva clarifies that this prohibition applies to one who calculates auspicious times, meaning that one should not make astrology a dominant influence in one's daily life, and predictions through astrology are forbidden. Therefore, one should not use horoscopes to determine one's future actions. It is however permitted to make character analyses through astrology. It is the prevalent custom that, on a happy occasion such as a birth, one wishes *mazal tov*, indicating the wish that the planetary influence on the child should be a good one. Therefore, as much as we do not utilize or calculate the *mazalos*, we do recognize their significance in the order of the world.

The Torah also states, "You shall be perfect with the L-rd your G-d." (Devarim 18:13) This means that the more we perfect our relationship with *Hashem*, growing in *middos*, *teshuvah*, Torah, *mitzvos* and prayer, the more G-d is going to reciprocate for us by changing the natural course of events, thus making any action based on astrological predictions superfluous.

It is written: "And the hosts of Heaven bow to You." (Nehemiah 9:6)

Reb Moshe Steinerman

Lesson 27: AlphaBeis Gematrias / *Atbash*

Gematrias

If you look into Sefer Yetzirah, one of the most Kabbalistic works in our possession, you will see that G-d actually made creation using the *Alef Beis*. Just as everything in the physical world, as wide and infinitely varied as it is, is only the result of different combinations of molecules, so too is the physical world just the result of different combinations of letters from the *Alef Beis*, as conceptually difficult as that is to imagine.

In the Hebrew language in which the Torah is written, there are no numbers. Instead, each letter possesses a numerical value (*Alef* = one, *Beis* = two, *Gimel* = three, etc.). The mystical tradition of *gematria* is the calculation of numerical equivalence of letters, words, or phrases, in the belief that words or phrases with identical numerical values, bears some relation to each other or bear some relation to the number itself as it may apply to a person's age, the calendar year, or the like.

In the Kabbalistic tradition, we find additional types of *gematria* which are used to gain even deeper insight into the nature and essence of words and concepts and their interrelation with each other.

In rare cases, certain letters of the Torah are written larger than others, four times as large to be exact. According to the Chasam Sofer, the *gematria* of those letters is also four times what it would normally be. With this is mind, we visit the large *Beis* of *Breisheis* - the first letter of the Torah, and the large *Ayin* and *Daled* of *Shema Yisrael* - to gain deeper insights into these key passages.

Thus, the Talmud even explains each letter of the *Alef Beis* in terms of the concept it represents (Shabbos 104a), even why certain letters were placed side-by-side. Kabbalah goes even further to show how the letters themselves are composites of other letters, except for the letter *Yud*. The letter *Alef* is composed of two *Yuds* and a *Vav*. Since each letter of the *Alef Beis* has a pre-assigned numerical value (*gematria*), and *Yud* equals 10 and *Vav* equal 6, the total numerical value of the letter *Alef* would be 10+10+6, or 26, the *gematria* of the Four-Letter Ineffable Name of G-d.

158

As a word, *Alef* is like the word *aluph*, which means chief, and its own *gematria* is one, and therefore alludes to THE One, the Chief of all chiefs, G-d Himself. This is why many Torah works, such as the Babylonian Talmud, do not begin with Page *Alef* (Page 1), but Page *Bais* (Page 2) instead, in deference to G-d. In fact, even the four-letter Name of G-d, when expanded (for example, the letter *Yud* is spelled *Yud-Vav-Daled*), results in different numerical totals, each one representing a different level of revelation of G-d's light, and these, the Names of G-d, are actually the true building blocks of all creation, including molecules.

The relationship between words or phrases that have the same *gematria* is one of the ways of expounding Torah. The source for this is found in the verse Devarim 32:47.

It is not an empty thing from you, for this is your life. כי לא דבר רק הוא מכם כי הוא חייכם.

Rabbi Jacob Ben Asher, commonly known as The Baal HaTurim, and Rabbi Aharon Rokeach, commonly known as the Rokeach, both point out that the numerical value of the first part of the verse כי לא דבר רק הוא מכם is 679. The *gematria* of *gematrios*, גימטריאות, the plural of *gematria*, is also 679.

What does this *gematria* equivalence mean? The Sages tell us that there is no superfluous word in Torah. Every word and every letter have meaning. The first part of the verse uses the word דבר which was translated as "thing", but דבר also means word. Thus, כי לא דבר רק הוא מכם literally means "for there are no empty words from you." From your mouth should come no empty words of Torah. Every letter has meaning. Words which have the same *gematria* will give you hints about the fullness of Torah.

There are many different methods to decipher the hidden *gematrias* and secrets of words. Here are some of these methods:

❖ **מספר הכרחי** *Mispar Hechrachi (Mispar ha-Panim,* **absolute, standard, normative value)** is the most commonly used method of calculating *gematria* where each of the 22 letters is assigned a basic value.

ת	ש	ר	ק	צ	פ	ע	ס	נ	מ	ל	כ	י	ט	ח	ז	ו	ה	ד	ג	ב	א
400	300	200	100	90	80	70	60	50	40	30	20	10	9	8	7	6	5	4	3	2	1

❖ **מספר גדול** *Mispar Gadol* **(large value)** is similar to the standard method, but final (*sofit*) letters are counted as a continuation of the alphabet and are valued from 500 to 900 instead of being included as the regular letter.

159

ת	ש	ר	ק	ץ	צ	ף	פ	ע	ס	ן	נ	ם	מ	ל	ך	כ	י	ט	ח	ז	ו	ה	ד	ג	ב	א
400	300	200	100	900	90	800	80	70	60	700	50	600	40	30	500	20	10	9	8	7	6	5	4	3	2	1

❖ **מספר סידורי** *Mispar Siduri* (ordinal value) assigns each letter a number ranging from 1 to 22 in the order of the alphabet.

ת	ש	ר	ק	צ	פ	ע	ס	נ	מ	ל	כ	י	ט	ח	ז	ו	ה	ד	ג	ב	א
22	21	20	19	18	17	16	15	14	13	12	11	10	9	8	7	6	5	4	3	2	1

❖ **מספר קטן** *Mispar Katan (Mispar Meugal,* **reduced value)** is the value of the letters but without the zeros after large numbers. (ex. *Lamed* is 3 instead of 30, *Shin* is 3 instead of 300).

ת	ש	ר	ק	צ	פ	ע	ס	נ	מ	ל	כ	י	ט	ח	ז	ו	ה	ד	ג	ב	א
4	3	2	1	9	8	7	6	5	4	3	2	1	9	8	7	6	5	4	3	2	1

❖ **מספר הפרטי** *Mispar Perati (Mispar HaMerubah HaPerati)* assigns each letter its standard value as a squared number. (ex. *Aleph* = 1 x 1 = 1, *Gimel* = 3 x 3 = 9).

ת	ש	ר	ק	צ	פ	ע	ס	נ	מ	ל	כ	י	ט	ח	ז	ו	ה	ד	ג	ב	א
16000	90000	40000	10000	8100	6400	4900	3600	2500	1600	900	400	100	81	64	49	36	25	16	9	4	1

❖ **מספר שמי\מילוי** *Mispar Shemi (Milui,* **full name value)** values each letter as the value of the letter's name. (ex. *Aleph* = 1 + 30 + 80 = 111). However, there is more than one way to spell each letter.

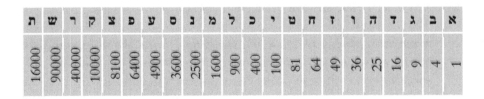

ת	ש	ר	ק	צ	פ	ע	ס	נ	מ	ל	כ	י	ט	ח	ז	ו	ה	ד	ג	ב	א
406	360	510	186	104	81	130	120	106	80	74	100	20	419	418	77	22	6	434	73	412	111

❖ מספר מוסף *Mispar Musafi* adds the number of letters in the word or phrase to the value.

❖ אתב״ש *AtBash* exchanges each letter's value for its opposite letter's value. (ex. *Aleph* switches values with *Taf*, *Daled* switches values with *Kuf*).

❖ אלב״ם *AlBam* splits the alphabet in half and letters from the first half switch values with letters from the second half. (ex. *Aleph* switches values with *Lamed*, *Vav* switches values with *Pey*).

❖ מספר בונה *Mispar Bone'eh* (building value) does exactly as the name describes. It adds the value of all previous letters in the word to the value of the current letter as the word is calculated. (ex. *echad* is $1 + (1 + 8) + (1 + 8 + 4) = 23$).

❖ מספר קדמי *Mispar Kidmi* (also called *Mispar Meshulash*, triangular value) adds the value of all preceding letters in the alphabet to each letter's value. (ex. *Aleph* = 1, *Beis* = 1 + 2 = 3, *Gimmel* = 1 + 2 + 3 = 6).

ת	ש	ר	ק	צ	פ	ע	ס	נ	מ	ל	כ	י	ט	ח	ז	ו	ה	ד	ג	ב	א
1495	1095	795	595	495	405	325	255	195	145	105	75	55	45	36	28	21	15	10	6	3	1

❖ מספר נעלם *Mispar Ne'elam* (hidden value) values each letter as the value of the letter's name excluding the letter itself. (ex. *Aleph* = 30 + 80 = 110).

ת	ש	ר	ק	צ	פ	ע	ס	נ	מ	ל	כ	י	ט	ח	ז	ו	ה	ד	ג	ב	א
6	60	310	86	14	—	60	60	56	40	44	80	10	410	410	70	16	—	430	70	410	110

- ❖ **מספר המרובע הכללי** *Mispar HaMerubah HaKlali* is the standard value squared.
- ❖ **מספר משולש** *Mispar Meshulash* (cubed value, triangular value) values each letter as its value cubed. (ex. *Aleph* = 1 x 1 x 1 = 1, *Beis* = 2 x 2 x 2 = 8).

ת	ש	ר	ק	צ	פ	ע	ס	נ	מ	ל	כ	י	ט	ח	ז	ו	ה	ד	ג	ב	א
64000000	27000000	8000000	1000000	729000	512000	343000	216000	125000	64000	27000	8000	1000	729	512	343	216	125	64	27	8	1

- ❖ **מספר האחור** *Mispar Ha'achor* (sometimes called *Mispar Meshulash*, **triangular value)** values each letter as its value multiplied by the position of the letter in the word or phrase.
- ❖ **מספר מספרי** *Mispar Mispari* spells out the Hebrew name of each of the letter's standard values and adds up their values. (ex. *Aleph* = one (*echad*) = 1 + 8 + 4 = 13).

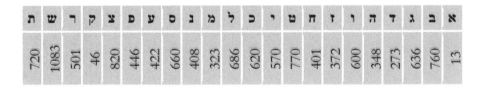

ת	ש	ר	ק	צ	פ	ע	ס	נ	מ	ל	כ	י	ט	ח	ז	ו	ה	ד	ג	ב	א
720	1083	501	46	820	446	422	660	408	323	686	620	570	770	401	372	600	348	273	636	760	13

- ❖ **מספר קטן מספרי** *Mispar Katan Mispari* (integral reduced value) is the digital root of the standard value. This is obtained by adding all the digits in the number until the number is a single digit. (ex. *echad* (13) --> 1 + 3 --> 4).
- ❖ **מספר כלל** *Mispar Kolel* is the value plus adding the number of words in the phrase.
- ❖ **אכב"י** *AchBi* splits the alphabet in half and within each group, the first letter switches with the last letter and the second with the tenth, etc. (ex. *Aleph* switches with *Chaf*, *Hey* switches with *Zayin*, *Mem* switches *Shin*).

❖ **אטב"ח** *AtBach* splits the alphabet into three groups of nine including the final *(sofit)* letters at the end. Within each group, the first letter switches with the last letter and the second with the eighth, etc. (ex. *Aleph* switches with *Tes, Lamed* switches with *Ayin, Yud* switches *Tzadi, Kuf* switches final *Tzadi*).

❖ **איי"ק בכ"ר** *Ayak Bachar* (or *Ayak Bakar*) splits the alphabet into three groups of nine including the final *(sofit)* letters at the end. The letters in the first group replace the ones in the second group, the letters in the second group replace the ones in the third group, and the letters in the third group replace the ones in the first group. (ex. *Aleph* takes the place of *Yud, Yud* takes the place of *Kuf, Kuf* takes the place of *Aleph, Beis* takes the place of *Chaf*, etc.).

❖ **אופנים** *Ofanim* replaces each letter with the last letter of its name. (ex. *Aleph* becomes *Fey, Lamed* becomes *Daled*).

❖ **אח"ס בט"ע** *Achas Beta* splits the alphabet into groups of 7, 7, and 8 letters. The letters in the first group exchange the ones in the second group, the letters in the second group swap the ones in the third group, and the letters in the third group replace the ones in the first group. The letter *Taf* does not change.

163

❖ **אבג"ד** *Avgad* trades each letter with the next one. (ex. *Aleph* becomes *Beis*, *Beis* becomes *Gimmel*, *Taf* becomes *Aleph*).

❖ **Reverse** *Avgad* swaps each letter with the previous one. (ex. *Beis* becomes *Aleph*, *Gimmel* becomes *Beis*, *Aleph* becomes *Taf*).

It is very exciting to use *gematrias* to open up insights into the Torah. Kabbalah is full of *gematrias* as it is part of the *sod*, secrets of the Torah. The holy Arizal teaches that when eating bread, one should dip the bread in salt three times, since *Hashem's* name, 26, three times equals 78, which is the *gematria* of salt, *melach* and bread, *lechem* 78. If you take father and mother, it equals the same *gematria* as child. 44 ילד = 3 אב + אם 41

Another example of how *gematria* works: consider the verse in Genesis 49:10, where it says:

"לא יסור שבט מיהידה ומחקק מבין רגליו עד כי יבא שילה ולו יקהת עמים."

"The scepter shall not depart from Judah nor a scholar from between his feet (among his descendants) until Shilo shall arrive and his will shall be an assemblage of nations."

Both Rashi and Onkelos deduce the phrase "until Shilo shall arrive" as meaning until the Messiah comes, to whom the kingdom belongs. The Sages have taught that this verse is a primary Torah source for the belief that the Messiah will come.

The *gematria* of the phrase יבא שילה, Shilo shall arrive, is 358. The Hebrew word for Messiah is משיח which also has *gematria* 358. The verse of Genesis 28:10 tells us:

"ויצא יעקב מבאר שבע וילך חרנה"

"And Jacob departed from Beersheva and went toward Haran."

He had lived with his family for about 63 years and having to leave was hard for him. The *gematria* of ויצא יעקב, and Jacob departed is 289, which is the same *gematria* as טרף meaning torn apart. Jacob was torn apart having to leave his family.

Lesson 28: Atbash

The ATBASH Cipher

א ב ג ד ה ו ז ח ט י כ ל מ נ ס ע פ צ ק ר ש ת

ת ש ר ק צ פ ע ס נ מ ל כ י ט ח ז ו ה ד ג ב א

My personal favorite *gematria* method is *Atbash*. It is quite amazing to take a letter and flip it, revealing tremendous insights into words. It is commonly used in Kabbalistic meditations, due to its being able to draw spiritual energy secretly without drawing attention from opposing forces. *Atbash* is really one of the greatest secrets of all the other methods taught.

There is a tremendous amount of life force that comes through any name, and when you reverse it in *Atbash* that energy remains; it just takes on a hidden form. It can't just be done randomly, though; it has to make some sense and stand for something when it's flipped.

At the bris of my first-born son, the Nikolsberg Rebbe of Monsey was able to tell over a *gematria* on the spot. For us regular people words are just that, words. To a tzaddik, everything in the world, every word, and every letter is just waiting for its code to be deciphered. When a tzaddik sees a word, he doesn't see that alone, but he also sees its root and its connections to other things.

When you look at the letter *Aleph*, do you see just this letter, or do you see two *Yuds* and a *Vav* which make it up? As you glance at the *Aleph*, do you see just the letter or does your mind start to delve deeper and see it spelled out: *Aleph Lamed, Peh* sofit?

We learn from the beauty of *gematrias* that the word is so much deeper. Thousands of Jews have returned to Torah and mitzvot because of the Torah codes or hidden gematrias that amazed them.

A friend of mine from Tzfat wrote an entire book on the *gematrias* from Rebbe Nachman's teachings. I used to pass by him on my way to the *mikvah* as he was composing the book. He would stop me and share with me how even a *rebbe* who writes a holy book can have secret messages in the holy Hebrew letters. Page by page, he went through the Likutey Moharan and uncovered combinations that showed the Divine spirit behind the *rebbe's* teachings. I wonder how many other *tzaddikim* left secret trails within their manuscripts that we have yet to uncover. You see for us, we just see a letter as a letter. For them, it is so much more.

Lesson 29: The Book of the Zohar

While I am a huge fan of preparing oneself properly before embarking on the path of Kabbalah, there is something quite unusual about the study of the Zohar. It is unlike any other book in Kabbalah literature. Its words are words of poetry taught by Rebbe Shimon Bar Yochai that awaken a person from the slumber of this world. The Zohar's words are actually purifying a person as they are studied, even if the learning is without understanding.

The study of Zohar is extremely beneficial. Through studying the Zohar, you can attain enthusiasm for all your sacred studies. The very language of the Zohar is so holy, it can motivate you to serve G-d. The Zohar uses most forceful expressions in speaking about our duty toward G-d. When speaking of a person who does good, the Zohar says "*zakah*...worthy is he!" On the other hand, it cries out against a sinner, "*Vai*... Woe! Woe is to him! Woe is to the soul who strays from serving G-d!" Reading such expressions can greatly influence you to serve G-d. When he used it in the Zohar, Rabbi Shimon bar Yochai made the Aramaic Targum language so holy that even other things written in this language have the power to arouse a person toward G-d. (Rabbi Nachman's Wisdom 108-109)

Rabbi Shimon ben Yochai gave assurances that through him the Torah would not be forgotten from the Jewish people. As our Sages teach, "When our *rabbis* entered the yeshivah in Yavneh, they said, "The Torah will one day be forgotten by the Jews." (Shabbos 138b). But Rabbi Shimon ben Yochai said that it would not be forgotten, as is written (Devarim 31:21), "It will not be forgotten from the mouth of his offspring." And, as is explained in the Zohar, "Because of this work, the Book of the Zohar, [the Jews] will be redeemed from exile." (Zohar 3, 124b)

The Zohar purifies the soul even when the reader doesn't understand what he says. This is like, a person who enters a perfume store; even if he doesn't buy any perfume, when he leaves the store he has the smell attached to him. (Degel Machane Ephraim to the Likutim, 5)

One who does not merit comprehension of the Zohar should nevertheless learn it because the language of the Zohar purifies the soul. (Ohr Tzaddikim by Rav Meir Papirash, a student of the Ari ha Kadosh, *siman* A, 16)

The *sefer* haZohar is full of *mussar*, and every letter comprises great *tikkunim* to the *neshamah* in order to correct *gilgulim* [reincarnations]. (Notzar Chessed Perek 4)

Reb Moshe Steinerman

One point of Torah study is that when your soul will cling to the books that deal with *yiras Hashem*, you will thereby realize at every moment the great debt you owe to the Creator of all worlds, and in particular through the Sefer ha Zohar, which is the most important of all, and it will cause your heart to flare up in flames of fire. The Sefer ha Zohar is [therefore an important] key to this. (*sefer* Sur Mera V'ase Tov)

[A story is told that] once our *rabbi* asked one of his important students why he doesn't learn the Zohar and the *tikkunim* and the writings of the Ari Hakadosh, and the student answered with a broken heart:

"*Rabbi*. What can I do? In order for this holy study, we need greater *kedusha* and purity, and I do not possess these, and how can I approach the *kodesh hakodashim* to study this?"

The *rabbi* then answered: "If you are not yet *kadosh* and *tahor* (holy and pure), go out and learn this holy study and cling to it, and through this, you will sanctify and purify yourself, for it is impossible in these generations to comprehend anything without this study. (Introduction to *sefer* Tzvi LaTzaddik*)*

In the introduction to the book Etz Chayim, our holy master Rabbi Chayim Vital, may his merit shield us, warned the students of the Torah, those who listen to the word of G-d, the great obligation they have to study the hidden Torah [Kabbalah], and the great punishment for neglecting its study, because one hour of this study does the same as thirty days of the study of *pshat* (plain meaning of the Torah). (Kise Melech on Tikune Zohar 30, 73b)

If the person does not occupy himself with the 4 levels of Torah study: *pshat, remez, drash,* and *sod* [*PARDES*- Simple meaning, allusion, homiletical level, and the secrets of the Torah] he is missing the *mitzvah* of Talmud Torah, which is great and equivalent to all other *mitzvos* in the Torah, and this person has to reincarnate until he will occupy himself with the four levels of *PARDES*. (Kitve Ari ha Kaddosh, Shaar ha Mitzvos Aleph)

As you can see, the Zohar is unique among all the holy books of Kabbalah. It is not a simple work to overlook or go through just once in your life. Yes, many other books may draw you closer to *Hashem*, but can they do what the Zohar can accomplish for its reader?

The Zohar is more a way of life than just a holy book. One of the main things I took out of learning the Zohar was the importance of nightly Torah study after *chatzos*. I haven't counted how many times Rebbe Shimon taught this important practice, but it could be more than any other concept in the Zohar. He teaches us that when we study Torah at night, *Hashem* and the *tzaddkim* in the Garden of Eden are listening to our study. This really isn't just a simple statement to overlook. Let us think for a few minutes what this truly means. An unimportant person such as I, am bringing enjoyment to the greatest scholars who ever lived. Not only enjoyment, but I am drawing the holiness of the Garden of Eden into my life and my Torah study. My Torah study is no longer about me but starts to reach levels of true *lishma*. The world is being elevated through this study; I am changing my ways; my soul is being purified, and I am a partner in the coming of

Moshiach. Then as the Zohar explains, I remain awake in study until sunrise, when I pray the morning prayers at *vesikin*, thereby elevating all the fallen sparks of the night to complete worlds above.

I believe that this is the most important idea to take away from the Zohar. How can a person study the Kabbalah and practice it without an understanding of the powerful watches of the night? To say *Tikkun Chatzos*, talk to *Hashem* in *hisbodedus*, pray at sunrise, this is one of the highest levels of *avodah*. You must have a very powerful soul in order to pull this off. The Zohar gives you this power. It gives you the *mussar* you need to hear to realize the importance of Torah study and true *avodas Hashem*. Yes, Talmud study is a priority but without the Zohar contributing its holiness to your soul, you might be missing out on some important revelations as your soul attempts to complete itself. There are hundreds of books on Kabbalah; we are not here saying that you should make them a required study. We are saying this about the Zohar: A book which is a light, a renewal for a person's soul. It is something extraordinary, maybe a bit scary at first during its first chapters, but which is afterward similar to studying the Midrash or *sifrei mussar*.

When the Biala Rebbe of New York was at my house for *Shabbos*, I asked him which *sefarim* he would like me to leave out on his desk. One of the books was the Zohar. It is known traditionally that studying the Zohar on Friday night can do wonders for a person's soul.

One thing about the Zohar is that you don't need to study a lot of it for it to affect your soul in great ways. Even twenty minutes of the Zohar is similar to hours of another study. You will find though that once you open this holy book, it becomes difficult to put down. This is because the soul yearns for sweet words to comfort it. Too much of anything isn't good and a person needs balance in his life. If you study the Zohar or any *kabbalah sefer*, make sure your priorities still lie in foundational books.

Lesson 30: The Mikvah

"אָמַר רַבִּי עֲקִיבָא: אַשְׁרֵיכֶם יִשְׂרָאֵל! לִפְנֵי מִי אַתֶּם מִיטַהֲרִין? מִי מְטַהֵר אֶתְכֶם? אֲבִיכֶם
שֶׁבַּשָּׁמַיִם! וְאוֹמֵר:"מִקְוֵה יִשְׂרָאֵל ה'." מַה מִּקְוֶה מְטַהֵר אֶת הַטְּמֵאִים, אַף הַקָּדוֹשׁ בָּרוּךְ הוּא מְטַהֵר
אֶת יִשְׂרָאֵל"

"Rabbi Akiva said: Fortunate are you Yisrael! Before Whom do you cleanse yourself? And who cleanses you? Your Father in Heaven! It also says: 'The *mikvah* of Yisrael is *Hashem.*' Just as a *mikvah* cleanses the contaminated, so does The Holy One Blessed Be He cleanse *Yisrael.*" (Yuma 85b-Mishna)

These words are commonly sung during *Lag B' Omer* and *Shabbos*. Why during such auspicious times of joy do we recite these words? Maybe because the idea of *mikvah* is one of redemption, as the Mashiach comes in the merit of the *mikvah*. Rabbi Akiva said: Happy are you, Israel. Before whom do you purify yourselves? Who purifies you? Your Father in Heaven! As it says, "I will sprinkle pure waters upon you, and you shall be clean." (Ezekiel 36:25) And in this merit the promise of, "And the spirit of *tumah* (impurity) I will remove from the land," will also be fulfilled. And this is what our holy *rabbis* taught regarding the verse "And the spirit of *Elokim* hovered on the face of the water." (Bereshis 1:2) The Sages said: "This spirit refers to the spirit of King Mashiach," meaning that in the merit of the purity brought by the *mikvah* we will merit the coming of the Mashiach. (The holy *rav* the Chozeh of Lublin *zt"l*, brought in the *sefer* Mayan Ganim)

Why is it referred to as "*mikvah Yisrael Hashem?*" On the second day He created the firmament to divide the waters from the waters, and in doing so He stipulated that they should separate between defilement and purity on behalf of Israel and be to them a means of purification. It says, on the second day of creation, when the holy One Blessed be He created the firmament to divide between the upper and lower waters, the holy One Blessed be He established a condition with the waters that they should serve to separate for Israel between *tumah* and *taharah*, so that Israel could achieve *tahara* (purity) through the waters, and as written in Bereshis 1:11, "*ulmikvah hamaim kara yami m vayaar Elokim ki tov.*" "And to the gathering of waters he called seas and *Elokim* saw that it was good." Therefore, the *mikvah* is called *mikvah Yisrael Hashem*. (The Holy Zohar 198b)

If a person were to head out into the rain, the rainwater wouldn't purify him. The *mikvah* has to be in a contained area of forty *seah*, a running stream, river, natural lake or an ocean. So, what does it mean when it says, "I will toss pure waters on all of you and you will be purified?" (Ezekiel 36:25) The passage is teaching us that *Hashem* is giving the purity of the *mikvah*, not the *mikvah* itself. It is just a tool used to connect to *Hashem*, without proper *kavanah* and the desire to change and become holy, the *mikvah* won't properly connect you to *Hashem*. And it says: "*Hashem* is the *mikvah* - bath of Israel." (Jeremiah 17:13) Just like a *mikvah* purifies the impure, the holy One blessed be He purifies Israel.

The letter *Mem* is the dominant letter in *mayim*, the Hebrew word for water. The numerical value of the letter *Mem* is *gematria* forty. The *halacha* states that the *mikvah* must contain a volume of 40 *seah* of water. Therefore, it is not very surprising to learn that the letter *Mem* is also said to represent the *mikvah*. (Tikkunei Zohar 19) *Mem* is also a closed letter, indicating containment and unity. It is also sounded with the mouth closed. (Bahir 85)

Without water, a person couldn't survive more than a few days. Life begins with water and ends with water. A baby, when in its mother's womb, exists in a sack of water. We find that the womb is also associated with the letter *Mem*. (Sefer Yetzirah 3:4) The closed (final) *Mem* is similar to the womb, which is closed during pregnancy, while the open *Mem* is like the open womb giving birth (Bahir 84). The numerical value forty, associated with *Mem*, also represents the forty days during which the embryo is formed. When a person dies, and he returns his soul to *Hashem*, he is purified by waters of a *taharah mikvah*. We, therefore, see that life and death are associated with cleansing waters.

The *sefirah* of *Chochmah* is connected to the idea of water and Torah. In Sefer Yetzirah it teaches, "The belly is created from water." (Sefer Yetzirah 3:6) The belly is man's receptive power, represented by water. In a deeper sense, the head is viewed as the center of *Binah* consciousness. It is the head that is the seat of the conscious stream of thought. The workings of the belly, on the other hand, are almost completely subconscious. The belly, therefore, parallels the *Mem*, which denotes *Chochmah* consciousness. Some mystics would contemplate their belly when attempting to attain *Chochmah* consciousness.

Breathing borders on both the conscious and the unconscious. One usually breathes unconsciously, but one can also control his breathing consciously. Breathing is therefore associated with both *Binah* and *Chochmah* consciousness. It is for this reason that controlled breathing techniques are important in making the transition between these two states. Breathing is centered in the chest (Sefer Yetzirah page 152).

"Behold, all who are thirsty, come to the water." (Yeshaya 55:1) The Rambam explains, "This passage is to teach you that, just as water does not collect on an incline but rather flows on its own and collects at a low place, similarly the words of Torah are not found among the haughty nor in hearts of the arrogant, but rather in the humble and the lowly person who sits in the dust at the feet of the sages and removes his desires and temporal pleasures from his heart. He does minimal work each day, enough for his livelihood if he has nothing to eat, and the rest of his time he involves himself in Torah study."

Just as water stretches from one end of the world to the other, so Torah reaches from one end of the world to the other. As water gives life to the world, so Torah gives life to the world. As water is given without cost to the world, so is Torah given without cost to the world. As water is given from Heaven, so Torah is given from Heaven.

Just as water is given with thunder, so to the Torah was given with the accompaniment of thunder (at *Har Sinai*). As water restores a person's spirit, so Torah restores a person's spirit.

Just as water cleanses a person from uncleanness, so Torah cleanses an impure person from his uncleanness. As rainwater comes down in many drops and becomes a mighty river, so Torah; today a person studies two *halachos*, tomorrow two more, and so on until he becomes like a bubbling brook. As water leaves an elevated place and flows to a low place, so Torah leaves one whose opinion of himself is high and attaches to one whose spirit is lowly.

Just as water is not held in vessels of silver or gold, but only in inexpensive vessels, so Torah abides only in one who regards himself as lowly as an earthenware vessel.

As when thirsty, a grownup is not ashamed to say to a child, "Let me have a drink of water," so in studying Torah a grown man who is unlearned should not be embarrassed to say to a child, "teach me a chapter or a verse or a word," or even, "teach me a single letter." As with water, if one does not know how to swim in it, he will end by drowning, so too with words of Torah; they must be studied under the guidance of one's *rabbi*.

The Shem MiShmuel *zt"l* explains, "Our sages explain that just as water flows from a high place to a low place, so too Torah only enters the understanding of one who is humble and lowly in his own eyes." It is conceivable to explain that this is the purification of the מי אתתם, which must be prepared with running water. Running water signifies one's constant inner motion of yearning for *Hashem*. But this must also be combined with the ashes of the red cow. We can further understand this from the words of the Kotzker Rebbe *zt"l*, who once said that it is easier to fast and inflict upon himself the toughest self-mortification in the world than to truly accept upon oneself the yoke of Heaven. "This is the symbolism of the ash of the red cow: one who has thoroughly nullified his ego by accepting the yoke of Heaven. The more one accepts this yoke as an ox who bears a burden, the more he thrusts away all impurity."

Wisdom is realizing that we know nothing. The *mikvah* connects us to *Hashem* so that we lose our ego and realize the only thing that matters is our connection to *Hashem*. We came down as a pure being and the impurities of this world attached to our body through our sins. This is negatively affecting our holy souls. The *mikvah* is reconnecting us to *Hashem* by helping us realize that only He gives wisdom, strength and the ability to breathe. He gives us the ability to be pure; we have to turn to Him to overcome all tests in life. The process of going to the *mikvah* is a symbolic change in our chronic negative nature when we are ready to start a new life.

Accepting positive changes in our life the process of *teshuvah*, the *mikvah* is the first step in and taking a new opens direction. The Arizal promised that anyone who would immerse in his *mikvah* in Tzfat would completely repent during his lifetime. Having lived virtually on top of the hill overlooking the *mikvah* Ari, I can attest that, not only does this holy water cause one to repent but also on days when I felt the lowest, I literally walked out of the *mikvah* a different person.

Once when I was heading to the Ari *mikvah*, I met Rav Mann *zt"l*, who was a special *tzaddik* in our generation. I had made some comment about the *mikvah* being difficult to attend daily, and he responded that he had not missed a day of immersion in five years. Whether he chose to immerse only in the Ari's *mikvah* I do not know, but as an elderly gentleman, I wonder how he tolerated this well-known freezing outdoor *mikvah*.

During the war in the north with Hezbollah, during a quiet day without bombings, I headed out to the *mikvah* Ari. While surrounded by the water, the city was bombarded with rockets. I was alone there since most of Tzfat had left the city for safety; I remained in the freezing *mikvah* waters until the bombing stopped. I felt the safest place to be at that moment was in the waters of purification. Maybe I was there for twenty minutes or half hour; I don't know how long it was, but too often we rush our time in the *mikvah* when its value is crucial to our repentance.

Being a *sofer*, scribe I decided to write myself a special pair of *tefillin* which would require immersing in the *mikvah* before writing each name of *Hashem*. There are approximately forty names of *Hashem*, so I began my venture immersing each time in the *mikvah* Ari. One day, I had immersed a total of six different times to complete this holy pair of *tefillin*. While quite out of the ordinary, I can't express in words the feeling I get when I put on this holy pair of *tefillin*. I can also tell you that the *mikvah* Ari took me to levels of *d'vekus* during that period that I could not place into words.

People from all around the world visit this special place and immerse, hoping that they will connect to the Arizal in some way, hoping that they will repent before they leave this world. As you can tell, I do believe in this miracle.

Having left the holy city of Tzfat for some years, I many times think of the *mikvah* Ari when immersing in other places. I meditate on the root of the *mikvah* and its purpose. Thinking that all *mikvahs* are connected from the same source, but to me, there will always be one *mikvah* Ari.

There definitely is something special about immersing in natural *mikvahs*. They are of a higher *kedusha* than a man-made *mikvah*. I feel so much more rejuvenated from the experience. Living in Jerusalem, we don't really have so many natural springs to take advantage of as when I was living in Tzfat. Most of my life, I made sure to immerse at least once a week in an outdoor *mikvah* in order to have a fuller experience and connection to the *mikvah*. That not being the case now, I have to make do; but looking back, there were some great times over the years, when discovering outdoor bodies of water.

In my early twenties, I lived in the mountains of Maryland. It was an hour away from a proper *mikvah*. So, I was forced to find alternatives in nature. Living all alone as a religious Jew in these parts wasn't simple, but a *mikvah* certainly made a difference. It was a beautiful experience, not only to go to the *mikvah* in the Blue Ridge Mountains but also to walk around later in *hisbodedus* and study Torah. My favorite *mikvah*, ironically, was in the Catoctin Mountains in Thurmont, Maryland. In the '90's this was a hotspot for anti-semitism and the Ku Klux Klan. Hundreds of times, I drove there to pray and immerse. Today this movement has died down; maybe my immersions there helped a bit; only *Hashem* knows, but I always found this ironic.

The winter months were very taxing on me. Trying to never go three days without a *mikvah* as the Baal Shem Tov suggested wasn't easy. Sometimes I drove an hour away just to pray with a *minyan* and immerse in the *mikvah*. At times my main *kavanah* for traveling was just to replenish my mindset in a *mikvah*. That was an hour in each direction just to dunk in the spiritual waters. Having been fed up with such an undertaking, I thought to myself that it might be easier to attempt the scary frozen lake *mikvah*, as had been done by so many masters.

So, that day I brushed off the snow on my car and started traveling down the snow-packed single-lane country roads. I brought an extra towel with me and heated the car up really warm, so I could bake in its warmth when I returned. Little did I know the dangers involved in such an attempt. In the Frederick watershed lay a frozen lake. I parked my car about 400 feet from the *mikvah*, excited by my new personal dare. Surrounded by ice, I slipped inside the lake, bearing nothing but the skin on my flesh. One, two, three times I immersed and then I went out into the land filled with snow. I was freezing and started shaking. My feet were covered in snow and I didn't have any nerve feelings to get dressed. I started running for my car. When I got to the door, I wasn't able to open it as my fingers were too frozen. After what seemed like forever, I managed to open the door, but the car wasn't warm as I expected. I turned on the heat and put my hand alongside the air vents. I started praying; I was so scared. This was the first and last time I attempted such a stunt. Now when I hear the stories of *Chassidic* masters immersing in sub-zero temperatures and breaking the ice, I truly believe their greatness. For me, I attained a lot that day; I went home and returned to my Torah study, freezing the rest of the day from the experience.

The Baal Shem Tov would often immerse in the *mikvah*, either before or after saying *Tikkun Chatzos*. Often this meant having to go to the river and *toivel* in it. During the frigid winter, that also meant first breaking through the ice on top of the river and making a large enough opening to immerse therein.

One such winter night, the Baal Shem Tov remained in the water much longer than usual and the *gabbai* noticed that the torch he was holding so they would have light, was about to flicker out. The fire of the torch not only illuminated their way, but it also served as a source of warmth for the Baal Shem Tov when he came out of the freezing water.

Chassidus, Kabbalah and Meditation

Nervously, he whispered out to the Baal Shem Tov that the torch was going to extinguish any moment. The Baal Shem Tov told him to take a large icicle and light it. The *gabbai* did so and it burned exactly as a regular torch.

Hashem quite obviously protected people who undertook to purify themselves. It is understood that for health reasons, it may be difficult for some to immerse in the *mikvah* but thankfully, today we have heated *mikvahs* to help with this. One should try to go at least once a week if not every three days as the Baal Shem Tov suggested. In the Soviet Union, the Communist regime forced the closure of all indoor *mikvos*, leaving the Jewish community with no alternative but to immerse themselves in outdoor pools of natural water.

When the Nazis, *yimach shemo*, were picking Jews off the streets, the Skolye Rebbe never missed going to the *mikvah* every morning. His *gabbai* would dress up in clothing similar to the Nazis and pretend he was taking the Skolye Rebbe away. In this way, they were never caught and the *rebbe* continued his practice of attending the *mikvah* every day. How amazing it is when a person works on his nature so much that he becomes a breathing *sefer* Torah! (Taken from my book Kavanos Halev)

I once asked the Hornsteipl Rebbe, Rabbi Shalom Friedman, how Rabbi Chaim Vital was able to become a fitting vessel to learn Torah from the Arizal HaKodesh. He answered with a serious stare in his eyes: "Every day he immersed in the *mikvah* without fail. He began by learning Tanach; he followed this by learning Mishna. Afterward, he learned Talmud, and only then did he learn Kabbalah." (Taken from my book, Kavanos Halev)

The *maggid* who would study with the Beis Yosef appeared to the holy Rabbi Tzvi Hirsch of Tzidichov and told him that he wanted to learn with him just as he had studied with the Beis Yosef. He said that the Beis Yosef had the *zechus* to study with him because of his deep study of the *halachos*. He further told Rabbi Tzvi Hirsch that it was in the merit of his immersions in the *mikvah* for the sake of Heaven (*lishma*). (Tzvi la Tzaddik 34)

My Teacher *zt"l* told me that for one who wishes to grasp this wisdom, there is nothing that will help him in the world so much as the *tevilah* in the *mikvah* so that no time will pass when he will not be in purity and holiness. This is so that his capacity of grasping wisdom will not depart from him and from the strength of the *tevilah* he will derive great illumination. (Etz Chaim Hakdama)

The Baal Shem Tov *zt"l* said that he merited great levels through constant immersions in the *mikvah*, and they are much better than mortifications like fasting, for this weakens the person and does not permit him to serve the holy One blessed be He. (Sefer Sha'are Parnassah Tova, Tehillim Ch. 51)

Through the *mikvah*, we can reach *ruach hakodesh*. It says, "And the spirit of *Elokim* hovered on the face of the waters."(Bereshis 1:2) We can find an allusion in this verse to what is written in the *baraisa* of Rabbi Pinchas ben Yair that says: "Watchfulness leads to zeal and zeal leads to cleanliness and cleanliness to purity, etc. until we reach *ruach hakodesh*. And this we find in the verse in Bereshis: 'And the spirit of *Elokim* (*ruach Elokim*),' meaning *ruach hakodesh*, 'hovers on the face of the waters', which means that through the waters of the *mikvah* a person can attain great levels, mainly *ruach hakodesh*." It is known about the Baal Shem Tov *zt"l* who once said that he merited great levels through constant immersions in the *mikvah*. (Nefesh Adam)

Rebbe Nachman gave us his perspective of the *mikvah* as well. He said, "Immersing in the *mikvah* is the cure for all troubles. The *mikvah* has the power to purify us from every kind of sin and impurity. The spiritual power of the *mikvah* is rooted in the most exalted levels of wisdom and love." (Likutey Etzos 56:7) Furthermore, immersing in a *mikvah* helps to make it easier to earn a living and receive the flow of blessing. Strife and anger are dissipated, and in their place come peace, love, deep wisdom and healing, the length of days and the power to arouse men to *Hashem*. (ibid 31:2)

He also said that "Immersing in the *mikvah* is an antidote to anger because immersing in the mikvah brings understanding." (Likutey Etzos, Mikvah)

The Baal Shem Tov used to say *tehillim* while inside the *mikvah* (Beis Aharon 145).

The Baal Shem Tov said: "I managed to achieve with the holy One blessed be He that the immersion in the *mikvah* that a person does every morning will be considered by the Holy One blessed be He as if that person had fasted for one day." (Sippurei Chasidim ha Chadash, Letter 16)

The Admor Meir Yechiel from Ostrovza *zt"l*, told what happened once when the Baal Shem Tov was asked by a magician the following: "I see the people leaving their houses early in the morning and they are followed by many *klipos* [Forces of evil] and when I see them return to their houses I don't see anything anymore." The Baal Shem Tov replied to him: "This is the result of immersing in the *mikvah*." (Nahar Yotze me Eden, 4:1)

We recall the merit of our forefathers through immersion in the *mikvah*, as it is written (Jeremiah 3:8): "The *mikvah* of your forefathers is *Hashem*." Meaning, that through the action of immersing in the *mikvah* we bring the remembrance of our forefathers before *Hashem*. (Sefer ha Middos)

It is written by the sages that even though there can be no prophecy outside Israel, in the *mikvah* of water there can be. Proof of this can be seen through Ezekiel because the word of *Hashem* came to him by the river even though he was outside the land of Israel. (Beis Aharon, Likkutim)

"And it shall be before evening, *erev*, comes he shall bathe in water." (Devarim 23:12) This means that in order to separate oneself from the darkness and the night, the person shall wash in water, referring to the *mikvah*, for it is the beginning of all *teshuvah*. (Divrie Emes, Parashas Tetze)

In order that there be no impediment to grasping the Torah, you should never miss, and it should never bother you, [the effort to be pure] through immersing in the *mikvah* for this is the most important thing for achieving purity. (Mishnas Chassidim)

A person should think about what is brought in the *baraisa* of the *Maase Merkava*. Those angels who are sent to this world to announce what has been decreed from Heaven, as they travel through the air of this world, they are not able to sing afterward when they again go up until they immerse themselves in the river *Dinur* 365 times and afterward they do *tevilah* seven times in white fire. They require all these *tevilos* for they came close to the vicinity of men. Therefore, if the higher creatures need so much purity to be holy in order to sing in front of the holy One blessed be He, how much more must a person have purity in order to pray before the Holy One Blessed be He... (Kav ha-Yashar Chap 11)

"Fortunate is he who accustoms himself to always go to the *mikvah* and it will be beneficial against all impurities and specifically against the impurity produced by sins. It will lead the person to purity, mainly purity of heart." (Shnei Luchos ha-Bris *zt"l*, Shaar ha Otyos, Letter *Tes*)

The Zohar states, "When *Shabbos* comes it is incumbent on the holy people to wash away (by immersing in the *mikvah*) from themselves the marks of their weekday labor. For what reason is this? Because during the weekdays a different spirit roams about and hovers over a person, and it is in order to divest himself of that spirit and invest himself with another spirit. A spirit which is sublime and holy, that he must wash away the stains of the weekday world (by immersing in the *mikvah*)." (Zohar 204a)

It is explained in the Zohar ha Kadosh that the benefit of the *mikvah* is to return the *neshamah* to its proper place, because the one who is impure has no *neshamah* and in particular the one who damages the Holy *brit*, his soul departs from him [in the book Shnei Luchot HaBris, letter *Kuf*]. The *rav* of Portugal says: "And don't take lightly the purity of your body because it will help you for the purity of your *neshamah*." (Derech Chayim 91b)

The measure of the waters of the *mikvah* is 40 *seahs* and the initial letters are *samech mem* (*Mem* is forty and *samech* is *seah*), to subjugate the *kelipos* of the *samech mem* (*Satan*). (Divre Chassidim brought in the *sefer* Mayan Ganim)

I heard about the students of the Baal Shem Tov that they were once congregating together and were discussing the thing upon which the head and leader of the generation must be most watchful of. Some of the students said that the most important thing is to supervise the slaughtering of animals (*zevicha*) that the *shoches* will be G-d fearing and that he would be careful in all the other details relating to the slaughter as well. This is because, G-d forbid, forbidden foods clog the heart and it becomes dull to the light of the Torah. Some of the students also said that the most important thing for the leader was to be diligent about the laws of the *eruv* (*eruvin*). This is because the laws of *Shabbos* are similar to mountains that hang on a hair strand (Chagiga 10a), and this prohibition is of grave importance. Some other students said that the most important thing is to supervise the *mikvaos* so they will be *kosher* without any doubt. This is because when the foundation of the building is built without *kashrus* then it will be very difficult for that man to be able to vanquish the evil side, *Hashem* save us. Following this discussion, the Baal Shem Tov said: "I give testimony that at this precise moment they were arguing in the *yeshiva* of the heavens which of these things was the most important and they concluded that all of them were and as a sign of these three things there is the verse, (Chabakuk 3:12) 'You marched through the land in indignation, you threshed the nations in anger.' And the word *zaam* has the first letters of the words *zevicha eruvin mikvaos.* All of these are the foundation of the world." (Birkas Avraham Parasha Vaetchanan brought in the *sefer* Baal Shem Tov on the Torah Parashas Yisro*)*

Do you realize that we entrust the prayer leader with such a great responsibility? (His job is to elevate our prayers to be accepted in Heaven.) "If all the *shalichei tzibbur* in all places would purify themselves this would accelerate the redemption." (Sheilos u Tshuvos Min haShamaim, *siman* 5, brought in Radbaz end *perek* 5)

While immersing in the *mikvah,* a person should accept upon himself to give up his life in order to sanctify the name of *Hashem,* as it is written (in the Otzar Sippurim *chelek* b *siman* 7), "by the one who would set the bonfire of *mesiras nefesh* in the *mikvah* day after day for the holy and most honored." (Rabbi Chayim of Tzantz *zt"l)* You should make yourself holy with sacred waters and take away the sins and transgressions so as to run from your sins and expiate your faults. In this way, you will be saved from 600,000 *mazikin* (damaging spirits) which are in the power of the *Yetzer Hara,* as it is brought in the introduction to the Tikkunei Zohar 11a. (Sefer Or Zarua La Tzaddik)

It is written in Shaar ha Yichudim: "The remedy to eliminate anger is immersion in the *mikvah* and to think there about the Name *E-H-Y-E*

ה-ה ה-ה יוד אלף when filled with the letter *Hey.* This is because it equals 151, similar to the word כעס *kaas,* anger [*Kaf Ayin Samech*] which equals 151 (adding one number for the word itself). Through the *tevilah* with proper concentration, the anger will depart from him. The remedy to eliminate anger is to immerse and think there that *mikvah* in *gematria* equals 151 which is also *kaas,* and through the *tevilah* he will eliminate the *kaas.*" (Sur Me Rah, Hosafos)

On the *chag* of *Succos,* the Jews are judged on water. This happens: "Because they make little of the *mitzvah* of *netillas yadaim* and they despise the *mikvaos* and the laws of purity that depend on water; therefore, they are judged on the water. For those people who did not immerse all year long in a *mikvah* of water, it is written '*kol Hashem bamayim.*' (Tehillim 29:4) The holy One blessed be He cries out loud and shakes the world because of the water that men treat lightly, the immersion in the *mikvah* [not taken seriously] (Tochen Divre Avrech Al Tehllim, Maamar Meir Loalam).

We have spoken about the greatness of the *mikvah* bringing a person to purity, but how do we avoid becoming impure in the first place? Who is a *tzaddik?* It is he who guards the *bris.* We learn this from Yosef who, by reason of his having guarded the covenant, is known as "Yosef the righteous." (Yosef Ha Tzaddik) (Zohar Ha Kadosh, I, 59b)

He who looks even at the small finger of a woman in order to derive pleasure from looking is like one who looks at her private place; even to listen to her voice (which is considered as looking at her nakedness) or to look at her hair is forbidden. (The Rambam Chapter 21, Hilchos Issure Biah)

The Chatam Sofer wrote: "The Jews, they are holy and should not stumble through looking at women, *chas-v'shalom*, for all who do this are lost in this world and in the World to Come." (Parshas Chaye Sarah)

Everything that a person looks at, the image penetrates and fixes itself in the mind. When he comes to pray or to study Torah, those material images appear in his mind, and they damage and invalidate his thoughts. Thereby he will not be able to concentrate as required, because the eyes only see through the power that resides in the soul, and the soul receives those images that come through the eyes. If the person looks at nakedness, he causes nakedness to penetrate in a high place. (Reshis Chochma, Sha'ar ha Kedusha)

You, my dear sons, if the blemish of wasting semen in vain is in your hands, and even if completely without intention on your part, be careful to purify yourselves in the waters of the *mikvah*. Do so according to the law without delay and *Hashem* forbid that you don't follow this rule. The seminal emission [*keri*] is not like having relations with your wife but, due to our many sins, it is like having relations with *lillis* the evil one and with the other forces of *tumah*. She clings to the man who sinned and wishes to separate him from the life of the world to come, *Hashem* save us from her. (Sefer Sheves Mussar Chapter 40)

The holy Arizal wrote that, if one has an emission G-d forbid and immerses himself on that same day and returns to *Hashem*, then the damage created from his sin is erased... (Pele Yoetz Tahara)

Rebbe Nachman taught a *tikkun* for such events and as a general remedy for all matters. He says, "A person who experiences a night time emission should recite the following ten Psalms on the same day: Psalms 16, 32, 41, 42, 59, 77, 90, 105, 137, 150. One who recites these Psalms on the same day need have no further fears about the harm such an emission can cause. Any damage will certainly be repaired through doing this. It is a very great *tikkun*." (Likutey Etzos 11, 92)

His *talmud muvak*, Rabbi Nosson, writes: "Before speaking of the Psalms, the *rebbe* said, 'The first remedy is *mikvah*. Das ersht is mikvah. You must first immerse yourself in a *mikvah*.'" Then he suggested you recite his *Tikkun*.

Another time the *rebbe* said, "You must be very careful to immerse in a *mikvah* on the same day that you have an unclean experience. If you cannot immerse the first thing in the morning, do so anytime during the day, even toward evening. It is most important to immerse on the very same day. Everyone experiences a nocturnal emission at one time or another. I call you to bear witness that these ten Psalms are a beneficial remedy for this unclean experience. They are an absolute remedy."

Indeed, the one who is meticulous regarding his soul and is careful to immerse after having a seminal emission even nowadays, he is doing a very praiseworthy action; he knows the right path and blessings will come to him. (Sefer haChinuch Mitzvah 104)

He would immerse himself afterward in the *mikvah* because it is considered as if one received the death penalty by strangulation. (Kav haYashar, Chapter 48) This is probably since when immersed under water for a long time, one looses their breath and this takes the place of actual punishment.

The holy Rabbi Mi Baranov told a story how once he wanted to see with his own eyes the service that the holy Rav Chaim Mi Tzantz *zt"l* performed for the Creator. So, he went into the *mikvah* at midnight and hid in the room there before the holy Rav Chaim came. He then glanced as his holy *rav* entered in with his wounded leg [which as it is known was always swollen full of blood and pus]. He started screaming, "Here I stand ready to receive upon me the four types of death administered by the *bes din* which are stoning, burning, beheading, and strangulation." He repeated these many times in both Hebrew and in Yiddish. With great pains he would immerse for each type of death, screaming and lamenting, and all the while the Rabbi Mi Baranov was hidden under a bench. He was terrified but unable to move for fear he would be seen by the holy Rav Chaim. After concluding all his immersions Rav Chaim came out of the *mikvah* and with great speed he got dressed in order to go home and recite the *Tikkun Chatzos* (the midnight prayer Jews say to lament over the destruction of the Temple of Jerusalem.) Those who heard the holy *rav* recite the *Tikkun Chatzos* know that he did so with tears and laments that pierced the heart. The holy Rav Mi Baranov *zt"l* testified that every time he would think about what he saw in the *mikvah*, he would tremble and quake. He would literally feel the sensation of actually receiving the four types of capital punishment prescribed by the *beis din*. (Darche Chayim, Hasafos)

When the Israelites said, "It is proper that we sing before You (*Hashem*); [they were stating that] we are now absolutely pure, totally free of all defilement. We marched into the sea until it covered our heads, and this was like the purifying immersion in a *mikvah*. This purified us of all the defilement of Egypt. We also submitted to circumcision on the night we left Egypt. We and our descendants until the end of all generations, therefore, deserve to sing to You when You do miracles for us. We can offer praise and song to Your great Name." (Yalkus Meam Loez Beshallach)

We find another allusion to the *mikvah* in a parable given by the Prophet Ezekiel. He likens Israel to an abandoned child, who was cast aside by her parents at birth. *Hashem* takes in this infant girl, caring for her and raising her to be a princess. *Hashem* then says (Ezekiel 16:8,9), "Your time was the time of love. I spread My garment over you and covered your nakedness. I swore to you, and I entered into a covenant with you - says the Lord G-d - and you became Mine. Then I washed you in the water..." This washing refers to the immersion of the Jews before the giving of the Ten Commandments. (Radak, Abarbanel) (Aryeh Kaplan, Waters of Eden)

"Let now a little water be taken, and wash your feet." The Zohar explains that this alluded to the fact that Abraham had a *mikvah* and immersed the strangers inside it. (Zohar 1:102)

Ultimately, all uncleanness is a result of Adam's sin. (Alshich on Vayikra 21)

Death and all other human imperfections were a result of this sin. If man would have remained in his elevated state in the Garden of Eden, nothing would exist that could cause uncleanness. This explains why a person who has been defiled by something unclean was not allowed to enter the grounds of the holy Temple. The Temple represents a miniature Garden of Eden. When Adam sinned, he was driven from this Garden. Therefore, anything associated with this sin prevents him from entering the miniature Garden of Eden that is the Temple. When a man is in a state of *tumah* or uncleanness, he may not enter the Temple grounds under the severest of penalties. (Alshich on Vayikra 21)

Even though a person cannot re-enter the Garden of Eden itself, whenever he associates himself with these rivers or with any other water, he is reestablishing his link with Eden. We thus find a Midrash which tells us that after Adam was driven from Eden, he repented by sitting in the river for 130 years. (Pirke de Rabbi Eliezer 20)

Although he had been permanently barred from the Garden itself, he tried to maintain a link through this river. Thus, when a person immerses in the waters of the *mikvah*, he is also reestablishing a link with man's perfected state. He then loses the status of uncleanness (*tumah*) and is reborn into a state of purity, where he is permitted to enter the Holy Temple. (Midrash Yalkus Reuveni Bereshis 2:10)

It is so important to make sure Jewish communities have *mikvaos*. You might assume that in some small communities, even if the *mikvah* was built, the people wouldn't come. However, we have seen over the years that this isn't the case. Even if only a few women would use the *mikvah*, it would save their family purity for generations thereafter. It is the only way a woman who experienced her cycle can return to holiness. It is no small matter.

The Holy Rav Nachum of Chernobyl *zt"l* came to a small city where there was no *mikvah*, and he sold his portion in *Olam Haba* for 300 pieces of silver and then gave the money to the people of the city, so they would build a *mikvah*. (Mifalos ha Tzaddikim)

All those who are watchful regarding *tevilah* will live long and good days. (Yerushalmi Berachos 3:4)

In place of the *mikvah*, when there's not enough time to immerse before saying the *berachos* of the Torah and the *kriyas Shema*, or when one can not immediately find a *mikvah*, there's a great piece of advice that will substitute the *mikvah*, and that is to stand under a shower as the equivalent of nine *kavim* pour down from the shower or using a large bucket of water. There are different opinions and *machlokes* on how much water, what method works and what level of purity is accomplished.

There is also an option of *netilas yadaim* in place of the *mikvah* when there's not enough time to immerse in the *mikvah* before saying the *berachos* of the Torah and the *kriyas shema*, here's a great piece of advice that will substitute the *mikvah*, and it consists of washing the hands with a vessel [*keli*] forty times. When the person will find a *mikvah*, then he must go and immerse. The order in which the hands should be washed is: following the letters of the expanded name of *Hashem* filled with *Yudim,* which adds up to seventy-two, יוד-הי-ויו-הי [have this in mind during the procedure].

There are ten letters in this holy Name. Then we must wash as follows:

1 - For each letter, we wash once each hand alternately so that we will need to wash twenty times, ten for each hand.

An example of this would be as follows: We take the vessel with the left hand and pour water on the right hand once, concentrating on the letter *Yud;* then we take the vessel in the right hand and pour water on the left, concentrating on the same letter *Yud.* Then we repeat this procedure for the next nine letters.

2 - Then we wash each hand ten times corresponding to the ten letters, but this we do as follows:

Ten times we wash the right hand, concentrating on one letter each time; the first time the *Yud,* second the *Vav,* third the *Daled,* and so on until we complete the ten times and we wash ten times the left hand in the same manner.

At the beginning, it may seem confusing and difficult, but after a few times it will become very easy to do and will only take one to two minutes. It would be a shame not to do it out of laziness, for the benefit is immeasurable. And it should afflict the person for the fact that he is not able to immerse in a *mikvah* as he should, and he should think at the time of the *netilah* that the *tumah* [impurity] is leaving him. This should be done only by one who can not go to a *mikvah* immediately and must wash before saying the *berachos* and the *kriyas shema.* But as soon as he is able to go to the *mikvah* he should do just that.

(The source for what we've said is the writings of the holy Maharam of Chernobyl *zt"l* printed in the beginning of the book *Chessed leAvraham* dealing with washing the hands when there's no *mikvah* available. Also, in the *sefer* Shulchan Hatahor, by the Gaon of Kamarna *(siman 88 saif beis),* it is written that the Baal Shem Tov established this. This advice is found in *sefer* Baal Shem Tov, who brings it from the *sefer* Emes leYaakov Ninio *zt"l* (page 117) as had been received from the Arizal. According to my knowledge this advice will be good to save us from the possibility that we may be saying *berachos* the Name of *Hashem,* and other things of *kedusha* in impurity before going to the *mikvah,* and sometimes some people will delay saying the *kriyas shema* until after its time, and this we know from many *acharonim* should not be done. (From the book 9 Kavim)

Lesson 31: The Garden of Eden / Pardes

One cannot overstate the emphasis the sages placed on living a life of Torah. Such learning does not even end in this world. The image of *Olam Haba*, the World to Come, is a great *yeshiva* where those who are worthy merit the right to sit at the table studying Torah with great masters.

The story is told of one man who was given a glimpse of the World to Come. Just a bit disappointed, he remarked. "Are these people in Heaven?" His host said: "These people who are studying Torah are not in Heaven; rather Heaven is in them!"

So why is there so much emphasis on *talmud* Torah? It is because learning Torah is the doorway to everything else in a Jewish person's life. That is why the Talmud says, "The study of Torah is equal to all the other commandments." (Shabbos 127a) Through Torah study, you have the desire to perform all the other commandments. Without the continuous study of Torah, you would otherwise overlook many of the commandments. The Torah makes the *mitzvos* real and alive in the heart of a person. To perform them, to teach them and learn more about them, this is heaven on earth.

So, why does the Torah start out with the story of Gan-Eden? The goal of man is to know *Hashem*. How does a person accomplish this? He lives a life of Gan-Eden. In Gan-Eden the righteous point and are able to say, "This is *Hashem*." But do you imagine that they really see *Hashem*? It can't be that they see *Hashem* as we understand vision. So, what is it that they really see?

After *Purim* I asked my friends, why do you feel down the day after *Purim*? Well on *Purim* you were not able to know the difference between Mordechai and Haman... how did you really accomplish this? You reached a level of *bitul*, nothingness. You see when you're *bitul*, you realize that *Hashem* is in control of everything and there is no good or bad... just *Hashem's* will. Now it's after *Purim* and your self-worth has returned. You no longer are able to see that *Hashem* is in control, so you feel you have lost control. Your world feels overwhelming because you haven't put *Hashem* inside it. So, *Purim* was a taste of how you are really supposed to trust in *Hashem*.

When the Talmud teaches that the beauty in the Garden of Eden is to know *Hashem*, this is what it means. The ultimate thought and peace of mind is realizing that *Hashem's* will is perfect.

This leads us to question as to why didn't Adam and Chava feel this was enough satisfaction? Why didn't they feel enough peace of mind in the holy Garden to just stay there and bask in the light of *Hashem*? Adam and Chava were instead thrown out of Gan-Eden because they chose to know good and evil (actually, Chava chose and she persuaded Adam). They rationalized that this would help them to know *Hashem* better. The logic of man is flawed, and they erred in not just trusting in *Hashem's* words.

It didn't take long for mankind, Adam and Chava, to realize their mistake and to make their only mission to return to the light of the Garden. Now that they tasted evil, the greatest pain in the world…they understood that to be separation from *Hashem*.

Why would anyone in their right mind choose to separate themselves from their light source and ultimate destiny, the Garden of Eden and knowing *Hashem*? This is the distilled essence of stubbornness. It prevents acceptance or "going with the flow". Being close to *Hashem* was very easy for the first couple in the world and it is quite simple even for today's generation of madness. This stubbornness is deeply cultural and subliminal.

In the worlds above, do you think there is not an idea of separation? There are many levels in the Garden of Eden. There is an upper Garden as well as a Lower Garden and inside these are many doors, chambers, and academies. If a person wants to find a pathway to *Hashem* in this world, he must separate from the norm of society and become sublime. He must find a *rav*, community, and friends whose only desire is to come close to *Hashem*. He should surround himself with good-hearted people who follow *halachos* and kind ways. This is only the first step towards setting oneself up in order to recapture the light of the Garden of Eden that we were shown before birth.

My father was in a state of locked-in syndrome; he couldn't speak and was paralyzed for years… As I stood by his bedside and cared for my holy father, reading the Tanya by his bedside, I understood that I was talking to an angel, not just a man stuck in a physical body. While people looked at him with pity, he returned this look with his shiny green eyes, a look that made us feel stupid that it wasn't he who was paralyzed but rather it was we. In those years we didn't have the technology to record all his thoughts, but currently, a *rabbi* sits in the same position as my father, locked in a world which to us is frightening but to him is a level of Gan-Eden on earth. His name if Rabbi Cahana who served as a chief *rabbi* of a synagogue in Canada, may *Hashem* restore his health.

Rabbi Cahana writes, "You have to believe you're paralyzed to play the part of a quadriplegic. I don't. In my mind and in my dreams, every night I am a *Chagall*-man; I float over the city, twirl, and swirl, with my toes kissing the floor. I know nothing about this statement of man without motion. Everything has motion. The heart pumps, the body heaves, the mouth moves, the eyes turn inside-out. We never stagnate. Life triumphs up and down."

Rabbi Cahana explains, "When my brain exploded my body flew apart onto my backyard, only ten times larger. My mind landed on top of the hedges. One arm a mile away, another arm over here. Legs here, legs there. The torso somewhere else. It was my job to somehow bring these all back together. To bring the body back to the head. This was my spiritual duty. I still believe I walk more gracefully. After all, who among us is really sure-footed?" However, in the World-to-Come, "*Ki anyin be'ayin yiru.* - We will see eye to eye." (Midrash Tehillim 13:2) In this world, the Divine Spirit revealed itself to specific individuals; but in the Future-to-Come, it says, "And the glory of *Hashem* shall be revealed, and all flesh shall see him." (Vayikra Rabbah 1:14)

So how do you get *Hashem* to uncover his face and not hide? How do you taste the World to Come while clothed in the physical? Well, we know that *Shabbos* is a taste of the Divine and so are *mitzvos,* also enclothed with sparks from Gan-Eden. When we do a *mitzvah lishmah,* we also attach ourselves to the realization of *Hashem's* ultimate will. We are thereby revealing His presence to the world. We are ridding ourselves of our ego, stubbornness, and selfishness, and closing the gap that separates us from *Hashem. Hashem* is thereby becoming less hidden.

The Zohar speaks about Rav Chiya's trip to Paradise. They ascended to Heaven by using the holy Name. There is a lot we can learn from the sages that entered the upper worlds while still clothed in a physical body. The Talmud (Chagigah 14b, Zohar I, 26b and Tikunei Zohar, Tikun 40) reports the following incident regarding four Mishnaic Sages:

The *rabbis* taught: Four [Sages] entered the *Pardes* [literally "the orchard."]. Rashi explains that they ascended to Heaven by utilizing the [Divine] Name [i.e., they achieved a spiritual elevation through intense meditation on G-d's Name] (Tosafos, *ad loc*). They were Ben Azzai, Ben Zoma, Acher [Elisha ben Avuya, called *Acher* (the other one) because of what happened to him after he entered the Pardes] and Rabbi Akiva. Rabbi Akiva said to them [prior to their ascension]: "When you come to the place of pure marble stones, do not say, 'Water! Water!' for it is said, 'He who speaks untruths shall not stand before My eyes.'" (Tehillim 101:7) Ben Azzai gazed [at the Divine Presence - Rashi] and died. Regarding him, the verse states, "Precious in the eyes of G-d is the death of His pious ones." (Tehillim 116:15) Ben Zoma gazed and was harmed [he lost his sanity - Rashi]. Regarding him, the verse states, "Did you find honey? Eat only as much as you need, lest you be overfilled and vomit it up." (Proverbs 25:16) Acher cut down the plantings [he became a heretic]. Rabbi Akiva entered in peace and left in peace.

Ramak now cites the Tikunei Zohar which adds some details not mentioned in the Talmud.

The ancient *saba* [an old man] stood up and said [to Rabbi Shimon bar Yochai], "Rabbi, Rabbi! What is the meaning of what Rabbi Akiva said to his students, 'When you come to the place of pure marble stones, do not say, 'Water! Water!' lest you place yourselves in danger, for it is said, 'He who speaks untruths shall not stand before My eyes.' But it is written, 'There shall be a firmament between the waters and it shall separate between water [above the firmament] and water [below the firmament].' (Genesis 1:6) The Torah describes the division of the waters into upper and lower; why should it be problematic to mention this division? Furthermore, since there are [in fact] upper and lower waters, why did Rabbi Akiva warn them, 'Do not say, 'Water! Water!'"

The holy Lamp [a title accorded to Rabbi Shimon bar Yochai] replied, "*Saba*, it is proper that you reveal this secret that the *chevraya* [Rabbi Shimon's circle of disciples] have not grasped clearly."

The ancient *saba* answered, "*Rabbi, rabbi,* holy Lamp. Surely the pure marble stones are the letter *Yud* - one the upper *Yud* of the letter *Aleph*, and one the lower *Yud* of the letter *Aleph* [an *Aleph* in script is formed by an upright *Yud* at the top to the right, and an upside-down *Yud* at the bottom to the left, joined by a *Vav*, the diagonal line between them]. Here there is no spiritual impurity; only pure marble stones, and so there is no separation between one kind of water and the other; they form a single unity from the aspect of the Tree of Life, which is the *Vav* in the midst of the letter *Aleph*." In this regard it states, "[lest he put forth his hand] and if he takes of the Tree of Life [and eat and live forever]." (Genesis 3:22)

Ramak now begins to analyze these passages.

The meaning of Rabbi Akiva's exhortation is that the sages should not declare that there are two types of water. Since there are not [two types of water] one would be causing a separation. This is the meaning of "do not say, 'water, water.'" Do not say that there are two types of water, lest you endanger yourself because of the sin of separation. For this reason, the old man asked two questions. "There shall be a firmament between the waters and it shall separate..." (Genesis 1:6). Thus, there are two types of water and a separation between them. In this case, does it not appear to be permissible to refer to two types of water? Even more problematic is that the Torah itself states, "It shall separate between water and water." The water above the firmament and the water below the firmament. This is a complete separation.

The marble stones represent the letter *Yud*.

The old man asked a second question - the waters are in fact of two types: water of the firmament and water below the firmament [in rivers, lakes, and seas]. Why then did Rabbi Akiva exhort them not to say "water, water", lest they endanger themselves? On the contrary, it should be permitted to mention two types of water, for this is no worse than the language used by the Torah, and this is also the situation in fact.

Now Rabbi Shimon did not wish to explain this matter himself; he wanted his disciples to hear it from the old man. The old man explained that each of the marble stones represents the letter *Yud*. As we have explained elsewhere this means a *Yud* at the beginning, and a *Yud* at the end, according to the mystical explanation of "I am first and I am last." (Isaiah 44:6) The first *Yud* represents *Chochmah*, and the second *Yud* represents *Malchus*, which is also *Chochmah* according to the mystical explanation of the light that returns from below to above (called *or chozer*). The upper *Yud* is the *Yud* of the Tetragrammaton (*Yud-Hey-Vav-Hey*) while the lower *Yud* is the *Yud* of the name *Alef-Daled-Nun-Yud*.

Chassidus, Kabbalah and Meditation

The latter is the concept of "female waters" (*Mayin Nukvin*), and the former the concept of "male waters" (*Mayin Dechurin*). They are called "female waters" because they receive from below, from the performance of the commandments, and through them, a person has the ability to affect the higher worlds so that the light will shine forth and become clothed in them, as in a palace. Thus, the light that is elicited [by the performance of the commandments is like] a king in his palace.

These are also the keys to the inner and outer aspects. The inner aspect is the light of the Tetragrammaton, which undoubtedly descends as *or yashar* from above to below. The outer aspect is that which returns according to the mystical explanation of *or chozer*. This is the meaning of the statement in regard to the *Sefiros*, "from below to above, and from above to below," as explained elsewhere. This is signified by the top and the bottom *Yuds* of the *Alef*. This is also the secret of the intertwining (*shiluv*) of the two names ‏י-ה-א-ה-ד-ו-נ-ה-י‏ - *Yud-Alef-Hey-Daled-Vov-Nun-Hey-Yud* - with the upper *Yud* at the beginning and the lower *Yud* at the end.

These two *Yuds* are referred to in the passage "pure marble stones." Each of the *Yuds* is a stone because its shape is round like a stone. It is called "marble" because marble is generally white, which is indicative of the attribute of Mercy (in Hebrew *rachamim*). In this sense, it is also similar to water [which represents kindness]. Now since these two *Yuds* are the aspect of compassion, just like water, which is called "waters of kindness," they are therefore referred to as "marble," as we just explained.

We can also explain this by way of [the science of] *tzeiruf* (letter combinations and permutations): The *Sefirah* of *Chochmah* is called *yesh* - "being" [since it is the first imminent *Sefirah*], spelled *Yud-Shin* in Hebrew. The lower *Chochmah* [i.e., *Malchus*] is called *shai* [*Shin-Yud* -- the identical letters, but in reverse order]. When both words are combined they form the word *shayish* -- *Shin-Yud-Shin* (marble). The *Yud* is *Chochmah*, the source, and the *shin* is the emanation of its branches [i.e., the branching out into *Sefiros* according to the mystical explanation of *or yashar*]. *Malchus* is called *shai* according to the mystical explanation of the light that reverses (*or chozer*). When these two words, signifying these two types of light, are combined to form the word *shayish* (the two *Yuds* combine into one).

They are the letter *Yud*... the upper and lower *Yuds* of the *Alef* are joined by a diagonal *Vav*.

They are called "pure", for there are a number of different types of water [mentioned in the Torah]; one of these is *mei nida* - literally waters of impurity [because they are used to purify a person after he became contaminated by contact with the dead. Water from a living spring is mixed with the ashes of the red heifer and is then sprinkled upon the impure person]. Separation and division are mentioned in regard to this type of water, as will be explained. These waters [of the pure] marble stones are completely pure and pertain to *Atzilus*.

"They are the letter *Yud* - one the upper *Yud* of the letter *Alef*..." We already

187

explained above that the Name ‫‬י-ה-נ-ו-ד-ה-א-י *Yud-Alef-Hey-Dalet-Vav-Nun-Hey-Yud* has the upper and lower aspects of *chochmah* [represented by the two *Yuds*] and six letters in between, alluding to the letter *Vav* [which has a numerical value of 6. Note that the upper and lower *Yuds* of the *Alef* are joined by a diagonal *Vav*.

This is the way a scribe traditionally writes the letter ‫א‬]. This symbolizes *Tiferes*, which branches out into six extremities [*Tiferes* is the central *Sefirah* of the six *Sefiros* of *Zeir Anpin*]. The *Vav* is situated between the *Yuds* in order to join them. That is to say, through *Tiferes* the daughter [*Malchus*] is able to ascend "to her father's house as in her youth."

It is for this reason that Rabbi Akiva warned his friends not to say that those two marble stones were separated from one another, G-d forbid, for this is not true. On the contrary, the firmament between them, which is *Tiferes*, actually unites them, and through it, they are joined together. There is no separation other than in a place of spiritual impurity, as it is written, "To separate between the impure and the pure." (Vayikra 11:47) However, in a place of purity - pure marble stones - "do not say, 'water, water.'" This is what the old man was explaining: "Here there is no spiritual impurity… they are from the aspect of the Tree of Life…" These waters are in *Atzilus* and therefore there is no separation between them… on the contrary, the firmament unites them…

[Translation and commentary by Moshe Miller from Pardes Rimonim, Sha'ar Arachei HaKinuim, s.v. Mayim]

In the Future-to-Come, the faces of the *tzaddikim* will be similar in appearance to the sun, moon, heaven, stars, lightning, roses, and the *menorah* of the *Bais Hamikdash*. (Sifre Devorim 1:10)

In the Future-to-Come, the *tzaddikim* will be clothed in fire and will enjoy its splendorous warmth as a man enjoys the warm rays of the sun on a cold wintery day. It will be sweet to them. (Pesikta Rabbasi 12:6)

[In Gan-Eden] the righteous are sitting clothed in splendid [spiritual] garments, enjoying many [spiritual] delights. Meanwhile, the wicked are standing outside, looking at them from afar. Unmitigated evildoers are not allowed to come close and have direct knowledge [of the delights of Gan-Eden]. They only learn [about Gan-Eden] from hearsay. Occasionally, they receive permission to surround the *tzaddikim* and peek at them through holes and cracks, as it says, "The wicked roam on all sides." (Tehillim 12:9) (Sefer Chassidim p. 103)

It is a wonder why any Jew would purposely oppose a Torah lifestyle. It is a very shortsighted vision apparently, as ultimately this world is simply a stepping stone to the main banquet.

The Talmud teaches, "All the world drinks from the surplus of Gan-Eden. (Ta'anis 10a) How much of this surplus you will drink is entirely up to you. The flow of blessing is endless to those who sacrifice their lives for *Hashem* and His will. It says, "This world is compared to the dry land; the World-to-Come, to the ocean. If one does not prepare on dry land, what will he eat upon the ocean?" (Midrash Mishlei 6:6).

Lesson 32: Ruach HaKodesh

Rabbi Yochanan said, "From the day that the holy Temple was destroyed [the power of] prophecy was taken from the prophets and given to deranged people and children." (Bava Basra 12b) The *rabbis* taught in a *braisa*, "When the latter prophets – Chaggai, Zechariah, and Malachi - died [at the beginning of the Second Temple era], Divine Spirit was withdrawn from the Jewish people." (Sanhedrin 11a)

The question then remains, how much Divine Spirit has been left for the righteous. While the generation might not be on the level of receiving this Holy Spirit, would *Hashem* still send down a lower form of it, called *ruach hakodesh* to still communicate with those pure at heart. There is a very big difference between *nevuah* and *ruach hakodesh*. The main one is that only a *navi* carries a message from *Hashem* to people, and can say, כה אמר השם. A *baal ruach hakodesh*, even when he has a clear knowledge of something, is never saying, I have a message to you from *Hashem*.

There's a famous story about the Noda Biyehuda that when he first became *rav* and had many opponents they kept trying to test him and trip him up. Once, by a *seudas bris*, they made something look like a questionable piece of meat and brought it up to him and asked what its *din* was. He started leaning towards one ruling and they all brought proofs to the contrary. He heard them out and started to agree with them. Then they brought proofs the other way around and he started leaning towards that. That is when he suddenly announced that this case is made up.

They knew he was right, but they wondered how he knew. He said when a *shaila* comes to a *rav* he gets *siatta diShmaya* to answer correctly. If I can't make up my mind, then it must not really be a question.

HaRav Chaim Kanievsky *shlit"a* went to visit Gaave'd Yerushalaim, HaRav Tuvia Wiess *shlit"a*. Rav Tuvia told Rav Chaim that he learns in the *sefer* Birchas Peretz of the Steipler *zt"l* (father of Rav Chaim) and the many *gematrios* mentioned in the *sefer* must be *ruach hakodesh*. Rav Chaim answered that it's not *ruach hakodesh* but rather *siyata diShmaya*.

I recall Rabbi Avigdor Miller saying on one of his tapes that *ruach hakodesh*, as it is used in post-Talmudic *seforim*, means a form of *siyata diShmaya* to make the right decisions and say the right *pshat*.

Reb Moshe Steinerman

Rabbi Baruch Ber Levovitz once told over to his students that he asked his *rebbe,* the great Rabbi Chaim Soloveitchik, "Does the Chafetz Chaim have *ruach hakodesh?*" Rabbi Chaim replied that the sages already taught, "When the later prophets died, Chagai, Zecharia, Malachi, *ruach hakodesh* departed from the Jewish people." (Sota 9b)

"However, we find in the Talmud (Eruvin 64b, referring to a later time) 'at that time Rabbi Yishmael answered with *ruach hakodesh.*' And many other times our sages taught that *ruach hakodesh* shone in their *bais midrash.*" (Toras Chaim - sec. Ruach Hakodesh)

The classic book Orchos Tzaddikim writes (Shaar Yiras Shamayaim): "Just as no being is capable of seeing G-d, so too no being is capable of seeing the soul. And just as G-d can see the future, so too, a man at the time when he is asleep (if he has succeeded in allowing his higher soul to control his lower soul), then he will see in his dreams future events. And he will see the spirits of the dead and places and people he never saw before, and he will see great things and forms, that which he is not capable of seeing while awake."

Chovos Halevavos brings down in the Sha'ar Cheshbon Hanefesh some interesting inside information: "And he will be on a high level, among the levels of the pious, and a high level among the *tzaddikim,* and he will be able to see without his physical eye, and hear without his physical ear, and speak without a tongue (for example, talk to others in their dreams), and he will sense things without his physical senses, and be able to picture them without need for a comparison." Tov HaLevanon commentary: "All this refers to deep, Divine matters, close to the level of *ruach hakodesh.*" (from Sha'ar Cheshbon HaNefesh #10)

Eliyahu Hanavi wrote: (Tana D'Bei Eliyahu 9) "I testify before Heaven and Earth, whether man or woman, whether Gentile or Jew, whether slave man or slave woman, everyone according to his actions, that *ruach hakodesh* will dwell on him." (i.e. anyone can reach *ruach hakodesh,* even women, slaves, or non-Jews)

Ruach hakodesh is the opposite of psychic. A psychic tries not to know anything about the topic he is divining. A *baal ruach hakodesh* asks many questions. Also, a psychic has a feeling or bias, which is assumed to be accurate when he has no prior bias. *ruach hakodesh* is unmistakable.

When I have told people that a certain *rebbe* or *tzaddik* I know has *ruach hakodesh,* many times I am shown a grin or strange response. Some say there is no *ruach hakodesh* today, while others are amazed at the insights of their *rav* and there is no way to explain it except to simply label it as *ruach hakodesh.*

Rabbi Avdimi of Haifa said, "From the day that the (first) Temple was destroyed, the prophetic gift was taken away from the prophets and given to the sages (*rabbis*)." The Gemara asks: "[Can it be] that before the destruction of the Temple, no sage was a prophet? What Rabbi Avdimi meant to say was that, when the Temple was destroyed, although prophecy was taken from the prophets (who were not sages), prophecy was not taken from the sages (i.e., they retained their prophetic power even after the Temple's destruction)." (Bava Basra 12a)

Chassidus, Kabbalah and Meditation

Knowing that a *rebbe* can see the past, present, and future may enhance one's appreciation of the *rebbe*, but that's not the main thrust of one's relationship with him. When a *chassid* seeks the advice and spiritual insight of a *tzaddik*, he knows the *tzaddik* is using *ruach hakodesh* or prophecy to communicate to him what G-d wants him to know. That's why a *chassid* is absolutely committed to following the *rebbe's* words because he is assured that G-d is personally communicating His desire and directive to him through the *tzaddik*. Although the average Jew may not perceive the spiritual forces present in the world, experiencing a *tzaddik's ruach hakodesh* gives him the spiritual confidence necessary to develop a love and passion for G-d. This elevates his Divine service to a whole new level. This is one of the most important functions of the *rebbe-chassid* relationship. (Rabbi Shloma Majeski)

How can you explain the time that I sat down with the Biala Rebbe *shlit"a*, of New York, and he knew how many candles my wife was lighting for *Shabbos*? He started out asking me what it was that my wife did specially for *Shabbos* every week. Not wanting to divulge the secret, I kept quiet. He then said, "Does she light extra candles?" Still, in a secretive mood, I responded, "Yes, she likes to light many candles." "How many?" he asked. Being stubborn, I still didn't come clean with the secret. Finally, he just came out with it: "Is she lighting thirty-six candles?" Having only just met the *rebbe* this time, it was impossible he could have guessed any of this. Could you explain it off as just *siyata diShmaya* or would you call this a lower level of *ruach hakodesh*?

Rabbi Mann of Tzfat *zt"l* was able to know exactly where I was holding in my spiritual level when I bumped into him in the courtyard of the *shul*. Sometimes, I would try to head quickly to my seat, so he wouldn't know what I was up to. Maybe he was able to read this from my forehead. In Kabbalah, it teaches that on the forehead of a pure person, you are able to see the name of *Hashem*. If someone is attached to evil, you can also see this. Would you call this *siyata diShmaya* also?

I once had a question in Kabbalah and I asked the Nikolsberg Rebbe for guidance. He told me to close my eyes and he explained it by showing it to me. How is that even possible without *ruach hakodesh*?

When I met the *rebbe* the first time with my family, he asked questions from all of us. "Who has stomach problems?" My mother raised her hand. "Who has sugar problems?" My hand went up... It continued on and on until most of our problems were brought to the fore.

We learn in the Talmud that even the lowest of Talmudists were able to perform reincarnation. They were able to give blessings that had amazing results. In our century, Baba Sali was able to restart the car on a bottle of water and drive out of the desert sun. He also gave a cup of water to ill patients, who were quickly healed.

Maybe it isn't that the sages are given special abilities alone, but rather the *Shechinah* that accompanies those who do the will of *Hashem* that reveals to them heavenly secrets. As generations pass, open miracles are fewer and pure *ruach hakodesh* is shown through more and more opaque glass. To such an extent that we can't call it outright *ruach hakodesh* as it was known to our ancestors, but nor can we call it *siyata diShmaya*, because it is so much deeper.

According to the Talmud, the *Urim* and *Tumim* were actually used as the subject of mystical contemplation. The High Priest would contemplate the stones of the *Urim* and *Tumim*, meditating until he reached the enlightened state of *ruach hakodesh*. He would then see the letters on the stones light up, spelling out the necessary message. (Yoma 73b)

This explains the meaning of the terms *Urim* and *Tumim*. The word *Urim* clearly comes from the word *or*, meaning "light." This indicates that the letters actually light up. The word *Tumim* is derived from the word *Tamim*, under discussion. This indicates that the *Tumim* would bring the High Priest to the level of *Tamim*, the completeness and perfection implied by *ruach haKodesh*.

Thus, when the 119th psalm speaks of those "complete on the way" (Tamim Derech), it is speaking of those who are seeking enlightenment and the transcendental experience. One gets a definite impression that it was actually a psalm used by people seeking enlightenment, perhaps even the disciples of the prophets in their quest for the prophetic experience. As such, it would have been a long mantra, chanted in a prescribed order until it brought the individual to a high meditative state. The Baal Shem Tov was taught by his spiritual master that if he said the 119th psalm every day, he would be able to speak to people while at the same time maintaining a transcendental state of attachment to the Divine. It is evident that many passages are highly suggestive of the mystical experience. The psalm speaks of a person walking the path of enlightenment, seeking higher states of consciousness, while at the same time asking to be delivered from error and other dangers facing those who ascend the spiritual heights. (Meditation and the Bible, Aryeh Kaplan 142)

The diviners meditate in their thoughts, fixing their full concentration on the subject they wish to know. As a result of their powerful meditation (*hisbodedus*), their mind is divested of all physical concepts. Their soul then communes with spiritual entities which can inform them of events in the near future. (Sefer HaChinuch 510)

One must learn these methods from a master, just as the "Sons of the prophets" who would prepare themselves for prophecy. They would also have to put themselves in a joyous mood. This is the significance of Elisha's remark, "Now bring me a musician." And it was when the musician played [and the hand of *Hashem* came upon him]." (2 Kings 3:15)

They would then meditate *(hisboded)* according to their knowledge of the meditative methods. Through this, they would attain wondrous levels, divesting themselves of the physical, and making the mind overcome the body completely. The mind becomes so overpowering that the physical senses are abandoned, and the prophet does not sense anything with them at all. The prophet's consciousness is then on that which he is seeking, climbing the steps on high. It was in this manner that they would meditate and divest themselves from the physical. (Rabbi Moses Cordevero, Shiur Komach 16)

The concept of a prophetic dream and that of a vision are so close to each other that they can be considered the same. The reason for this is that they both have the same source. Such a prophetic dream comes through meditation (*hisbodedus*) involving the mind and consciousness. As a result of this meditation on a subject in the mind, a strong impression is made on the soul. Through this meditation, the soul elevates itself, just as if it were separated from the body, and is not restrained by the physical.

This is actually the meaning of the word *chalom*, meaning dream. It comes from the root *chalam*, meaning to strengthen, as in "You strengthened me (*tachlimeni*) and gave me life." (Isaiah 38:16) The reason for this is that a dream is caused by the strength (*chalam*) and vitality of the soul when it overcomes the body. When one is in a state of preparation through meditation (*hisbodedus*), he is strengthened through a prophetic dream.

A prophetic vision is also the result of meditation. The prophet mentally gazes at glorious visions involving the mystery of the Chambers on high, binding them together and unifying them on high with their cause. His mind soars among the fearsome Forms which are in each Chamber, and his consciousness is bound to them and unified with them.

Through this the prophet divests himself of the physical, abandoning all feelings and sensations associated with the body. He dissolves himself in those Forms, and his consciousness becomes clothed in them. Through these forms he experiences his vision, seeing according to the level of his perception. It is in this manner that one receives a prophetic message, and the words are engraved (*chakak*) in his heart in a spiritual manner.

After the vision leaves him, he divests himself of the Form in which he was garbed through the power of his own original form. This is alluded to in the *Torah*, which says, "*Hashem* left when he finished speaking to Avraham, and Avraham returned to his original level, where he was before he had this vision."

I have seen a similar concept in the teachings of the Masters of Truth, who received it from the *Gaonim*. They write all the faculties of the prophet and seer faint, and they are transmitted from Form to Form until the individual is clothed in the power of the Form that is revealed to him. This power is then transmitted to an angelic Form, and when that Form is transmuted in the prophet, it gives him the power to receive the prophetic potential. This is then engraved in his heart with a spiritual form. After this agent overwhelms him, thus performing its function, the prophet then divests himself of the power of the Form revealed to him and grabs himself in the power of his normal form. It is as if he divests himself of one form and invests himself in another. The parts of the prophet's mind are then reunited, and his physical faculties once again return, as they were originally. Then, when he is in a normal human state, he speaks the words of his prophecy. These are the words that I found. (Rabbi Meir Ibn Gabbai, Hakodesh, Sitrey Torah 27)

We find in the Talmud, "Everything that Ezekiel saw, Isaiah saw as well."

(Chagigah 13b Rashi, Tosafos) Moreover, we know that the Israelites visualized the entire *Merkavah* at the Red Sea and Mount Sinai. They were shown the same system through which *Hashem* brought the universe into existence. Still, Ezekiel was the only one to describe it explicitly. The details that Ezekiel wrote are not just descriptive. Besides alluding to the complete system through which *Hashem* runs the universe, it contains the meditative techniques for setting up a *Merkavah* and attaining this spiritual experience. According to the Kabbalists, hidden in this first chapter lies the entire methodology through which all the prophets attained prophecy. It contains the key to all the secrets of prophecy and to almost all of Kabbalah as well. (Inner Space page 139)

The mystery of *ruach hakodesh* is this: It is a voice sent from on high to speak to one worthy of *ruach hakodesh*. Such a voice is purely spiritual, and such a voice cannot enter the prophet's ear until it clothes itself in a physical voice.

The physical voice in which it clothes itself is the voice of the prophet himself when he is involved in prayer or Torah study. This voice clothes itself in his voice and is attached to it. It then enters the prophet's ear so that he can hear it. Without the physical voice of the individual himself, this could not possibly take place.

The explanation is as follows: First, there is an earlier voice, from which the angel or Holy Spirit was created. This is the voice of prophecy. When this voice comes to reveal the prophecy, it must clothe itself in that individual's present physical voice. This must be a voice expressed by the individual at the very moment he is experiencing the prophecy.

This is the mystery of the verse, "The spirit of *Hashem* speaks in me, and His word is on my tongue." (2 Samuel 23:2) The "spirit" and "word" are the original voice, created through his deeds. This is now resting on his tongue. It is literally emanating from his mouth, expressed in his speech, and therefore it literally speaks with his mouth. It is only then that he can hear it. This involves many details.

This can also occur in another manner. The supernal voice can clothe itself in the voices of other saints, from earlier generations. The two voices then come together and speak to the individual.

It is impossible for the voice of such a saint to speak to the individual unless the two share the same soul root. Sometimes, however, it can also occur when the individual has done some deed that is associated with that saint in particular.

When the voice is clothed in the individual's own speech, this is certainly a much higher level than when it is clothed in the speech of another saint. When one needs another saint, this is an indication that his own speech does not have the power to induce prophecy.

This explains the difference between prophecy and *ruach hakodesh*. Prophecy is from the male aspect, while *ruach hakodesh* is from the female. (Torah from the Arizal)

Now if *ruach hakodesh* is from the side of the female, then the *Shechinah* is also the feminine aspect. Therefore, the key to *ruach hakodesh* is connecting to the

Shechinah continuously.

Who is a *chassid?* He who acts with love for his Creator, striving to give Him pleasure, and whose whole intention is to cleave to Him in *d'vekus* for the sake of His great Name, becoming thereby a chariot for *Hashem.* (Rabbi Isaiah Horowitz, Kitzur Shnei Luchos Ha-Bris, Sh'ar HaAhavah, p. 11)

In the previous gate, we have warned the initiate regarding the pitfalls that lie in the road leading to enlightenment. Still, he should not give up. Commenting on the verse, "Devorah was a prophetess" (Judges 4:4), the prophet Elijah taught his disciples, "I call Heaven and Earth to witness, that any individual, man or woman, Jew or Gentile, freeman or slave, can have *ruach hakodesh* come upon him. It all depends on his deeds."

Our own eyes have seen, and our own ears have heard distinguished individuals who have attained the level of *ruach hakodesh*, even in our times. Some of these individuals can predict the future. Others have mastered wisdom that had never been revealed to previous generations.

In order that those who wish to enter the Sanctuary not be discouraged, I will explain a few concepts, opening the door like the eye of a needle; "For *Hashem* will not withhold good from those who walk uprightly." First, I will explain a few general principles involving enlightenment. Then, in the Eighth gate, I will discuss a number of specific practices.

The best way of all is that taught by Elijah. This was the way of the early righteous (*chassidim rishonim*), also known as the Pharisees. The technique is as follows:

One must first repent every sin he has ever done, rectifying all the spiritual damage he has caused. He must then perfect his soul through concentration in prayer and diligent Torah study without ulterior motives. He must continue like an ox under its yoke until the physical becomes weak. This should also include such disciplines as minimizing the amount of food one eats, waking up at midnight, shunning all unworthy traits, separating oneself from other people, and not speaking unnecessary words. One must also constantly purify his body through immersion in the *mikvah.*

After this, one should meditate occasionally on the fear of *Hashem.* He should mentally depict the letters of the Tetragrammaton. At this time, he should be careful to keep his thoughts away from all worldly vanities, binding himself to the love of *Hashem* with great passion.

Through this, one can be worthy of *ruach hakodesh* in one of the following aspects:

The first aspect consists of a transmission of the highest Light, from the root of the highest levels of his soul to the individual. Such a revelation is *ruach hakodesh* in its purest form.

The second aspect comes about through the study of Torah or observance of some commandment. Our sages taught, "When a person keeps a commandment, he earns an advocate [angel]." This actually means that an angel is created through one's actions. If the individual does this consistently according to the law, with great *kavanah*, then this angel will reveal itself to him. This is the meaning of those angels called *maggidim*, which are mentioned in various writings, but if the commandment is not kept according to the law (*halacha*), then this angel will be made up of good and evil, combining truth and falsehood.

The third aspect is that, as a result of one's piety, Elijah will reveal himself to him. The greater one's piety, the greater will be his enlightenment.

The fourth aspect is greater than [the previous two]. This involves the revelation of the soul of a *tzaddik* who has already passed away. This *tzaddik* may share the same root with the individual's soul or may come from other roots. This aspect can come about through the proper observance of a commandment, just like the previous aspects. People who are worthy of this attain a level where they gain knowledge of high wisdom and the hidden mysteries of the Torah. This, too, depends on one's deeds.

The fifth aspect is the lowest of them all. This involves dreams where the future and other knowledge is revealed to the individual. This is also close to *ruach hakodesh*.

The method discussed earlier brings one onto a straight path. The individual does not use mystical oaths to bind the Supernal Beings, but only resorts to the power of his good deeds and sanctification of the self. He can then be assured that the *ruach hakodesh* he attains will be pure, without any admixture of evil whatsoever.

This, however, is not true when a person attempts to coerce the Supernal Beings. It is true that one may have success through methods involving mystical oaths, specific actions, prayers, and *yichudim*, but if one makes the slightest error, it is possible that his revelation will be intermingled with Outside Forces.

There are also other methods involving specific techniques, which will be discussed in the Fourth Section and can bring the above-mentioned aspects to a person, even when they do not come automatically. These methods, however, require great holiness and purity, since otherwise, they will give rise to a mixed revelation, as mentioned above.

The first way that we have discussed, however, is the path taken by the earlier generations. It is the path referred to by the Ramban in his commentary on the Torah. This is also the significance of Ben Azzai's experience, when he would [simply] study and would be surrounded by burning flames, as the Ramban explains in his Iggeres Hakodesh. (Excerpts from Shaarey Kedushah, The Seventh Gate)

One must purify himself in four ways:

First, one must repent all of his sins, whether they involve violating the Torah's prohibitions, neglecting its positive commandments or even transgressing Rabbinical laws or adhering to unworthy traits. Such repentance must include a resolve never to repeat the sin or return to the bad trait. Such repentance is especially important for sins for which the Torah prescribes a penalty of being [spiritually] "cut off," or those which involve a desecration of *Hashem's* Name. This includes violation of the *Shabbos*, the menstrual rules, sexual pollution, oaths--even if they involve the truth, gazing at forbidden members of the opposite sex, malicious gossip, tale bearing, mockery and idle chatter. One must also keep himself from pride, anger, oversensitivity, and depression, behaving with modesty and humility and rejoicing in his portion.

The second purification involves the meticulous observance of all 248 commandments of the Torah [which parallel the 248 parts of the human body], as well as the legislated commandments. Particularly, it involves keeping set times for Torah study, praying with *kavanah*, reciting all blessings and the grace after meals with *kavanah*, loving one's fellow man, and honoring the *Shabbos* in every detail. One should also wake up each night at midnight to study Torah and mourn for Jerusalem. Whatever one does should be with love, for the sake of Heaven.

The third and fourth purifications involve specific preparations through which one sanctifies himself for *ruach hakodesh*.

The first of these involves purification of the body, through immersion in the *mikvah*, and clean clothing.

The second should be done when one actually prepares to receive *ruach hakodesh* after the other good traits have become part of his nature.

You should be in a room by yourself, after immersion and sanctification. It should be a place where you will not be distracted by the sound of human voices or the chirping of birds. The best time to do this is shortly after midnight.

Close your eyes and divest your thoughts of all worldly things. It should be as if your soul had left your body, and you should be as devoid of sensation as a corpse. Then strengthen yourself with a powerful yearning, meditating on the supernal universe. There you should attach yourself to the root of your soul and to the Supernal Lights.

It should seem as if your soul had left your body and had ascended on high. Imagine yourself standing in the supernal universes.

If you make use of a *Yichud*, have in mind that through it, you are transmitting light and sustenance to all universes. Keep in mind that you, too, will receive your portion in the end.

When the Spirit rests on you, you must still discern if it is pure and clean, or from the Other Side, a mixture of good and evil. Keep in mind what happened to Ben Zoma and Ben Azzai when they ascended to the Orchard. You can discern this through what is revealed. It can consist completely of truth, or it can be truth mixed with falsehood. Occasionally, the revelation will consist of idle concepts, dealing with worldly vanities, or ideas that do not conform to the teachings of the Torah. When this occurs, you must repel yourself from it. You must then continue to fortify yourself with worship, until the revelation is faithful, based on the fear of heaven.

At first, the Spirit [of *ruach hakodesh*] will rest on you occasionally, at distant intervals. The revelation will only involve simple concepts and not deep ideas. Very little will be revealed, but as you progress, your power will likewise increase. (Excerpts from Sha'arey Kedushah, The Eighth Gate)

As you can see from our holy sages, working on one's character traits is the first step towards attaining enlightenment. You would think that something as pure and holy as Divine inspiration would require hours of *Yichudim* but, though this will be beneficial, the most important elements are the intentions and pureness of one's character traits.

Someone once asked the Nikolsberg Rebbe, "How is it that you are able to see into a person's soul and know so much about him?" He responded, "If you look at everyone with an *ayin tov*, a good eye, then *Hashem* reveals things to you." Once when I was feeling a bit shy to open up to the *rebbe*, he told me, "A *rebbe* doesn't see bad things; he only sees good."

Why would *Hashem* reveal anything to a sage unless it is for the purpose of helping someone's soul? The sage who is pure has no desire to randomly visualize things. In fact, the Hornosyple Rebbe of Jerusalem once revealed to me that insights and the problems that other people have confuse his prayers and are overwhelming.

There was a holy sage who was blessed with *ruach hakodesh* after years of praying for this ability. When he finally received it, he saw so much about people and their sufferings that he could no longer take it. He prayed that his revelations would cease.

It is said about the Seer of Lubin, the holy *chozeh*, that he was able to see from one end of the world to the other. So, the question is why can we not see even minuscule distances on Earth, and why was the *Chozeh* able to? I think we can all answer this question fairly easily. Have you ever been really frustrated looking for something at home or in the grocery that was right in front of your eyes? Why didn't you see it? Because eyes don't act alone. They are connected to a brain. In order to see, the eye must look, and the brain must perceive.

We can all see *Hashem's* presence in everything with our eyes, but it won't help if we are looking but not seeing. *Eiynayim lahem v'lo yiru*, you can have eyes that don't see anything. It takes the *kedusha* of a *chozeh* to see the light emanating from every action and every part of the *bria*.

However, there are things that cast a bright light much closer to home that we don't really have an excuse not to see. We should easily be able to see the brilliantly lit *neshamos* of the people around us. Everybody we know, or meet has surely done enough good to make their holy neshamos light up an entire universe. How strange that often we only notice the few specks of dirt that they have accumulated. We manage not to notice the incredible light that emanates from them.

We could easily see the glow of a person passing us in the street or the new face in *shul*, feeling that someone cared enough to say good morning or hello. We can't possibly miss the burning sensation of our children who feel neglected by a person so integral to their lives when our busy schedules leave them off our agenda for extended periods. We shouldn't miss the searing fire that we set off in the people closest to us, including our spouses, with some of our actions and behaviors.

We may not be able to see around the world, but because we are capable of seeing things quadrillions of miles away, we should really open up our eyes to the things that are even brighter than a star and right under our nose. (Revach L'Neshama)

Clairvoyance comes through purifying oneself from all negative traits. *Ruach hakodesh,* which is far higher, comes as Rav Elyah Lopian said (Lev Eliyahu; Rabbi Lopian himself was known as one who acquired *ruach hakodesh*): "By the forty-eight ways through which the Torah is acquired," as brought down in the end of Pirkei Avos. The first is Talmud - diligence in Torah study; then "a listening ear"; listening thirstily and plumbing the depths of the Talmud.

The Talmud has a special energy with which to enlighten a person. This especially holds true if one studies seven *blatt* of Talmud a day. I have found in my own studies that conversations or things that happened during my day could be seen in my Talmud study that same day, but this only happened when I studied many, many pages of Talmud that particular day. I also noticed something special within the *sefer* Ayin Yaakov, many times I was able to open the pages of this book randomly to answer my questions.

Opening a Torah book from your personal *rebbe,* or any Torah book can spark a lower revelation of *ruach hakodesh.* In *Chabad,* for example, many will tell stories suggesting the *rebbe* had *ruach hakodesh.* One such example is a story I read this week of a woman who went to the *rebbe* because she was not Jewish (she came from a Roman-Catholic home) but wanted to marry a Jewish man. The man refused to marry her if she did not convert to Judaism, but the woman was afraid that converting would devastate her family. Two minutes into her visit with the *rebbe,* he told her not to worry because she was Jewish. When she protested, the *rebbe* said to ask her mother if she was Jewish. It turned out that the girl's parents had hidden their Jewish identity after the war, even from their own daughter. The *rebbe* knew what the girl herself did not.

One *motzoei Shabbos,* which was also *erev Rosh Chodesh,* Rabbi Pinye Althaus was standing by the elevator in 770. As the *rebbe* walked past him, he immediately noticed that Reb Pinye was not in a good mood.

"Pinye, you must have forgotten to say *yaaleh veyavo* during Maariv," the *rebbe* remarked. Reb Pinye recalled that this was the case, and he replied, "That's true." With a smile, the *rebbe* added, "You see what I need to use my *ruach hakodesh* for, Pinye?" (Translated from the Kfar Chabad Magazine)

A *yungerman* who did not have children and has been married for ten years has been visiting Rav Chaim Kanievksy regularly for a *beracha* and guidance as to what he and his wife should do to be *zoche* to have children. Each time the *yungerman* would visit, Rav Chaim would respond with his standard refrain of "*Beracha vehatzlacha,*" and would then add, cryptically, that the *yungerman* should "check what needs to be checked."

The *yungerman* never understood what Rav Chaim meant and did not know what to check.

At the beginning of this week, the *yungerman* once again went to Rav Chaim for a *beracha* and an *eitzah.* Rav Chaim responded, "*Bracha vehatzlacha,*" and once again added, "Check what needs to be checked."

Finally, the *yungerman* couldn't restrain himself and asked Rav Chaim, "What should I check? What should I look into?"

"Check your *mezuzos*," said Rav Chaim.

The *yungerman* ran home and sent all of his *mezuzos* to be checked. On Tuesday, he returned to Rav Chaim, shaking. He related that he had sent all his *mezuzos* to be checked and virtually all of them were perfectly kosher. One of them, however, was not. The *mezuzah* that had been hanging on his bedroom doorpost had the words "*veshinantom levanecha*" connected, without the proper space between the words.

Rav Chaim listened and smiled, and then once again wished the *yungerman*, "*Bracha vehatzlacha.*"

Without this impediment, the *yungerman* and his wife continue to hope and pray that they will parent a child *bekarov*.

May they and all of *Klal Yisrael* only celebrate good times together. (Yair Alpert-Matzav.com Israel)

A wealthy person would often come to the Baal Shem Tov and beg him relentlessly for a blessing for children. Finally, the Baal Shem Tov told him, "If you want such a blessing, you'll have to accept the fact that if you have a child you will lose all your wealth." The person mulled it over and finally agreed; and indeed, that is what happened: a baby was born but the man lost all his wealth.

The Baal Shem Tov explained that in heaven, the amount of *chessed* (kindness) the man was destined to receive was limited - enough for either children or wealth, but not both. Seeing this, the Baal Shem Tov was able to provide the man with a choice, which ultimately led to the fulfillment of his desire for children. (Derech Mitzvosecha)

In another story, a *chassid* in the publishing business wanted to publish and print Torah books but needed a permit from the Russian Minister of Education. Since the Russian government was not too favorably inclined toward the Jews, and how much more so when it came to publishing Jewish books, the *chassid* was very concerned.

Not knowing what to do, he went to the Alter Rebbe for a blessing and advice. The Alter Rebbe told him to go to the city of Vilna and speak to a certain Torah teacher (*melamed*) who taught first grade in the city.

The *chassid* was puzzled because not only was the Minister of Education located in Petersburg and not Vilna, he also could not imagine how a simple individual like a *melamed* could possibly be of help in this situation. Nevertheless, since the *rebbe* sent him to Vilna, he went, and after much searching found the *melamed*.

"Why on earth did the *rebbe* send you to me?" asked the bewildered *melamed*. "I am an ordinary person with no connections and no knowledge of politics at all!" Stumped, the two of them went to a third *chassid*, one of the leaders of the Vilna community, to make a plan. Although this *chassid* did have some political connections, he also did not understand why the *rebbe* would send the publisher to Vilna. Nevertheless, all three decided that if the *rebbe* sent him there, something would eventually turn out.

Tired of sitting around for days waiting for something to happen, they walked to the center of town and wandered aimlessly around a local park to discuss their possible next steps. They noticed a well-dressed Russian official scrutinizing the *melamed*, and before they knew it, the official approached them and asked the *melamed* to meet him the next day at his hotel.

With trepidation, the *melamed* arrived at the hotel the following day, and to his surprise, the official was awaiting him with a warm smile. He asked the *melamed* if he recognized him, but the *melamed* had no idea how or where he would have met a Russian official of such high stature.

"Do you remember the town of Shklov, where you lived as a child? There was a boy in your town who was a bit wild, and after he violated the Torah in a very serious way, the community decided to punish him. In order to publicly embarrass the boy, they put him in a sort of cagelike structure and placed it in a well-trafficked section of town where everyone could see him. Needless to say, it was devastatingly humiliating for the boy. Finally, some kind soul broke the lock on the box which allowed the boy to run away."

Hearing this sparked the *melamed's* memory and he, in fact, did remember that he was the one who showed such kindness to the boy. Then, to his shock, the official identified himself. "I was that little boy. I have felt indebted to you all my life and wanted to pay you back, but I didn't know your name or where to find you. As Minister of Education, I am in a position of great power and wealth and can arrange for you to have anything you want. Please allow me to pay you back for what you did for me."

When the *melamed* heard these words, he almost fell off his chair. He told the minister that he didn't want anything for himself but would like a favor for one of the friends who had accompanied him to the park. He proceeded to relate the story of how the Alter Rebbe sent this publisher to Vilna to obtain a permit for his printing house, knowing in advance how it would all work out.

Needless to say, all involved were overwhelmed by the great vision of the Alter Rebbe, who foresaw every detail of this whole episode. Able to see the future, he knew that the Minister of Education would not be in Petersburg but in the city of Vilna and that he had a debt to pay this *melamed*. And able to see the past, the Alter Rebbe knew the story of how the *melamed* freed the prisoner as if the whole thing happened right before his eyes.

The ability to do this is only because of the *ruach hakodesh*, the spiritual capacity, of the *tzaddik*.

Every morning we say: "*Hanosein lasechvi vinoh l'havchin beyn yom ouveyn loyloh.*" (*Shachris* Prayers) Sometimes, while outside it's still dark, the rooster crows. With our physical eyes, it's still dark, but the rooster knows that the sun will soon rise or is already rising up.

How, by feeling with its deeper understanding, discernment, and judgment. The same is true with someone who possesses *ruach hakodesh*. He sees and comprehends with his spiritual eyes what the physical eyes are unable to see or grasp. We may doubt what he perceives or comprehends, but he is so connected with the above (and so humble) that what he sees is a total reality.

The Ba'al Shem Tov says that a righteous person who has *ruach hakodesh* does not initially know what to do with it, or how much he can rely upon it. He gradually learns through experience how much he can rely on his intuition in life situations. In other words, he learns from his experience how much is really Divine intuition.

Moshe claimed that he was not "a man of words". He was certainly aware of his stature as a prophet. Maimonides teaches that a prophet "recognizes that he is no longer as he once was; but rather that he has been elevated above the level of otherwise individuals." Moshe was aware of his spiritual level - but only as one worthy of *ruach hakodesh*, of a prophetic mental state. He assumed that the greater level of *nevu'ah* would be similarly recognizable by one who merited it. Since Moshe did not sense this level of prophecy within himself, he declared that he was not a "man of words" - i.e., one meriting prophecy expressed in speech.

Moshe's reasoning, however, was flawed. The inner prophecy of thought is a natural talent of the soul and a result of the prophet's spiritual efforts. Thus, the prophet is aware that he merits *ruach hakodesh*. The external prophecy of *nevu'ah*, on the other hand, depends on *Hashem's* will, according to the dictates of Divine Providence at that time. The first level is comparable to the laws of nature in the world, while the second is like supernatural miracles performed on special occasions. *Nevu'ah* does not reflect the inner qualities of the prophet's soul.

Hashem's response to Moshe is now clearer. "Who gave man a mouth? Who made him blind? Was it not I, the L-rd?" (Shemos 4:11) The world has two sides, the natural and the supernatural. The mouth is part of the natural realm, whereas blindness is a special condition. G-d told Moshe, come from Me. Just as you attained the natural level of *ruach hakodesh*, so too, it is My will that you will be granted the supernatural level of *nevu'ah*. (Rav Kook)

One thing is for sure: If *Hashem* wants *nevu'ah* or *ruach hakodesh* to return to mankind, it is not difficult for Him to make this happen. More important than actual attainment is the pathway towards the perfection of the soul. We spoke about the importance of cleanliness, fixing all one's character traits, and judging others favorably. Further, we went into meditations, the importance of Torah study, humility, repentance, and *d'vekus*. Each person should strive to be a complete vessel before *Hashem*, that he should be blessed with *siatta diShmaya* that has sparks of *ruach hakodesh*.

Rabbi Chaim Vital taught in the name of his teacher the Arizal: "Very important is the study of Torah. One's main intent when studying Torah should be to bring enlightenment and the highest holiness to himself. One must, therefore, concentrate on binding his soul to its highest root through the Torah and attaching it there. His intent should be that through this, the rectification of the Supernal Man should be completed. This was *Hashem's* ultimate intent when He created man and commanded him to study the Torah.

Chassidus, Kabbalah and Meditation

"There are other qualities that one must cultivate. These include humbleness, humility and the fear of sin. These three traits should be cultivated to the ultimate degree. There are also traits that should be avoided to the ultimate degree. These include pride, anger, temper, frivolity, and malicious gossip. Even if one has good reason to display his temper, he should avoid it.

"One should also avoid idle chatter, although it is not as serious as the five things mentioned above. One should not display temper, even to members of his family. Keep the *Shabbos* in action and speech, with all its particulars. This is very helpful for enlightenment. Sit in the synagogue with awe and trembling. The special meditation for this is of great help in attaining *ruach hakodesh*.

"That prime path of *ruach hakodesh* is through care and *kavanah* in the blessing over food. In this manner, one dispels the power of the husks (*klipos*) that have a hold on food and attach themselves to the person who eats. When a person recites a blessing over food with *kavanah*, he removes these [evil spiritual] husks. In this manner, an individual purifies his body, making it [spiritually] transparent, prepared to receive holiness.

"It is also important to wake up at midnight and recite the 111th Psalm. While reciting this, one should meditate on the letters מנצפך *MNTzPKh*, as discussed elsewhere. This is very helpful for enlightenment.

"When you wear *tefillin*, mediate that the four parchments of the head parallel the four letters of the Tetragrammaton.

"It is also important to have a set order of study each day and not miss it. This should include Tenach, Mishna, Talmud and the Kabbalah, together with proper meditations, as discussed elsewhere. It is important to be very careful regarding this.

"It is good for a person to live in a house with windows open to the heavens so that he can always lift his eyes to the heavens and gaze at them. He can then meditate on the miracle of *Hashem's* creation, as it is written, 'When I look at Your heavens, the work of Your fingers...' (Tehillim 8:4) The Zohar also says this about Nebuchadnezzar, who stated, 'At the end of the days, I Nebuchadnezzar lifted my eyes to Heaven, [and my understanding returned to me, and I blessed the Most High].' (Daniel 4:31) It is therefore good for a person to constantly gaze at the heavens." This is something that will bring him wisdom, holiness, and fear of *Hashem*.

"The root of all when it comes to enlightenment is the study of *halachah*. When a person delves deeply into a question of Jewish law, he should meditate how the shell (*klipah*) of a nut covers the kernel. The kernel is the concept of holiness. The shell consists of the questions that one has with regard to that question of Jewish law. This shell surrounds the law and does not permit the person to understand it.

"When he then resolves the question, he should have in mind that he is breaking the power of that shell and removing it from the holiness. The kernel, which is the law, is then revealed.

"If a person does not study the law, and thereby break the shells, how can

203

he come to the kernel, which consists of the wisdom of Kabbalah and the secrets of the Torah? One must, therefore, strive very much, studying and meditating in the above manner."

"I also heard that my master would always interpret each law in six ways. Then he would give it a seventh interpretation which would involve its hidden mystery. This is related to the mystery of the six weekdays which precede the seventh, which is the *Shabbos*." (Shaar Ruach Hakodesh)

Rabbi Jonathan Sagis said in the name of his master that nothing is more important for a person who seeks enlightenment than immersion [in the *mikvah*] since one must be pure at all times.

Rabbi Avraham HaLevi [Berukhim] said in the name of his master that he once gave him advice regarding enlightenment. He was told to avoid idle knowledge. He was also instructed to go through the Zohar, hesitating only to understand the text, but not probing it in depth. In this manner, he was to cover forty or fifty pages a day until he had gone through the entire Zohar many times.

It is often said in motivational speeches that you should find the hardest working, and most successful person, and then work even harder than them. Do you realize how difficult it is to accomplish this in Judaism? Do you realize how hard your *rabbi* works for what he has attained? Even so, we must strive to accomplish the highest spirituality that we can. We must strive with humility to give one hundred percent. If that means sleeping less, taking fewer breaks, not socializing as much, then so be it. The reward for being close to *Hashem* outweighs everything else.

The Arizal was asked why he was worthy of all this wisdom. He replied that he had worked very hard at it. I countered, "The Ramak and I, Chaim, also worked very hard." He answered, "Yes you worked very hard, more than anyone else in this generation, but you did not work as hard as I did."

On many occasions he would stay up all night, pondering a single passage in Zohar. At such times, he would virtually go without sleep completely.

Rabbi Samuel Uceda said that he heard his master say that if a person does not engage in any mundane speech whatsoever for forty days, he will attain wisdom and enlightenment.

I also heard from my master the mystery of "entrusting the soul." This involves the ascent of the soul at night in the mystery of, "Into Your Hand, I entrust my spirit." (Tehillim 31:6) There is no question that if a person is a *tzaddik*, and is perfect in all his deeds, then his soul will ascend on high each night. This is stated explicitly in the Zohar.

Even if a person is not perfect, there are some practices that have the specific power to elevate his soul at night. One need not do them all; only one done properly is sufficient. If one does this, then his soul will ascend on high for that night alone. The only time that this will fail is if he has some major [unrepented] sin, which prevents him from ascending, but we are only speaking about the individual who walks in the ways of *Hashem* and does not sin purposefully.

There are a few methods for enlightenment, and each one is sufficient by itself if done properly.

The first method is that on that particular day, the individual should have perfect *kavanah* in his prayers. If he does this, then in the "Falling on the Face" in the morning prayer, he will bring about the supernal coupling. This is the mystery of the verse, "Who shall ascend to *Hashem*'s mountain." (Tehillim 24:3) The verse is speaking of the person who can ascend at night to the Upper Garden of Eden, this being "*Hashem*'s Mountain." The verse itself then replies, "He of clean hands and a pure heart, who does not lift his soul in vain." This is speaking of the person who lifts his soul through the mystery of the Feminine Waters in the "Falling on the Face", when he says [in that prayer], "to You oh *Hashem* I lift my soul." (Tehillim 25:1) The individual [who does this with *kavanah*] does not "lift his soul in vain." He is literally lifting his soul, and through this, bringing about the supernal coupling.

Such an individual can certainly have his soul rise at night, ascending to "*Hashem*'s mountain, His holy place." This is because he had brought about the supernal coupling between Yaakov and Leah, which takes place each night after midnight. Then, through the mystery of the Feminine Waters, his soul also ascends to this place, as we have explained elsewhere.

The second method involves giving charity properly on that day. This means that he should not know to whom he is giving, and the recipient should not know from whom he is receiving. It is also necessary that such charity is given to a proper individual, one who is truly in need and worthy of it.

The third method involves wearing *tefillin* the entire day. One must not take his mind off from them during this entire period. While wearing them, he should meditate on the short meditation for *tefillin*, which we have presented elsewhere.

The fourth method involves bringing merit to the guilty. On that day, one should prevent a wicked person from committing some sin and bring him to repent that one sin. Alternatively, he should speak to that person about repenting. This will bear fruit that will be of great benefit.

The fifth method involves concentrating and recalling every sin that one has done the entire day. This should be done when the individual is lying in bed. All of his sins should be before his eyes, and he should repent them all. After saying the bedtime *Shema*, he should also confess them verbally, as explained in our writings. The Zohar speaks of individuals who use this method, calling them, "masters of nightly reckonings."

It is important not to omit even a single sin or fine point that one transgressed on that particular day. When going to sleep, he should confess them all [before *Hashem*] and not forget even a single one. It appears that I heard from my master, however, that it is not necessary to review all that one had done that day since this would be an endless task. But one must strive to do so, setting his heart to remember all that he had done wrong that day. This is sufficient. (Rabbi Chaim Vital teaching Torah from the Arizal)

Reb Moshe Steinerman

In the Sha'ar Hakavonos of the Arizal, it says that when the *chazzan* lingers on the words *Ayei Mikom Kivodo* in *kedusha* of *musaf* you can have in mind one of three wishes that will be granted. You can ask for *ruach hakodesh,* great wealth, or children who are *tzaddikim.*

The Arizal cautions that you can only ask for one and not all three, so you must choose carefully. Rav Shimshon Pincus gives advice to those who are stumped by the dilemma. First of all, he says do not spend your precious request asking for *ruach hakodesh.* Even if you were granted *ruach hakodesh,* since we are not worthy enough it would not settle on us, much like if someone were to pour a gallon of cola into a five-ounce cup. It is pointless.

Children or money? That is up to you. What did Rav Pincus choose? He used to tell his kids, "Please be good; I gave up a great fortune for you!" (Revach L'Neshama)

Rabbi Yisrael Baal Shem Tov said that when he is attached to *Hashem* and a thought falls into his mind, this is a minor level of *ruach hakodesh.* (Likutey Yekarim #12) When a person writes *divrey* Torah, it is also a spark of *ruach hakodesh* explaining to him this Torah idea. Sometimes the soul of a person sees something subconsciously in a person's mind. They, therefore, change their plans based on this thought without realizing that *Hashem* blessed them with a spiritual insight into their life.

Whether you believe in *ruach hakodesh* being manifested in your life or in our sages of today is entirely up to you, but one thing is for certain: Divine inspiration has existed and will come to fruition once again during the messianic age. Taking the necessary steps towards purity and *ruach hakodesh* isn't just left for the *tzaddikim;* it is available to each and every one of us. Through this pathway, you will certainly find *Hashem* and truth.

Lesson 33: Seclusion and D'vekus

This material world is transient, but there is another, spiritual, world which is eternal and always present. So, you should separate yourself altogether from the things of this world; from its pleasures, from its hatred and its fierce competitiveness, and even from speaking about worldly matters. And when you think that you no longer belong to this [lower] world, you will not speak about it; rather, all your conversation will be about Torah and *mitzvos*, for they are of the upper, spiritual world. So, too, will all your thoughts be in the Upper World, for that is what is important to the soul. Why should you trouble your mind about things that not only are of no value or benefit to your soul but will also cause it harm? It is good for a person [to practice being in this state, and] when he is involved in prayer or Torah to think that he is not [standing] in this material world, but rather in the spiritual world, in the Garden of Eden, before the Divine Presence--and through this he will purify his mind [until that is his actual experience always]. (Reshis Chochmah, Sha'ar ha-Kedushah, chap. 4, #23)

The holiness we are to have vis-à-vis this world is to separate from the things of this world and be sanctified to spirituality--as if we were not part of this world at all. But the higher level of holiness depends on the sanctification [not only of our action but also] of our mind, that it be totally involved in spiritual things and clinging in *d'vekus* to the upper, spiritual world. Those who attain this higher state are not on the same level as the rest of the people who just do Torah and *mitzvos* without the inner elevation and are on the level of the Lower Garden of Eden; for these other *tzaddikim* ascend [to the Upper Garden of Eden] (ibid. chap. 4, #21).

Rabbi Elimelech of Lizensk said, "The *tzaddik* attaches himself way above, to eternal life, and even when he is in this world he experiences the delight of the Upper World and of eternal life. That is what the Gemara means when it says [as an expression of blessing], 'May you see your [eternal] world in your lifetime' - that through all these deeds and movements being done with holiness and purity, with *d'vekus* and joy, and with love and fear of *Hashem*, he will experience the delight of the Upper World in this world." (Noam Elimelech, Bereshis, p. 1a)

He further teaches, "There is a *tzaddik* who serves *Hashem* with *mitzvos*, and guards himself from transgressing, *Hashem* forbid, any small *mitzvah*, and exerts himself to do it as it should be done. But he is not on the level where, by means of the *mitzvos*, he can come to *d'vekus* with *Hashem*, blessed be He. A *tzaddik* like this will look forward to his reward in the World to Come.

The other kind of *tzaddik* serves *Hashem* with thoughts altogether pure, and by means of the *mitzvos* cleaves to *Hashem*, blessed be He, with *d'vekus*, and great love and longing; he always sees *Hashem's* exaltedness, blessed be He. A *tzaddik* like this draws to himself the delights of the World to Come, for him, as it were, enjoys the radiance of the *Shechinah* in this world. So, he does not look forward to the World to Come, for he experiences the delights of the Wolrd to Come in this world. This is what is said in Berachos, where the *rabbis* give the blessing, "May you see your world in your lifetime," that you merit to be such a *tzaddik*, that you will be in *d'vekus* always, and experience the delights of the World to Come in your lifetime. (Noam Elimelech Terumah, p. 41b)

Speaking of great light, Reb Arele Roth says for example, "A person does a great *mitzvah* and, as it is well known, at the time when he is involved in it, he is clothed in a surrounding light, an aura, a great and wonderful light. But often, due to his lower state, and the decent into materiality caused by his involvement in low bodily desires, this light is hidden from him, and he does not feel it or experience it--until the future time in the World to Come...when the lights of everyone's good deeds will be revealed to him."

All this is not true of the *tzaddik* of whom it said, "May you see your world in your lifetime." [Berachos 17a] For him, while he is alive, experiences the surrounding light, that pure and sweet light, which comes with the fulfillment of the *mitzvos* of *Hashem*. And all the physical delights and pleasures of this world do not even begin to touch the wonderful delights that the *tzaddik* feels in serving *Hashem*. About this, the verse says, "Taste and see that the *Hashem* is good." [Tehillim 34:9] Happy are those who seek Him and revere Him. (Shomer Emunim, p. 139a)

Moshe was able to understand what was required to attain enlightenment, realizing that the path was through meditation (*hisbodedus*). He, therefore, chose to separate himself from all who would disturb him and reject all physical desires, choosing to be a shepherd in the desert, where no people are to be found. While he was there he unquestionably attained a great attachment to the conceptual, divesting himself of all bodily desires, until he was able to remain for forty days and nights without eating or drinking. (Rabbi Simon ben Tzemach Duran)

When I was a young man, I lived a life of forced seclusion. We lived in the rural town of Walkersville, Maryland, surrounded by the Blue Ridge Mountains, non-Jews, and farms. As a religious boy all my life, I traveled one hour each way as a daily commute to *cheder*. Even though I grew up with many friends, I viewed the world as an outsider. There were always lines I kept for myself to separate from the non-Jewish neighbors I would play with, and even the Jews I would come to befriend in the big city where we usually spent *Shabbos* as *orchim*.

Growing older, I decided to take this separation one step further and for almost two years I studied by myself. For weeks, I would unplug the phone wire to better separate myself from the world and commune only with *Hashem*. I would take trips to the streams in the mountains to immerse in the *mikvah* and immersed myself in Torah all day. These years were some of the most beneficial of my life. Deciding to pursue *shidduchim*, I had to come out of my little box but was able to always take with me the benefits of seclusion and not get drawn into the many mistakes of Jewish communities. When I stumbled upon deep Torah teachings, it was as if I received them directly from *Shamayim* and they benefitted me greatly.

The Baal Shem Tov took this idea of seclusion much further. He would spend the entire week in a cabin in the forest and he would talk to *Hashem*. I heard that Rabbi Kook of Tiberias, a holy Kabbalist of our generation, makes sure every week to go out one or two days in seclusion. Where he goes, he doesn't tell his students.

As important as the idea of community is and it is very important for the *kedusha* of one's family to have a *shul* one belongs too, still there has to be some form of private *avodas Hashem* in one's life. This private *avodas Hashem* gives a person the ability to look outside the pressures of society and paint themselves a purer picture of life's purpose. The pursuit of money and fame really has little meaning when one views the world's obsessions from afar.

So, does seclusion bring you closer to *Hashem*? Yes, if you don't allow yourself to become depressed or anti-social because of it. Everything needs balance. A person who truly wants to come close to *Hashem*, can't have many friends. They will only distract him from the true purpose and the friends he does keep must also share a true desire for closeness to *Hashem*. Allowing many souls who are beginning in Judaism to attach themselves to you can also draw you even closer to *Hashem*, but it isn't without risk.

You must rejoice in serving *Hashem* more than when you profit with "The abundance of all the money in the world." (The holy Arizal)

When an individual is worthy of the mystery of attachment (*d'vekus*), he can also be worthy of stoicism (*hishtavus*). After he is worthy of stoicism, he can also be worthy of meditation. And after he is worthy of meditation, he can be worthy of *ruach hakodesh* (Holy Spirit, enlightenment). From there, he can reach the level of prophecy, where he can actually predict the future. (Meir Eynayim, Ekev, Shaarey Kedushah, Part 4)

Lesson 34: Music and Joy

The trait of sadness is a very bad quality, especially for one who wishes to attain wisdom and *ruach hakodesh*. There is nothing that prevents enlightenment more than depression, even for those who are worthy. We find evidence for this from the verse, "And now bring a minstrel, and when the minstrel played, the hand of *Hashem* came upon him." (2 Kings 3:15) [The music was needed to dispel his sadness. It was also only used in the initial stages of meditation before the revelations would take place]. (Shabbos 30b, Pesachim 117a, Sha'arey Kedusha, Part Four, p. 15b)

The same is true of anger, which can prevent enlightenment completely. The sages thus teach, "If a person becomes angry, if he is a prophet, his prophecy is taken away." (Pesachim 66b)

Song has the capacity to open new wellsprings beyond the limitations of intelligence, for the *nigun* is grasped within one's heart; the heart surely is capable of a fuller and more sublime understanding than one's brain. This is the power of faith and *teshuvah*, of repentance, which is elevated above knowledge and logic, and comprehended through one's heart. This will explain why a *nigun* can arouse a person to do *teshuvah*. This we witnessed in the times of the holy Temple, for when the Levites sang their songs of praise, the people were inspired to do *teshuvah*.

This is the power of the *nigun*, for listening to a pure melody can create encircling lights of *teshuvah*. Yes, the world of the *nigun* is surely the realm of repentance. *Nigunim* enthuse the listener with a revitalized power of faith and repentance, with *emunah* and *teshuvah* that goes far beyond the boundaries of intelligence, reason, and words. (Shiras HaLev [The Song of the Heart] by Shmuel Stern - Translated by Gita Levi)

Rebbe Naftali Tzvi of Ropshitz proclaimed that the *Heichal Hanegina* (the heavenly Mansion of Melody) was next to the *Heichal HaTeshuvah* (the heavenly Mansion of Return or "Repentance"), and the person who did not jump from the former into the latter was an absolute fool because the doors were interconnected. Regarding this statement, the Divrei Yisrael [of Modzitz] added: "Everybody says that the *Heichal HaNegina* is next to the *Heichal HaTeshuvah*, but I say that the *Heichal HaNegina* itself is the *Heichal HaTeshuvah*" [Found in *sefer* Imrei Shaul, p. 309].

Chassidus, Kabbalah and Meditation

What is a *chassid*? Someone who possesses a precious key, a key that opens all the doors, even those that G-d keeps closed. And the key is the *nigun*, the song of joy that makes our hearts thrill. The *nigun* opens the gates of Heaven. Melancholy closes them. (A Simple Jew blog)

The Radak and Rav Saadia Gaon said that the *zemer* is a giraffe. I find it very fascinating that the word for giraffe describes Jewish song – *zemer*. The interpretation is suggested as follows:

Notice that, in the *Alef Beis*, the letters following *zemer* spell *nachash*. For after the letter *Zayin* is a *Ches*; after the letter *Mem* is a *Nun*, and after the letter *Raish* is a *Shin*. To go yet a step further, the letters in the *Alef Beis* preceding *zemer* spell *kol*. For before the letter *Zayin* is a *Vov*, before the letter *Mem* is a *Lamed*, and before the letter *Raish* is a *Kuf*.

Song and music can go two ways. It can elevate the spirit and even the body if the source is "*Hakol kol Yaakov.*" Yet, on the other hand, it can lower the *neshamah* and body if the source is from the *nachash* and *tumah*. It can either bring out G-dliness within man or bestiality. It can stir one to yearn for closeness to *Hashem* and the heavens, or it can gravitate the soul and body to gratify the cravings of physical appetites and fleeting earthliness.

Rav Shimon Susholtz from Beis Medrash Keren Orah shared with me the observation that, especially when *bochurim* dance, one can tell whether the accompanying song is rooted in *nachash* or *kedusha*. The litmus test is to look at the position of their heads. If the heads face downwards towards the floor and feet, it is non-*kedushah* material. If their heads are straight, then it is holiness, for it arouses the soul and not the body. When I first heard this, I couldn't believe that this was the barometer of the music's source. Well, guess what? I found it to be true every time. [First, observe the phenomenon before you start writing any commentary to the opposite.]

While we are on the topic, here's another revealing observation. All the disco tech stuff awakens within an individual the desire to dance by oneself with oneself. It suddenly becomes show-off time, even if you don't find yourself in the center being *mesameach* the *choson*. With this type of music, the circle in which one was once holding hands with other *Yidden* peters out. Not so with the more traditional beats and *chassidishe* music. Why?

Kedusha, by definition, brings to unity and wholesomeness, while *tumah*, by its very nature, accommodates separateness and fragmentation. For if the soul is dancing, then all *Yidden* naturally tend to connect, since in the world of soul we are all one. If the body alone is dancing, then we tend to dance alone, for each individual has his own individual body.

We now might be able to answer why the giraffe is the symbol of the Jewish kosher *zemer*. The giraffe is unique by the fact that its head is raised above the rest of its body. The head of the giraffe towers towards the heavens to symbolize that the Jewish *nigun* must raise one's head towards *Hashem*, bringing man to a consciousness that distances him from the pursuit of material lusts that lie close to Earth.

The word *zemer* itself – identical to the letters of *remez* – hints to this concept. For *zemer* also spells *ram zayin*. *Ram* translates "to be lofty and high." The letter *zayin* symbolizes nature, for nature was created in seven days. The *zemer* must raise one above the seven to yearn to be otherworldly even though these feelings might only last for a few moments. However, impressions do last forever!

Chazal say concerning Adam Harishon that before the sin he was able to see from one end of the world to the other. His head and *daas* were clear and indelible. After the *nachash* seduced them to eat from the *eitz hadaas*, he lost that *madraiga* of *daas*. *Hashem* placed His hand on man's head and dwarfed his dimensions. The *nachash* brought sadness into the world, as evidently seen from the curses given to Adam and Chava. The purpose of the *zemer* is to bring happiness, the opposite of which was brought by its neighboring letters *nachash*. Specifically, it refers to the happiness that brings about clarity of mission and not cloudiness of mind; the light of meaning, not the darkness of chaos; and the direction of purpose, not the choreographic fluff that leads to dead ends. (Rav Brazil)

"A holy melody gives strength to the forces of holiness, but the music of the *sitra achra*, the other side, damages these forces and lengthens the exile. It makes people stumble and traps them like birds in a snare. Be very careful never to listen to this kind of music at all. The musicians and singers who produce it have no religious intentions whatsoever. On the contrary, they only want to make money or become famous. Listening to this kind of music can seriously weaken your devotion to G-d, but the melodies played by a truly religious, G-d-fearing musician can be very inspiring. They can strengthen your devotion immensely." (Likutey Moharan I, 3)

One rabbi takes a somewhat opposite approach to music. "Through song, the gates of Heaven can be opened. Sadness closes them. The origin of all songs is holy, for impurity has no song. It is the root of all sadness." (R. Velvel Pasternak)

Rebbe Nachman of Breslov wrote (Likutei Moharan, Part II, Paragraph 63) that every shepherd has his own unique melody, his own *nigun*, born of the grass, and the place to where he leads his flock to graze, and so forth. The shepherd himself is benefitted by this *nigun*. This is because spending so much of his time amidst the herd could result in a descent of the shepherd from his standing as a man down to the level of a beast. The *nigun* spares him from this descent. The *nigun* is surely a spiritual distillation, refining man's spirit from that of the beasts. As the Ramban writes, "There is nothing as subtle within the realm of physicality as music." That is to say, the *nigun* is found on the borderline of physicality, at the point of connection with the spiritual. Therefore, the *nigun* is bestowed with the power to raise us from the material and physical to the realm of spirituality. To enable ascent from the level of the beast to the level of human.

Rebbe Shneur Zalman of Liadi interpreted the Talmudic passage, "All bearers of (animal) collars go out with a collar and are drawn by a collar," (Shabbat 51b) to imply that humans, the singers of songs, are drawn out from beastliness through song. Similar to an animal that is draw outside through being pulled. [In the Talmudic text the word shir is used for "collar", this Hebrew word also means song.]

In the Holy Temple, the *Leviyim* would sing their song, accompanying the sacrificial animal's ascent towards Heaven. For through sacrifice, the animalistic ascends to a level of spirituality. The song of the *Leviyim* accompanied and facilitated this ascent of the bearer of the sacrifice. Through the *Levites'* song, the man offering the sacrifice was aroused to absolute *teshuvah* [repentance] and thus approached his Maker.

The journey from Egypt, where they Jews had sunk to the forty-ninth level of *tumah* [impurity], to the level of *kedusha* [holiness] necessary to receive the Torah, required forty-nine days of preparation, which is the forty-nine days of *Sefiras HaOmer* - the counting of the *Omer*. Similarly, a woman needs seven 'clean' days to purify herself from ritual impurity each month.

Rebbe Naftali Tzvi of Ropshitz informs us that the descent into the Reed Sea on the seventh day following the Shemos from Egypt was a form of purification that was accomplished through the singing of the Song of the Sea [*Shiras HaYam*]. It was through song that the forces of evil and impurity were subjugated and cleared away so that the Jewish people could receive *kedusha*, as one receives *tahara* [ritual purity].

He continues that this can be compared to one who comes to immerse himself in a river during the winter, only to discover that the river is frozen over. He cannot immerse himself and attain purity unless he breaks through the ice that covers the waters.

Similarly, each morning we recite *Pesukei d'Zimra* – verses of Song – before we accept the Kingdom of Heaven upon ourselves with the prayer of *Shema* and ask for all our needs in *Shemoneh Esrey*. Indeed, the *Pesukei d'Zimra* culminates in *Shiras HaYam*. For it is the *Pesukei d'Zimra* that cut through *[l'zamer* means to sing, and also to prune or cut] all the thorns and forces of evil that are in the way of the *kedusha* and Divine bounty to flow from above.

One who leads the prayers with song and praise in a pleasant voice and with joy and exultation cuts down and removes all the barriers that are in the way, so the prayers ascend on High. (Zera Kodesh al HaMoadim)

There are "Ten Types of Songs"

The ten types of songs are:

1. *Ashrei* - Joy
2. *Beracha* - Blessing
3. *Lamenazeach* - For the conductor
4. *Maskil* - Making wise
5. *Mizmor* - Psalm
6. *Hodiya* - Thanksgiving

7. *Shir* - Song
8. *Nigun* - Melody
9. *Tefillah* - Prayer
10. *Hallelu-yah* - Praise

Shmuel Stern teaches us that the ten signifies wholeness. As such, an entire tier of creation incorporates ten aspects. Our sages teach us that the world was created through ten utterances. Esoteric teachings reveal that the human soul also encompasses ten parts. The ten kinds of song, of *nigun*, correspond to these ten spiritual Spheres of the soul. (The ten-stringed harp mentioned in the book of Tehillim).

The book of Tehillim was composed through these ten kinds of *nigun*. As R' Yehoshua ben Levi explicates: "The book of Tehillim was spoken through the ten utterances of praise." These are the songs sung by King David. Therefore, most of the psalms included in the book of Tehillim begin with one of these ten kinds of song, e.g. *hallelu-yah*, *mizmor*, etc. These opening phrases reveal which of the ten kinds of song the particular psalm belongs to.

Tikkun HaKlali [The General Remedy]

The ten kinds of songs are the ten languages of praise through which the holy One should be praised, and that is why the book of Tehillim was composed through these ten kinds of songs.

When a person praises his Maker, he rectifies his soul and also restores all the elements of his soul that have fallen into impurity. Through the praise he extols upon his Maker, he admits that he is truly dispassionate for evil and yearns only for righteousness. Through this longing, he will cling to the good and surely, evil will then inevitably fade away.

Corresponding to the ten Spheres of the human soul are the respective ten kinds of *nigun*. When one praises and glorifies the Maker through one these kinds of song, the part of his soul connected to that kind of song is rectified and restored to holiness. So too, when one glorifies G-d with all ten kinds of songs, all ten parts of the soul will be returned to holiness.

Rebbe Nachman took this idea and through his vast knowledge of Torah came up with the Tikkun Haklali prayer consisting of ten Psalms. Through this, one envokes the power of the entire Tehillim and brings a *tikkun* to his soul. A general remedy for all problems, especially to increase one's purity of mind. The Psalms are recited in order as follows: 16,32,41,42,59,77,90,105,137,150.

The Nigun and Tefillah [Prayer]

Our sages have taught us that *tefillah*, prayer, is, in essence, the toil of one's heart. The *gematria* [numerical equivalence] of the word *tefillah* is *shira* [song], i.e. 515. So, we learn that true song is prayer, and true prayer is a song; that both, surely, are dependent upon one's heart.

In the Book of Chassidim, it is written: "Seek out the *nigunim*. When you pray, sing your prayers in the *nigun* that is pleasant and sweet to you, and thus pray with sincerity and dedication so that your mouth shall speak words of appeal and submission. The *nigun* prepares the heart to speak genuine words of praise; it cheers the heart until one's words are overflowing with love and joy."

The *Beis Hamikdash*, "heart of the world" (see Likutei Moharan 49) is a place of prayer, as it is written "...and My house will be a house of prayer for all the nations." And that is why the foremost singing of *am Yisrael*, the song of the *Levites*, was sung in the Holy Temple. For this song is dependent upon and intertwined with the heart, and the *Beis Hamikdash* is the heart of the world.

Our sages teach, "The holy One blessed be He would not have created this world, were it not for the song and praise sung anew each day." For He desires our hearts; when we sing before Him we reveal the genuine joy as we serve Him and seek out His holy light. This truly is our purpose, and therein lays the infinite significance of prayer and song before G-d [Likutei Moharan 42: It is written that through song, one creates a garment of light for the *Shechinah,* the Divine Presence].

This is why the *tzaddikim*, the righteous ones, have always chosen a path of singing before the holy One. King David, called the Sweet Singer of Israel, sang his Psalms before his Maker every day of his life. And when the Messiah, Moshiach ben David, will come, he will restore the songs of the holy Temple; he will teach us the songs and melodies of King David, for this, is the song proclaiming the eternal Kingdom of Israel. Then the righteous Moshiach will sing with us; he will instruct us how to serve G-d through song and *nigun*. May this day come soon, *amen*.

The Power of the Imagination

The power of the imagination is one of the primary forces of the *neshamah* [the soul] functioning within the realm of the *nigun*. When the *nigun* is a good one, that is to say, played for the sake of glorifying His name, it stimulates in the listener a wondrous imagination which connects him to his Creator and enables him to ascend to higher and higher spiritual levels. If a listener finds that the music leads him to negative imaginings and stirs in him earthly passions, he can then know that the music is not played for the sake of G-d. This is the great pleasure of the *nigun*: to arouse the power of the imagination.

The Power of the Intelligence

The capacity of intelligence in the context of *nigun* is found in the holy

Torah, and therefore through study, a person may rectify the *nigun*.

The supplementary aspect of intelligence, with regards to *nigun*, is the lyrics. This is what is alluded to in the book of Psalms when King David wrote "Song of the *Maskil*". We learn that the words accompanying the musical notes of the melody should employ the wisdom of the holy Torah and thus stir hearts to serve G-d.

The notes and the melody awaken the heart, while the words arouse the mind. When the musician plays his *nigun* with the wisdom of the Torah and sings words of holiness and Torah, the listener is inspired to a great awe of G-d, by way of the mind (through the words) and his heart (the melody). With this inspiration, the listener is brought to a genuine clinging to *Hashem*, both in heart and mind. So, it is befitting that King David, the Sweet Singer of Israel, composer of the book of Psalms, instructs the "Song of the *Maskil*" to play the sweet melodies and sing the sweet words that are absolute holiness.

When G-d forbid, the lyrics and/or melody are created out of wickedness and defilement, both the musician and his listener can be brought down to unspeakable lows. One should surely distance one's self from such music. For just as pure *nigunim* are born of holiness, so impure melodies/words find their source and vitality from the unholy. This explains the inner holiness of the cantillation notes as explained by the Arizal. Through holy and sublime *nigunim*, one can attain great spiritual ascents.

Nigun Above the Words

Words make up the language of our intelligence, while music is the language of the soul. That is why the language of the *nigunim* is at times more spiritually elevated than words, just as the *emunah* [the faith] rooted in one's heart ascends the limits of knowledge and rationality.

It is true that a great portion of a Jew's labor is to lead the mind to command and control one's heart and lead with intelligence [Torah] to control one's emotion. When a person achieves true wholeness, his emotions will nurture all of his deeds. His deeds, enacted then according to Divine will, will be performed with the utmost intensity of emotion.

The *nigun* signifies such wholeness. For when a person has achieved this level of perfection, he is motivated to sing. Then his wisdom and intelligence navigate towards a desire to sing and dance. As such, he can achieve an understanding and comprehension on a level higher than intelligence itself. This is the "encircling light" [or *makif*] that cannot be grasped by one's intelligence, but only on a higher level through the faculties of emotion and heart. When a person sings and dances with an abundance of joy and cheerfulness, he can surely attain lofty spiritual levels. Subsequently, this transforms the sparks of holiness that enter one's mind and are then truly understood.

All of this can explain why a person who is in a difficult spiritual state can attain joy and new spiritual strength through music and dance. It is through the 'encircling light' that the 'inner light' will be grasped by both his intelligence and his heart; this is the true source of joy.

So, we see that *nigun* and dance allow one to attain levels denied him by mere intelligence. It is told of the Alter Rebbe, Rebbe Shneur Zalman of Lyadi, that when he arrived at the city of Shkolov, he was addressed by the wise men of the town with a series of difficult questions. The *rebbe*, instead of replying to these questions with words, began to sing a *nigun*. He sang with an unsurpassed love and cleaving to the holy One blessed be He, and as he sang, the scholars felt how each one of their challenging questions was being answered. (This *nigun* is called "The *nigun* of *matan* Torah," The *nigun* of the Giving of the Torah).

The Power of Prophecy

The true purpose of the *nigun*, the genuine perfection of the song, is to achieve the power of prophecy. As is written in the book of Kings II: "As the musician played, G-d's hand came upon him." That is to say, that the musician was blessed with the spirit of prophecy. In the book of Shmuel, it is written: "…you will meet a group of prophets descending from the high place, preceded by a lyre, a timbrel, a flute and a harp, and they will be prophesying."

Rambam taught that the prophets were empowered with the spirit of prophecy only when they were intensely contemplative and meditative, their hearts abundant with joy. Prophecy is never the consequence of sadness or despair or lethargy, but rather of joy and celebration. Therefore, prophecy is led by song and the playing of musical instruments.

This then is the level of perfection in the realm of *nigun* and song, when music generates the spirit of prophecy through attainment of the highest spiritual levels of clinging to G-d. As is written in the book, The Gates of Holiness: "Even if one is worthy, if he has not accustomed himself to reveal his soul he will not merit receiving this power of prophecy. Therefore, the prophets mentioned above used the playing of musical instruments to achieve the soul-baring necessary for the attaining the sublime devotion that enabled the power of prophecies."

Such was the "school" for the *Levites* who dedicated themselves to five years of instruction before entering their service in the *Beis Hamikdash*. The Midrash teaches us that it was Moses of blessed memory who taught the song to the *Levites*, as is written in Midrash Raba, Genesis 54, "what efforts the son of Amram toiled until he taught the song to the *Levites*." This explains the reasoning as to why King David and Shmuel chose the *Levite* prophets. For the *Levites* had attained a perfection in music - the song of prophecy, the song capable of leading a person to a truly inspirational clinging to *Hashem* and the revelation of His light.

This is the Song of *Shabbos*, as we sit at the *Shabbos* table and sing songs that arouse our devotion and our clinging to the holy One. This song is born of the aspect of the *Levites'* song. For as we eat the *Shabbos* meal, it is as if we are partaking of the sacrifices in the holy Temple, and our song is like the song of the *Levites* accompanying the ascent of the sacrifice. Through the songs we sing on *Shabbos*, we experience the sweet taste of the pleasantness of *Shabbos*. Consequently, we influence the entire world of creation in a positive way, for all is surely dependent upon the joy and pleasantness of the *Shabbos*. This is why Rebbe Nachman was so adamant that his disciples sing the songs of *Shabbos* with utmost simplicity and sincerity.

Dance - The Tikkun of the Feet

Following the heart and the hands [clapping], the *nigun* travels to the feet; this is dance. In many ways, the ultimate purpose of the *nigun* is to reach the realm of dance, for then truly all of the physical body is attached to joy. The *nigun* extends to the whole body; it lifts the feet, and in that raising of the feet one is in absolute joy and shakes off the evil (the impure husks) within him. The dancer jumps and dances in supreme cleaving to the sublime purpose - the clinging to his Maker.

The dance of holiness is directed towards Heaven. When a person dances for the sake of filling himself with joy, joy in *Hashem* and the holy Torah, this is a great *mitzvah*, for it is a great *mitzvah* to always be in *simcha*, in joy, as it is written: "Serve the L-rd with joy." Joy brings a person closer to the Holy One and to act according to His Will. Dancing assists a person to be saved from iniquity and to free us from the sadness and evil within us, as Rebbe Nachman teaches in Likutei Moharan II: Torah 23. In this teaching Rebbe Nachman illuminates his teaching through a parable: Sometimes a group of people gathered together in joy and dance bring into their circle a person who is standing outside, who has fallen into sadness; they may pull him into their circle of dance even if at first it is against his will, and compel him to join in the dance, etc. (The rule being that one has to make a great effort with all one's strengths to overcome any and all obstacles to be in a state of happiness, to be always in a state of joy. For the nature of a person is really to draw himself towards melancholy and sadness consequent to the events of time, his trials and tribulations; and therefore, it is only with great effort that we can coerce ourselves to be in a state of constant joy).

Therefore, when we dance in the presence of a bride and groom in order to make them happy, this leads to the couple's building a home rooted in happiness. This is a great *mitzvah*; this is the dance for the sake of holiness. We find in Talmudic literature many examples of great Torah scholars dancing wondrous dances in front of the bride and groom for the sake of their joy.

Dance brings a person to self-nullification; a person, while dancing wildly, swiveling, leaping, etc., is not in a position of honor. In the holy tongue, the word *kavod* [honor] shares the root of the word *kaved* [heaviness], i.e., heaviness, lethargy. So, we find King David danced in attending the holy Ark as it was brought to the City of David. And as it is written: "Michal the daughter of Saul peered through the window, and she saw King David leaping and dancing before the L-rd, and she loathed him in her heart." And therefore, King David said: "Before *Hashem*, who chose me above your father, and above all his house, to appoint me prince over the people of *Hashem*, over Israel; therefore, I have made merry before *Hashem*. And if I am demeaned more than this, and be abashed in mine own eyes, [yet] of the maidservants of whom you have spoken, with them will I get me honor.' In fact, the dancing and leaping and hopping before *Hashem* was his honor."

And for this reason, the Rambam teaches in Hilchos Lulav that it is a great *mitzvah* to be joyous. The great sages, the heads of *yeshivos* and the *Sanhedrin*, the *chassidim* and the elders all sang and danced and made merriment; and in contrast, those who restricted themselves in concern over their own honor erred and sinned. He who is willing to humiliate himself is truly honorable and serves *Hashem* in joy. And that is why King David said, "And if I am demeaned more than this, and be abashed in mine own eyes..." for there is no greater honor than rejoicing in front of *Hashem*.

Hence the genuine purpose of dance is to bring a person to a state of joy, to attain true self-nullification before G-d. The true dance is the dance for the sake of Heaven, through which one merits worshipping *Hashem* in sincere service. This is why the great sages wrote: "In the future the holy One blessed be He will make a circle of *tzaddikim* and He will sit with them in Gan Eden." (Tannis 31a) For the true *tzaddikim* have attained absolute self-nullification before *Hashem*. They have reached the level of the aspect of the holy dance, and therefore, they will merit dancing in the presence of *Hashem* in the World to Come.

And through dancing *b'kedusha* [in holiness] it is possible to rise above reason and logic. Within the circles of dance, it is possible to attain higher levels of *emunah* and *devekus* [cleaving to *Hashem*] beyond the realm of logic and intellect, just as the dancers feet are functioning without intellect. When one dances for a purely holy purpose, for the sake of Heaven, and merits consequently to achieve *d'vekus*, then through his dance he can indeed go beyond reason and intellect and reach a higher level of holy faith and cleave to *Hashem*.

Through dancing for the sake of Heaven one conquers the primeval snake that has hold over the feet, as it is written: "He will crush your head, and you will bite his heel." When the dancer lifts his heels for the sake of Heaven, with his dance he crushes the head of the snake. Through dancing on behalf of holiness he indeed conquers the snake, the physical body made of the skin of the snake. Through *nigun*, through the swirling and holy dancing to the *nigun*, he transforms his body from corporeal skin to purified untainted light. And, G-d forbid, the opposite is also true – if one dances a dance connected to his evil inclination, a dance of impurity, it is as "And satyrs shall dance there." (Isaiah 13)

Yet through the escalation of the *rikud d'kedusha* [the holy dance] in the world, the level of 'feet' will be rectified until the words of the holy Zohar shall be fulfilled: "Until the feet come to the feet," which is, in truth, the final and complete redemption. (Shiras HaLev by Shmuel Stern - Translated by Gita Levi.)

The Alter Rebbe of *Chabad*, the Ba'al HaTanya, Reb Shneur Zalman of Liadi, in the early years of his leadership, would make unique chassidic interpretations of simple *passukim* from Chumash and passages from the Gemarah. On one occasion, he took the following statement from the Mishna:

"כל בעלי השיר יוצאין בשיר ונמשכין בשיר."

And all animals bearing a chain or ring may go out wearing the chain and may be led along by it.

The Mishna addresses under what circumstances a person may move his animals from the private domain to the public domain on *Shabbos*. The Ba'al HaTanya interpreted the Mishna uniquely: All the masters of song - the angels and souls - go out in song and are drawn in song.

Many of the Ba'al HaTanya's unique *pshatim*, like the one above, stirred the ire of many in the non-*chassidic* world. The inhabitants of the town of Shklov recognized the Ba'al HaTanya's greatness in Torah and asked him many questions. Each time, the Ba'al HaTanya refused to answer. The *misnagdim* in Shklov decided to organize a conference and invite the Alter Rebbe to give a dissertation and to finally answer their questions. Reb Shneur Zalman accepted the invitation.

Ascending to the podium, the Ba'al HaTanya began: "Instead of delivering a discourse and answering questions, I shall sing a *nigun*. For there is a Mishna that says:

כל בעלי השיר יוצאין בשיר ונמשכין בשיר

And all animals bearing a chain or ring may go out wearing the chain and may be led along by it, meaning that souls and angels from the World Above may be both elevated and drawn down into this world through the singing of a nigun."

The Alter Rebbe began to sing his *nigun*. A sweet stillness entered into the heart of every man there. All of their questions and problems that brought them to the conference were answered. With the Ba'al HaTanya's voice helping everyone achieve a state of *d'vekus*, all of the attendee's minds were refreshed from the wellsprings of Torah wisdom and their eyes looked anew at *Hashem's* Torah.

On 3rd day of *Sukkos*, 1966, the *rebbe* quoted the previous *rebbe's* saying that the tongue is the pen of the heart while a *nigun* is the pen of the soul. It expresses the soul of the one who composed it and reaches the soul of the one who is singing it.

During *parshas* Ba'aloscha 1967, the *rebbe* said to begin the *nigun* of *gimel tenuos* from the Baal Shem Tov. While they were singing, there were people speaking in the background. The *rebbe* said it is known that by singing a *nigun*, one connects with a deeper *hiskashrus* to the *rabbeim* than through their Torah. It is like he is standing in front of you.

On *shvei shel Pesach* 5707, the previous *rebbe* explained that a *nigun* has the power to pull a person out of where he is and bring him to *teshuvah*. (Rabbi Shmuel Gurary)

One thing to note about music is that each person has his own individual revelation when it comes to songs. You don't meet anyone who doesn't appreciate some form of music. Different sounds affect each of us in unique ways.

Over the years I have made my own little *Shabbos tishes*, sometimes with a few in attendance but mostly by myself. This started when I was living in Maryland after my father passed away. My mother and sister in attendance, I led the *Shabbos* meals with endless music. I found that living in this rural community with no other Jews to share *Shabbos* with, found its light only through the power of *nigunim*.

I would sing the *kiddush* slowly and with concentration, to the point that you could feel the uneasiness in the room of those who wanted this drawn out prayer to conclude so they could eat. Then the songs came. I figured out the great secret of *nigunim* since it was really all I had to make me happy about *Shabbos* with just two other people the entire twenty-five-hour day. So, when it came to the time to sing, I would sing the same song over and over again. I would not limit it to the standard three to four minutes. Sometimes I would sing the same song of Rebbe Nachman for twenty minutes. I found myself alone after awhile as everyone had left, but the *nigun* had opened up the very heavens before me.

I've heard so many beautiful songs sung during *Shabbos*, but they abruptly come to a close, just when they were about to open all the gates for one's holy soul to enter. A *nigun* is like a meditation to *Hashem*; it is a mantra that is supposed to assist a person to exit the physical plane and enter a completely spiritual one.

A *nigun* also has the power to bring people together. If you have a beautiful tune, you can virtually sing it in any language and it will sound beautiful. This is because song is full of peace and tranquility. Song arouses the heart and withers away all sadness.

Sitting there all alone in Maryland, I was able to feel hope and would no longer feel the loneliness when I would sing. In fact, I wasn't alone at all. I could feel my ancestors around me and the realness of *Hashem echad*.

When people "go off the *derech*", usually a few steps before this disappointing life change, comes the change in music and dress. It is because music is one of the most powerful gifts and curses to mankind. Everything in holiness must have an opposite nature in evil. Music is the key to prophetic visions and closeness to *Hashem*. What do the angels do all day before *Hashem*? They sing songs. You know what Gan Eden is? It is one big orchestra of Torah study, prayer, singing and understanding the will of *Hashem*.

Sometimes when I have a song in my head and I am walking outside, I am able to see nature dancing in rhythm to the very song I am listening to. Birds are flying by and chirping on the beat.

In my lowest hour, the day my father passed away, I recorded in my memoirs how in this deepest painful hour of my life, everything around me seemed like music orchestrated by *Hashem*. It was unreal. It wasn't that I actually heard a song; I rather felt song around me.

Rabbi Noson Maimon *shlit"a* taught, "When a person leaves this world and enters the next one if they understand how to read notes and music, they will enjoy a better revelation in *Olom Habah.*" This is because music is the very key to the *Sefiros* and entering the Inner Chambers. It is the skeleton key that opens all doors.

Do deaf people hear music? As long as they can feel vibrations, they can feel the rhythm of music and enjoy music just as hearing people do. "The perception of the musical vibrations by the deaf is likely every bit as real as the equivalent sounds since they are ultimately processed in the same part of the brain." (WebMD)

Therefore, music isn't just about hearing sounds; it is the inner realization that the world is an orchestra. The great composers of classical music must have understood this connection between hearing, feeling and seeing the entire world as one orchestrated by sounds, motion, life, and movement.

I heard from the Nikolsberg Rebbe's son that he asked his father, "Aren't you upset that Jewish artists aren't giving you credit for the songs you wrote that they are using to become famous?"

"My son," he responded, "I hope I came into this world for more than just creating a song." The Rebbe who composed hundreds of songs understood that even his music, which was revealed to him through *ruach hakodesh*, does not compare to the music his Torah teachings creates. The *rebbe's* entire life is an orchestra of goodness to *Klal Yisrael.* He is music. His songs are just sparks from the beauty of his soul, but his Toros are all music at the highest levels.

You see, the prophet only used the idea of song to enter the higher worlds. A song can take a person to places that they otherwise would have no access too. Once there, it was no longer needed because everything is the song of *Hashem.*

Lesson 35: Drawing Down Shefa

One who wishes to perceive Eternal Life should attach himself to the attribute of *E-l Chai* (living *Hashem*), [which is associated with the *Sefirah* of *Yesod*-Foundation].

This means that through his prayers, one should bring *E-l Chai* into *Adna*. It was regarding this that King David had passion and desire when he said, "My soul thirsts for *Hashem*, for *E-l Chai*." (Tehillim 42:3)

When the attribute (*Yesod*), which is called *E-l Chai*, is bound to *Adna* (*Malchus*), then one can draw down all his needs. He can overcome his enemies, and no one can stand up to him.

We must bind the *Sefiros* together, attaching all levels through the attribute of *Adna* (*Malchus*-Kingship). We say, "He chooses a song of praise, King (*Malchus*), Life (*Yesod*) of the world." If one wishes to seek a good life, he should bind himself to the attribute of *E-l Chai*.

When a person is attached to *Adna* in purity, then he is also attached to *E-l Chai*. It is thus written, "And you, who are attached to *YKVK* your *Hashem*, you are all alive (*Chai*) today." (Devarim 4:4) (Sha'arey Orah 2, p.18a)

If one wishes to attain these three things [life, food or children], he cannot attain them as a matter of right in this world. They cannot be attained through merit, which [involves] the Tribunal on high. How then can he attain these things?

One must elevate his concentration (*kavanah*) higher and higher. He must probe deeper than the future world (*Binah*-Understanding) until he reaches the level of *Keter*-Crown, which is *Ekyeh*, which is [associated with] the Infinite (*Ain Sof*).

One thus reaches the level of the Thirteen Attributes of Mercy. One of these Thirteen Attributes is called destiny (*mazal*). The sages, therefore, teach, "Life, children, and food do not depend on merit, but on destiny."

There is one thing that you must know and understand. Even though we say that one who wishes to attain what he desires from *Hashem* should concentrate on a particular Divine Name, this does not mean that he should concentrate on that name and go no farther.

But the true intent is this: One must concentrate on the Name associated with the thing that he needs. He must then elevate this concentration on that Name until the top of the ten *Sefiros*. He then reaches the highest ource, which is called the source of desire. When one reaches the source of desire, then his request and the desire of his heart are fulfilled.

This is the meaning of the verse, "You open Your hand (*yad-ekha*) and satisfy all life desire." (Tehillim 145:16) Do not read *Yadekha* as Your hand but as *Yud-ekha* Your *Yid (Your Yud)*. (Tikuney Zohar 8b) This means that *Hashem* opens the mystery of the *Yud* in the name *YKVK*, which is the source of desire. He then fulfills the desire of all who ask.

One who wishes to attain from *Hashem* what he desires must contemplate the ten *Sefiros*. He must transmit will and desire from the highest to lowest until he brings it to the final desire, which is the name *Adna*. The *Sefiros* are then blessed through him, and he is blessed through the *Sefiros*.

This is the mystery of the verse, "He who blessed himself on earth (*Malchus*), blesses himself by the *Hashem* of *Amen*." (Isaiah 65:16) The word *Amen* alludes to the mystery through which blessing is transmitted from the names *Ekyeh* and *YKVK* to the name *Adna*.

From this, you learn that when one prays, he must concentrate in the manner that I have described. He must unify the *Sefiros* and bring them close to each other.

When a person prays, he must concentrate and ascend from *Sefirah* to *Sefirah*, from desire to desire. He must continue in this manner until in his heart he reaches the Source of the Highest Will which is called the Infinite.

King David, therefore, said, "A song of steps; from the depths I call You, Oh *Hashem* (*YKVK*)." (Tehillim 130:1) He is saying that he is calling *Hashem* from His depths, that is, from the highest source, which is called the *Ain Sof*. This is the depth which is the apex of the *Yud* of *YKVK*. He, therefore, said, "From the depths, I call you *YKVK*."

And how does one concentrate? One does so through a series of steps in an upward direction. He enters through the final *Hey* of the Name [which is associated with *Malchus*-Kingship]. He then ascends from attribute to attribute, from *Sefirah* to *Sefirah*, until his mind elevates itself to the apex of the *Yud*, which is *Keter*-Crown. This is called the *Ain Sof*, and it is the mystery of "the depths." [King David, therefore, called this] "a song of steps."

These "depths" denote everything that is hidden, concealed, and difficult to grasp. It is therefore written, "That which was, is far off, deep, deep, who can find it." (Ecclesiastes 7:24) The great mystery that includes all this is the verse, "Very deep are Your thoughts." (Tehillim 92:6) You already know that the mystery of thought is the *Yud* of the name *YKVK*.

Now that we have taught you this, we can return to the main idea. When one concentrates, he must focus all his thoughts, until with absolute concentration he reaches the source of will. This is the apex of the *Yud*, and it is the depth of thought. Regarding this, it is written: "From the depths, I call You, Oh *Hashem*." (Sha'arey Orah 3,4, p.39b)

This idea of the apex of the *Yud* is very important in the meditative process. It is the line of *Tzimtzum*, it reaches to levels beyond our comprehension, but it is still a rope to climb. Let us go a bit further inside the mind of the great Kabbalist Rav Gikatalia for more clarification.

The *Sefirah* [of *Chochmah*-Wisdom] is called somethingness in the Torah. The reason for this is that the first *Sefirah*, *Keter*-Crown, is hidden from the eyes of all. Since no one can contemplate it, it is called nothingness.

If a person seeks [*Keter*-Crown] he will find nothingness. No one can contemplate the depth of its depth and excellence. It is for this reason it is not connotated by any letter in the alphabet, but only by the apex of the *Yud*.

The beginning of thought, and the first revelation of the array is the second *Sefirah*, which is called *Chochmah*-Wisdom. (Sha'arey Orah 9, p.93a)

We see from these important Torahs that the realm of *Keter*, which is higher than we can really understand, is the entrance point to nothingness. The goal of mankind is to reach this point of nothingness, where we are simply void in the light of *Hashem*. It is at this point that one reaches the source of *shefa* and blessing.

"*Hashem* wrapped Himself with light like a garment." (Tehillim 104:2) When He then constricted this light, further concealing Himself, He created the Vacated Space. This is alluded to in the verse: "He made darkness His hiding place." (Tehillim 18:12)

The reason for the *Tzimtzum* stems from a basic paradox: *Hashem* must be in the world, yet, if He does not restrict Himself from it, all creation would be overwhelmed by His essence. The paradox is that since *Hashem* removed His light from the vacated space, it must be empty of His essence. Still, *Hashem* must also fill this space, since "there is no place empty of Him."

If one were to climb Mount Everest, eventually after weeks and weeks he will arrive at the top. It is there that he will feel he is at the top of the world, but can you imagine if he got there and realized that the mountain has barely started?

This is what is so beautiful about the meditative process in Kabbalah and the *Sefiros*. There is no point beyond where there isn't more spiritual growth. So, let us say that we have climbed all the way to the apex of the *Yud*. At this point, we could just turn our mind into a streamline for *shefa* to descend to the world through us, or we could continue higher. The more we ascend, the greater the revelation; but at this point, should a person reach here, there is no ego left; one is only concerned about *shefa* reaching the world. So, one could attempt to continue the same meditation that got him to this point and repeat it since the systematic architecture at this point could still repeat itself unto infinity. However, one could also float up to the apex line through meditation on nothingness alone.

When a person ascends from one level to the next, but still wants to attain more, then he has no limits and is literally like the Infinite. This person then has the attribute with which to grasp the seed transmitted from the Infinite Being.

But when a person says, "That which I can grasp is sufficient for me," he then only aspires to the straw and chaff, which are the Husks. (Or Torah, p.72a)

From the apex, one could turn left or right, spiritually speaking, and enter into the Garden of Eden to observe the goings-on. Just as *Hashem* enters the Garden every night, one could also observe at his own level some happenings.

This is what Rav Chiya and a very select few did.

In the Garden of Eden are rooms after rooms of souls who are studying the holy Torah. It is easiest to connect to one's parents and grandparents in this place if they were sages in their lifetime. Souls from this world are generally not so welcome there unless their hearts are completely pure. There are thousands of rooms filled with light and holy souls learning Torah together. Depending on what a person studied in this world, he is granted admittance to attend classes in the Garden of Eden that specializes in those same teachings. The Talmud says, "Happy is he who enters the next world with the Talmud in his hand." (Kesubos 77b) This means that how you prepare yourself in study in this world will help you open more holy doors and chambers in Gan Eden.

Besides observing the study, those select few who are lucky can learn and remember teachings from this ascent. Others can visit certain holy sages to receive blessings and guidance, but this is all very complicated and not a simple matter.

We are forbidden to arouse the dead and speak to them. It takes a great deal of exertion for the dead to communicate [with the living]. Therefore, it is forbidden to call up spirits and inquire of them about the future. "You must be totally faithful to *Hashem* your G-d." (Devarim 18:13)

The saints are buried in the cemetery, which is, therefore, a holy and undefiled place. Since it is holy ground, prayer is more acceptable there. When one prays on the graves of saints he should not direct his prayers toward the dead who are buried there. Rather, he should ask that *Hashem* grants mercy in the merit of the saints who lie in the dust. (Rabbi Yaakov Moellin, *sefer* Maharil, Taanis 37a)

It is different though from the plateau of the apex, and when it comes to connecting to holy sages who are in constant prayer for our wellbeing. "In their death, the righteous are called living." (Berachos 18a) However, one does not pray to them but connects to them in order to attain more purity. Therefore, it is the custom of some to request at the gravesite of the sage for him to intervene and pray on one's behalf. Rav Chaim Vital would lay his body on top of the grave of a *tzaddik* upon the instruction of his master the Arizal, in order to completely connect his soul to the sage. If the sage was of the same soul root as the one attempting this, the revelation would be all the greater. Kabbalistically, this binding to the *tzaddikim* can be done even from afar by those with great purity, as mentioned earlier in this *sefer*. One can also connect his soul to the current *gedolim* of the generation, as mentioned.

It is written, "You plucked a grapevine out of Egypt." (Tehillim 80:9) Why is Israel likened to a grapevine? Just as a grapevine rests on dead trees, so Israel, who lives and survives, depends on the dead, the Patriarchs.

Elijah said many prayers on Mount Carmel, asking that the fire should descend, as it is written, "Answer me, Oh *Hashem*, answer me." (Kings 18:37) Still, he was only answered after he said, "Oh Hashem, G-d of Abraham, Isaac, and Israel." (I Kings 18:36)

The same is true of Moshe. When Israel sinned with the golden calf, he prayed on their behalf for forty days and forty nights, and he was not answered. But as soon as he recalled the dead, he was immediately answered. It is thus written, "Remember Abraham, Isaac and Israel," (Shemos 32:13), and immediately afterward, "*Hashem* regretted the evil that He had said He would do to His people." (Shemos 32:14) (Midrash, Shemos Rabbah 44:1)

When the world is in anguish, and people go to pray at the graves, all the dead are aroused...The souls speak up to *HaShem*, and He has mercy on His world (Zohar 1:225a).

It is important to understand the power of the *tzaddikim* even after their death. *Rabbeinu hakadosh* (Rabbi Yehudah Hanasi) used to visit his earthly home at twilight every *Shabbos* eve. He appeared in his best clothes, the ones he used to wear on *Shabbos*, and not in his death shrouds, to show his family that he still had his strength. (Sefer Chassidim)

Lesson 36: Nothingness

When your thoughts ascend on high to the Supernal Universes, you must strengthen your mind. You will then be able to stroll through these Universes just as a person strolls from one room to the next. (Likutei Yekarim #175)

To properly understand this idea, one must understand what it truly means to be nothing. The Baal Shem Tov taught, "Nothing can change from one thing to another [without first losing its original identity]. Thus, for example, before an egg can grow into a chicken, it must first cease totally to be an egg. Each thing must lose its original identity before it can be something else. Therefore, before a thing is transformed into something else, it must come to the level of nothingness."

This is how a miracle comes about, by changing the laws of nature. First, the thing must be elevated to the emanation of nothingness. Influence then comes from that emanation to produce the miracle.

When a person gazes at an object, he elevates it into his thought. If his thought is then attached to the Supernal Thought, he can elevate it to the supernal Thought. From there it can be elevated to the level of nothingness, where the object itself becomes absolute nothingness.

This person can then lower it once again to the level of Thought, which is something. At the end of all levels, he can transform it into gold. (Imrey Tzaddikim p.19c)

Rabbi Levi Yitzchok taught, "The most important thing to realize is that *Hashem* created all and that He is all. *Hashem's* influence never ceases. At every instant, He gives existence to His creation, to all universes, to the heavenly chambers, and to all the angels."

We, therefore, say [in the prayer before the *Shema*], "He forms light and creates darkness" [in the present tense], and not "He formed light and created darkness" [in the past tense]. We say that *Hashem* creates in the present tense because every second He creates and gives existence to all that is. Everything comes from *Hashem*. He is perfect, and He includes all things.

When a person attains the attribute of nothingness, he realizes that he is nothing and that *Hashem* is giving him existence. He can then say that *Hashem* creates – in the present tense. This means that *Hashem* is creating, even at this very moment.

When a person looks at himself, and not at nothingness, then he is on a level of "something" [an independent existence]. He then says that *Hashem* created – in the past tense. This means that *Hashem* created him earlier [but that he now has independent existence].

We, therefore, say the blessing, "[Blessed are You, Oh *Hashem*...] who created man with wisdom." [We use the past tense] since Wisdom is on a level of something."

We, therefore, find in the writings of the Ari that the expression, "*Hashem* is King", is an aspect of Nothingness. For when we say that "*Hashem* is King", [in the present tense] it means that He is presently giving us existence. This is the aspect of nothingness - we are nothing, and it is *Hashem* who is giving us the power [to exist].

On the level of nothingness, everything is above the laws of nature. On the level of something, on the other hand, all things are bound by nature.

The way in which we bind something to nothingness is through the Torah and commandments. This is the meaning of the verse, "The living angels ran and returned" (Ezekiel 1:14) - [that is, from a level of nothingness to one of something].

The Zohar teaches that the commandments and Torah are both hidden and revealed. Hidden alludes to nothingness, while revealed applies to something. They thus bind something to nothingness, and nothingness to something.

This is the meaning of the word *mitzvah*, meaning commandment. When we reverse the Hebrew alphabet through the *Atbash* cipher, then *Alef* becomes *Tav*, *Bais* becomes *Shin*, and so on [Through this cipher, the *Mem* of *mitzvah* becomes a *Yud*, while the *Tzadi* becomes a *Hey*].

[The first two letters of *mitzvah*, therefore] are *Yud - Hey*, the first two letters of the Tetragrammaton, *YKVK*. This is an aspect of nothingness.

The last two letters of the word *mitzvah* are *Vav - Hey* [the last two letters of the Tetragrammation]. This is an aspect of something.

The letters *Yud - Hey* [in the word *mitzvah*] are hidden, just like the concept of nothingness. [The letters *Vav - Hey*, on the other hand, are written directly, and are revealed, just like something.]

The commandments thus have a hidden part and a revealed part. The hidden part is bringing pleasure to *Hashem* through our observance of the commandments since we have no way of detecting this. [The revealed part is] when we benefit ourselves since this is visible.

This is the meaning of the verse, "Hidden things belong to *Hashem* our *Hashem*, [but revealed things belong to us and to our children forever]." (Devarim 34:22)

"Hidden things" allude to the hidden part of the commandment, and these "belong to *Hashem* our G-d." What we accomplish with relation to *Hashem* is hidden from us.

"Revealed things belong to us and to our children," however, since the Divine influence that we bring about is revealed to us. (Kedushas Levi, Bereshis p.1)

At every instant, all universes receive sustenance and Life Force from *Hashem*. Man, however, is the one who motivates this sustenance and transmits it to all worlds.

When a person wants to bring new sustenance to all universes, he must attach himself to the level of nothingness. This is the level in all universes that were not constricted.

When man nullifies himself completely and attaches his thoughts to nothingness, then a new substance flows to all universes. This is a sustenance that did not exist previously.

A person must fear *Hashem* so much that his ego is totally nullified. Only then can he attach himself to nothingness. Sustenance, filled with all good, then flows to all universes.

The individual thus attaches the Life Force of all universes to nothingness, which is higher than all worlds. On the level where this [Life Force] had not yet been constricted into the universes, it is attached to the nothingness, which is called the *Hyle*. (Likutey Moharan Tinyana 97)

Space is only dark and vacated with respect to us. The Lamp of Darkness mentioned in the Zohar is darkness to us, but in relation to *Hashem*, it too is a "lamp". With respect to *Hashem*, it is actually light, since, for Him, it is as if the *Tzimtzum* never took place. The reason for *Tzimtzum*-Constriction was so that creation could take place, and this is required for us, not for *Hashem*. This is expressed by the psalmist in the verse: "Even darkness is not dark to You. Night shines like the day – light and darkness are the same." (Tehillim 139:12)

Between each of the Spheres, there is a kind of no man's land where *Hashem* is completely hidden, and where one who does not know how to look would say that *Hashem* is not there.

Each prophet experienced this in his own way, as the prophetic experience involved moving from one universe to another in order to perceive *Hashem's* glory. For many seeking the spiritual experience, when they reach this empty feeling, this is when they would be frightened or turn around.

Rebbe Nachman explains this as the regular barrier one feels when he tries to draw closer to *Hashem* and make any spiritual advancement in his life. One feels frightened and finds many pitfalls of life in his way. He is about to give up as he is standing on the threshold of a new level, feeling completely abandoned and alone. But this is the prerequisite for any kind of serious growth.

Many times, people will try a new *Yichud* and find that they feel nothing from it. What they are feeling could actually be the nothingness of the revelation. Should a person know how to feel and perceive something which is beyond him? Rather, his *Tikkun* has actually worked because the idea of *tikkun* isn't always about having a personal revelation or experience. It may simply be the idea of climbing and descending, drawing *shefa* from nothingness down to the world of *Asiyah*.

So, when a person feels dejected and depressed about his spiritual failures, this descent is actually part of the experience of growth. It is part of the *Ma'aseh Merkavah* and *chashmal*. This is why it is so important for us to change our life perspective and to never allow any sadness or negativity to enter our minds.

According to the Talmud, *chashmal* comes from two words: *shash*, meaning silent, and *mal*, meaning to speak. *Chashmal* is the "speaking silence". This is where the meditator is trying to get to a level of nothingness where everything is tuned out but the image he wants to see. When Ezekiel tries to describe this phenomenon, he says that nothingness is the color of silence.

You see in this realm, we are divorcing ourselves from all worldly conceptions. Since our minds can only deal with worldly conceptions, the closer you get to *Hashem* the more you have to discard your normal categories of light, space and time, even thought. All you experience is nothingness, yet this is not a negative thought but rather quite productive.

But unfortunately, without a proper foundation in one's *Yiddishkeit*, this feeling can be too dejected. One can feel as if *Hashem* is rejecting him and casting him away. He may feel as if he is not welcome to be near to *Hashem*. Therefore, he feels dejected. He falls into a depression and may even come to sin *chas v'shalom*, all because he didn't understand the idea of coming close to *Hashem*, that the feeling of emptiness is actually a positive experience that is beneficial to his service of *Hashem*. It is actually a sign of closeness to *Hashem*.

The experience could maybe be explained in relation to the climber. He gets to the top of the mountain and then takes a moment to look around. He has overcome so many obstacles that he feels relieved, yet he is exhausted from his journey. His revelations might feel overwhelming, sometimes filled with joy, while at other times the climber could feel confused. Do you know how many climbers made it to the top, only to fall and die during the fast descent? This is why it is so important to climb with the right tools and guidance, to plan what you will do during your descent. This is why the sages meditated for one hour after their prayers, in order to train themselves to structure their spiritual experiences.

So, you made an ascent up the *Merkavah*; you feel nothingness and you meditated that blessings should draw down to *Asiyah* and *Malchus*. You have awakened to regular consciousness, or so you think. Now you should busy yourself with *mitzvos* and kindness to others. When you give of yourself to others, you don't have time to reflect on negative things. You should take this light and now share it with others. If you had a spiritual revelation that you can take away, that is great. However, if it was an empty feeling, that too is fine. All is well because, at the level of Nothingness, there is no evil. That is if you reached that point, the apex of the *Yud*.

Lesson 37: In Your Precepts, I will Meditate

Introduction

Every person has his own unique experience in what he feels or sees spiritually. *Hashem* made each of us completely different for a reason. Much of how we imagine things spiritually is based on our upbringing and prior experience. Wisdom too is a big part of having a clearer revelation into the spiritual. Someone who learned the story of Ezekiel many times over with commentaries will naturally have a clearer revelation into the spiritual. This is because he knows what to look for, which gives his imagination a basis to see correctly. I thought it would be special to share with you some of my own mediations since usually these things are not spoken about or shared. My spiritual interpretation is based on my own personal life experiences and I share with you just a small window into my meditations on *mitzvos* so that you too can embark on a personal journey into the unknown.

Wake up Meditation

Thoughts:
As you open your eyes in the morning (besides the *modei Ani* prayer and washing of the hands), the first thing you should do is think of a *passuk*. This is very holy for the soul and will help you be closer to *Hashem*.

Meditation:
Throughout the day, remind yourself of that *passuk* and how it may apply to the events of the day. Eventually, you will wake up naturally with *passukim* in your mind each day.

Thoughts:
A positive thought in the morning is like medicine for the soul.

Meditation:
Think to yourself how this day will be successful and how everything is going to work out easily for you.

Thoughts:
The first thing you see in the morning is very important to help with purity and fear of heaven the rest of the day.

Meditation:
Keep your eyes closed throughout the *Modei Ani* and washing of the hands. Afterward, open your eyes to look upon a card with *Hashem's* name on it as the first thing you see upon awakening. Think how the name is drawing its light into your soul and how all you want is to be a true servant of *Hashem* this new day.

Learning Yechudim

Thoughts:
A way to learn *yichudim* is to break them down slowly in parts. Studying the Rashash prayers should be done in the same way. Most people get overwhelmed seeing so many combinations of letters that everything becomes a blur; therefore, take each part in pieces and work on them for one day, even one week. Even if it's just one line, that's also okay.

Meditation:
Take one small piece at a time and commit it to memory before moving on to the next. Taking a photo of one part and using it as a screensaver (If done carefully with modesty), helps your mind to break down the details and commit them to memory. Don't allow yourself to get frustrated; look closely at the letters and allow the *yichud* and its holiness to talk to you so that you understand it. Your soul already understands more than you realize; you just need to calmly let the holiness of the letters and combinations enter into your soul. Thinking of their greatness alone is very good.

Looking at the Sky

Thoughts:
Every so often, it is good to look at the sky and think about fear of *Hashem.*

Meditation:
Glance at the sky, observe the varied colors of the clouds and think how

Hashem controls the entire world. Not only this, but *Hashem* also is there watching over you so that everything will work out as it should. Start to feel His presence in your bones; imagine the *Shechinah* around you holding you as if hugging you.

Slow Down Our Prayers

Thoughts:

Too often we rush into the prayers without composure. Therefore, it's very good to say the karbonos, because it reminds us that our prayer is much higher than we think and can accomplish a lot.

Meditation:

If you see yourself rushing your prayers, take a deep breath in and out. Stop for a moment and remind yourself that you're standing before the Almighty *Hashem* and that one word said with *kavanah* can do wonders. Think of how blessing is flowing down from *Shamayim* as you recite the words.

Lighting the Nair Tamid / Candle

Thoughts:

The *kohen* would light the candelabra in the *Bais Hamikdash* daily. So too, it's good to light a candle, preferably one of olive oil, before you pray or at night in order to increase the *kedusha* in the home

Meditation:

Already when you pour the olive oil into the glass, have in mind you're doing this service for *Hashem*. As you pour the oil, you are doing a service to show honor to *Hashem* and the *tzaddikim*. Even preparing the wick is holy. Before you light the candle, think of a sage you wish to connect with spiritually. If it's the memorial of a sage, it is good to light the candle for him. You might find a more contemporary sage easier to connect to.

Now begin to light the candle. Think of what *Sefirah* that *tzaddik* represented best with his *midos* and then meditate from one *Sefirah* to the next, connecting to his soul. For instance, Avraham is connected to the *Sefirah* of *Chesed*. Imagine that you are climbing along with him from the *Sefirah* of *Chesed* to *Binah*. Do this until the *Sefirah* of *Binah;* at that point, there is a big *aliyah* for both your souls.

The Karbonos

Thoughts:

Reciting the prayer of the *karbonos* is a very humbling experience. Here we are humbling ourselves to *Hashem* to serve Him. *Chazal* teach us that the recitation actually takes the place of giving the real offerings and it is as if we had actually brought the offerings themselves.

Meditation:

Incense: Begin by placing your thoughts as if you are standing in the *Bais Hamikdash* in the holy city of Jerusalem. You are the holy *kohen* with the *karbonos* mixture in front of you. The fire is lit, and you just need to sprinkle the first species of herbs. You can feel the warmth of the fire surrounding your body, even to the point that your limbs begin to feel the warmth. Now sprinkle 1. Stacte into the fire; as it drops into the flames, the flames become larger with black smoke arising straight up. Not only do you feel the warmth of the flames, but you also can smell its sweet flavor. Now you go on to the next spice, 2. Onycha: The flame increases and so does its warmth. Its smell is even more endearing. You drop the third one 3. Galbanum: the fourth 4. Frankincense: You mix them all together and the smoke rises to the heavens. You stand there before *Hashem*, in total selflessness. You now drop the 5. Myrrh, 6. Cassia, 7. Spikenard, 8. Saffron, 9. Costus, 10. Aromatic bark, 11. Cinnamon. Lastly, you drop the most treasured *malos ashan*, smoke-raising herb and the sparks from the incense fly straight up through all the gates of *shamayim*. Now you stand before *Hashem* with the arising, pleasant smoke, ready to pray.

Meditation

Ketores, is 715, equal to 11 times that of the Name *A-D-N-Y*.

Tzitzis

Thoughts:

The *tzitzis* is a reminder of all the commandments given to us by *Hashem*. This *mitzvah* is carried with a person throughout the day and its power is complete protection from all matters. However, as simple as it might seem, most of us don't receive its full power or appreciate how holy and remarkable the *mitzvah* of *tzitzis* really is.

Meditation:

Think of the *tzitzis* or *talis* as a garment on fire. Its knots, its strings are all flames of holiness surrounding your body. Dwell on how holy and pure your *neshama* is. How you want to be pure with the *bris milah*. Think about the holiness of *Eretz Yisrael* and how you want to benefit from its *kedusha*. The *Shechinah* surrounds you and is being lifted up through the *tzitzis* strings and you both are being elevated together.

Tefillin

Thoughts:

The *tefillin* are really boxes of light and *yiras Hashem*. The desire to learn Torah and perform *mitzvos* are contained inside. One just has to connect to its holiness and receive light.

Meditation:

Think to yourself how the boxes of the *tefillin* represent the first three upper *Sefiros*. Then as you wind the strap, imagine you are winding straps of fire around your arm. You put on the head *tefillin*, the *Shin* is on fire, black fire and red flames surround your head. Then you begin to wrap the straps around your hand spelling out *ShaKai*, you are wrapping the flames around you and drawing down all the light of the higher *Sefiros* into *Malchus*.

Thoughts:

The *parshios* of the *tefillin* represent the Divine Name, *YKVK*; also, the idea of fear of *Hashem*. It is also important to note that the Talmud says that *Hashem* Himself wears *tefillin* every day.

Meditation:

Think of how the 4 compartments of the *tefillin* represent the name *YKVK*. It is broken down as follows:

Yud – First *parsha* – "Sanctify to me all the first-born, etc." (Shemos 13:2)

Hey – Second *parsha* – "And it shall be when *Hashem* shall bring you, etc." (Shemos 13:5)

Vav – Third *parsha* – "Hear, Oh Israel, etc." (Devarim 6:4)

Hey – Forth *parsha* – "And it shall come to pass if you shall hearken, etc." (Devarim 11:13-21)

Imagine each letter in each *parsha* shining forth in red fire. Start with the first letter and then move on to each letter until you think of each holy letter on fire. Then imagine the whole name *YKVK* in red fire. Then switch to black fire with gray smoke arising from the letters. Think of fear of *Hashem*. How you stand before Him, in total subjugation to serve Him.

Giving Charity

Thoughts:

Giving charity is a great *tikkun* for the soul.

Meditation:

When putting the coin in the hand of the poor, think of how you are uniting the holy name of *Hashem*, *YK* with *VK*. The name of *Hashem* is otherwise broken so to speak in that blessing has trouble descending below due to our many sins. When you unite *YK* with *VK*, with giving the coin to charity, you are uniting the

Sefiros above so that blessing now pours forth from above to below.

For Anxiety and Fear of Hashem

Thoughts:

Sometimes a person just needs to stop and regain his focus. Controlling one's breathing can help with this and with bringing a person more fear of *Hashem*. After all, Who is it that gives us the breath of life?

Meditation:

Breathe in deeply and count to: 1. Exhale slowly, about double the time as your inhale time. Count to two. Then breathe in again deeply and count to three. Continue this technique until you count to 10. Then count down, 9, 8, 7, etc. till 1 and then start again. You don't need to do this for a long period; it is only in order to refocus and calm down. While breathing, think about fear of *Hashem* and how everything is okay because Hashem is with you.

While Getting Dressed for Shabbos

Thoughts:

Just like we have special clothing set aside for the *kedusha* of *Shabbos,* so too *Hashem* clothes Himself in special light for *Shabbos.*

Meditation:

ל-א-י-ר-ר-ה-א

or

ל-א-י-ר-ר-ה-ז

Name of *Hashem's* spiritual clothing for *Shabbos.* It is good to meditate on this while getting dressed for *Shabbos* (When one is already modest, not in a dressing room). Also, one can meditate on this throughout the day while wearing one's special *Shabbos* clothes.

Lighting Shabbos Candles

Thoughts:
When a woman lights her *Shabbos* candles, it brings a great light into the home. The *Shabbos* Queen, the *Shechinah* enters and a sense of restfulness is felt.

Meditation:
Think of how you are drawing down holiness into this world as you raise your hands as is common during the *Shabbos* lighting. Feel the holiness surrounding you and the room around you is filling up with spiritual light.

Thoughts:
Rav Pinchas of Koretz said that a person if he is holy enough can even foretell everything that will happen to him the next week. I'd like to add to this that if you meditate on the candles while they burn Friday night, you can think how you want to draw holiness into each day of the week.

Meditation:
Throughout the night, look at the candles and think about the specific tasks that you regularly do during the week. Draw light into them and think how you will be successful. Imagine that each day of the week works out perfectly with grace, happiness, and success.

Kiddush

Thoughts:
All the holiness and blessing for the entire week stems from our recitation of the *Shabbos kiddush*.

Meditations:
Think of all the people you know that need Divine assistance in their life. Think of all their needs and think how spiritual light is flowing down from all the worlds into their life to fix their problems. Think of each member of your family, what they need in order to be close to *Hashem*. Meditate for yourself, all the things that are important to you and what you need success with.

Thoughts:
Pouring the wine is very important and not to be overlooked.

Meditation:
Having a little water in one's cup, drop three drops of water into the wine bottle. Then pour the wine three times until your cup is filled. These three times with water and wine, represent the *Sefiros* of *Keter*, *Chochmah*, and *Binah* or *Chochmah*, *Binah*, *Daas* (As explained to be by the Baila Rebbe of New York *shlit"a*). Meditate on the *passuk*, *kosi revaya*, that *Hashem* fills up one's life with deliverance. That *Hashem* should overflow your life with blessing. Imagine the

wine coming from the very Garden of Eden flowing down into your cup.

Thoughts:
How you hold and pick up the cup of blessing is very important

Meditations:
The cup is picked up with the right hand supported by the left ever slightly. Think how the left *Gevurah* is drawing from the right of *Chesed*. That holiness surrounds the cup. The cup represents the *Shechinah* and all of Israel. All the suffering, all the generations of trials and suffering. In your hand lies the responsibility to bless all of Israel and draw them closer to *Hashem*. Now you let go of your left hand and hold the cup completely alone in the right hand commencing with the blessing.

Drawing Down Shefa, Blessing

Thoughts:
ג-ב-י-ל-ו-ן

This holy Name is a holy name connected to the idea of drawing blessing from Heaven to earth. It is also good to think about this name many times during *kiddush* Friday night.

Meditation:
ג-ב-י-ל-ו-ן

Imagine this name how it draws down *shefa* to all of *Klal Yisrael*.

Blessing Over Washing the Hands for Bread

Thoughts:
Without getting too deep, in a simple way, the washing of the hands is like the actions in the *Bais HaMikdash*.

Meditation:
Think of how your washing of the hands represents the *kohen*, how he would wash before preparing the sacrifice. So too, your actions are a holy service of Hashem.

Blessing Over Bread on Shabbos

Thoughts:
The shewbread was called *Lechem Hapanim*. It was twelve loaves of bread

offered in the *Bais HaMikdash*. "On the table, the shewbread should be placed before Me at all times." (Shemos 25:30)

Meditation:
Place 12 loaves of *challah* of any size on your table under the *challah* cover. Have in mind that these loaves are taking the place of the *Lechem Hapanim* as it was offered in the *Bais HaMikdash*.

Laying Down to Sleep

Thoughts:
Going to bed and sleeping can be turned into a *mitzvah*.

Meditation:
As you lay in bed, think of all the sins you committed that day and whisper them to *Hashem*. State with a firm belief that you are going to sleep only in order to better serve *Hashem* with a new vitality tomorrow.

Meditation for Smoking

Thoughts:
Even though it's not a good habit to start, if one is already smoking, at least it can be used to elevate the soul. The *rebbe's* used to elevate the Worlds through the smoke. (Let's hope you don't need this)

Meditation:
Think of how the smoke is arising like the smoke from the sacrifices in the *Bais HaMikdash*. Imagine the smoke going up through the worlds of *Asiyah, Beriyah, Yetzirah,* and *Atzulos*. While arising, it is taking your prayers with it through the gates of Heaven. You can also think of a friend and his troubles. How the smoke is taking up his plea through the gates and passing all the angels till it reaches the Throne of Glory.

The Blessings Over Torah Study for the Day

Thoughts:
There is an obligation to make a blessing before learning Torah each day. Usually, we just recited this in the morning prayers.

Meditation:
Think about how much you love the Torah and how much you want *Hashem* to give you a complete understanding of what you learn today. Crave the Torah

with your very being and yearn for its light. You can imagine how you are standing on *Har Sinai*, the holy mountain, accepting the Torah from *Hashem* this very day. Surrounding you are all the Jewish people and Moshe Rabbeinu is there with the *luchos*, tablets in his hands. Imagine the sound of thunder radiating through your bones and lightning flashing before your eyes. You can even imagine yourself as being Moshe Rabbeinu himself and how you desire to receive the Torah in order to share it to others.

To Help Another Overcome Din or a Difficulty

Thoughts:
When you look upon another Jew with favor, you can actually change his *mazal* for the good.

Meditation:
When you see a person on the street or think of a friend who needs prayers, imagine the name *YKVK* in white letters and or with the Hebrew vowels of *Segal*. Think of how the light of compassion should come forth from the holy Name and draw down *Chesed*, kindness from the heavenly *Sefirah* of *Chesed* upon them.

While Learning Talmud

Thoughts:
When a *chassidic* master learns a *blatt* of *Gemara*, he is also connecting himself to the *Tanaim* in the page of the Talmud to such an extent that it is as if they are standing there with him, teaching him the page. This teaching is brought down in the Talmud itself. (Yevamos 97a) (From my book, The True Intentions of the Baal Shem Tov)

Meditation:
Imagine as you read the names of the *tzaddikim* mentioned in the *Gemarah* that they are there discussing the specific idea in your presence. If it mentions that one rabbi said this in the name of another, imagine both of them there in front of you. Put your mindset there inside the *Gemara* as if you personally are a bystander experiencing the story being told as if it is actually happening this very moment. That you are also there while the Rabbis are discussing the Torah.

Reciting Tehilim

Thoughts:
David Hamelech wrote Tehillim with *ruach hakodesh*. (Likutei Mohoran 156) When one recites *tehillim*, it is as great as if Dovid Hamelech himself is saying it.

The *ruach hakodesh* is still in the words of *tehilim*. When you recite *tehilim*, your own breath arouses the Holy Breath in these words. Therefore, when you recite *tehillim*, it is as if Dovid Hamelech himself is reciting it. (Sichos HaRan 98) In the *Yehi Rotzon* before *Tehillim*, we ask that our recital of *tehillim* should be as if Dovid Hamelech himself is reciting it.

Meditation:
Recite: I bind myself to Dovid Hamelech in the *Sefirah* of *Malchus*. May it be as if Dovid Hamelech himself is reciting the prayers along with me. May *Hashem* answer my prayers and bring salvation.

While Writing Tefillin

The *klaf* is white fire and the letters (ink) are black fire. When you dip the *kulmas* into the ink, you are not just taking ink but also light from on high and putting this energy into the *tefillin*.

Thoughts:
It is good to go to the *mikvah* not only before writing *tefillin* that day but also before each holy Name of *Hashem* when you can. A good stopping point for concluding your writing for the day is a word before the name of *Hashem* so at the next writing session you can immerse before putting down Hashem's holy Name.

Meditation:
At the *mikvah*, immerse and think about all the *kavanos* you know that have to do with the holy Name you're going to write. Especially good is the *kavanah* with the name *YKVK*, the *uketz* of the *Yud* representing the *Sefirah* of *Keter*. The *Yud* itself represents *Chochmah*; *Hey* represents *Binah*. *Vav* represents *Chesed, Gevurah, Tiferes, Netzach, Hod, Yesod,* and the final *Hey* represents *Malchus*. As you think about this combination, *shefa* is descending through the worlds to mankind and into the *tefillin*, you're writing. As you leave the *mikvah*, don't look at anyone or talk but walk straight home to write.

Thoughts:
It is good to meditate on this holy name while writing *tefillin*, as brought in *sefer* Sharshay Shaimos.

Meditation:
דמודטירון

During a Tish

Thoughts:

During a *tish*, the *rebbe* sits at the head of the table and the *chassidim* gather around the table intently and silently watch the *rebbe* eating the meal.

Meditation:

When you attend a *tish*, one of the most important aspects is humility before the *tzaddik*. Without this, you will not experience the elevation of the soul. Therefore, at the *tish*, meditate on your lowliness and the pureness of the *tzaddik*. Think how he has ascended to Heaven to draw down blessings to Israel and how you are beside him as his assistant blocking away all the impurities wishing to throw him off course. Ascend with his soul the best that your spiritual understanding allows you. Imagine that his table has a spiritual counterpart in Gan Eden and that it is there that you stand near him offering this meal to *HaShem*. Bring yourself to even deeper levels of humility and you too can draw down light along with him. (The main reason people don't feel anything at a *tish* is that they don't understand the necessity of humility and the simple happenings mentioned above.)

Thoughts:

Chassidim at the *tish* wait to receive *shirayim* (leftovers), of the *rebbe's* courses of food, believing it to be a great merit (*zechus*) to eat something from the leftovers of a *tzaddik's* meal. Many *chassidim* claim that miracles can take place in the merit of partaking of the *shirayim*, such as miraculous healing or blessings of wealth or piety.

Meditation:

When you receive *shirayim*, imagine that this piece of food has within it all the sparks to fix any empty parts of your soul. While you eat it, imagine that this food has been given to you by the *Kohen Gadol* as part of the sacrifices to *Hashem*.

Burning Nails Friday

Thoughts:

The Shulchan Aruch (O.C. 260:1) writes that it is a *mitzvah* to cut one's nails on Friday in order to honor *Shabbos*. It further says that the pious would burn their nails and this would bring an increase of fear of *Hashem*.

Meditation:

Think how the nails represent the *klipah*, impurities that attached themselves to you throughout the week, causing you to sin and not do *Hashem's* will. Imagine, as they are consumed by the fire, that you are being completely removed from the impurity of the body and you are repenting for all your misdeeds. Through the burning, you are receiving a clean slate to serve *Hashem* anew.

While at Work

Thoughts:
In whatever we are doing, whether it is work, housework or learning, we must find *Hashem* and feel His presence with us.

Meditation:
While doing simple tasks, think about *Hashem*. Try to connect the task to relate to some *mitzvah* in the Torah. It is known that our forefathers would perform the commandments through spiritually connecting mundane actions to their *mitzvah* counterparts. Think how *Hashem* is in all things, giving them light to sustain them and how through this task, someone will be helped, so therefore, really you are practicing the *mitzvah* of loving your fellow man.

While Talking to Others

Thoughts:
A person should at all times be connected to *Hashem*. This is most difficult while interacting with others. Therefore, talking should only be with a purpose.

Meditation:
While talking to a person, think of humility. Think of how this person is much greater than you in so many ways. Think of how the things he is talking about relates to Torah lessons you have learned. Thereby, you elevate his words. When you speak, count the very words you say and articulate them with precision, valuing each word you speak as a gift from heaven. Talk only in positivity and for the purpose of helping this person with his life. If you have to use mundane words, let them be riddles or have within them hidden messages of Torah and *d'vekus* to *Hashem*. Think of how these words you just spoke relate to concepts in the Torah. The key to speaking to others is to never lose your *d'vekus* and attachment to *Hashem* but to silently be thinking how this conversation too is holy. All the while, during your speech, you can also be meditating on holy names of *Hashem* and praying to *Hashem* in your mind.

Dancing

Thoughts:
What could be greater than dancing in complete simplicity before *Hashem* with *d'vekus* and love in your heart?

Meditation:
You can use whatever meditations you have learned that draw you closer to

Hashem. Then once you are humbly standing before *Hashem*, imagine that you are there in front of the *Kisay HaKavod*, dancing before the King of Kings. It is just you there, alone before Him, or you can imagine others joining you. But in the simplest way, you a pauper and lowly Jew, are just dancing in appreciation of your Creator, blessed be He. When you do this, the holy *Shechinah* will attach itself to you.

Thoughts:

Through dancing, Rebbe Nachman teaches, you can elevate evil decrees and remove sadness from your heart. He teaches that a person usually feels *din*, judgment, in his legs. That is why you feel heavy when you're sad and you can't seem to move. By dancing, you remove this heaviness.

Meditation:

The legs are represented by the *Sefiros* of *Netzach* and *Hod*. The feet are compared to *Malchus*. Think of this while you're dancing and elevate the light in the lower *Sefiros* to *Binah* which is the heart of gladness. In *Binah*, the *din*, heaviness can be repaired. The idea of jumping up and down in dance is the idea that these lower *Sefiros* will go upwards, returning light towards *Binah*.

Singing

Thoughts:

Through singing with pure intentions to come close to *Hashem*, one attaches himself to the *Shechinah*. Singing is a great tool for *d'vekus*. Everyone loves to sing, and *Hashem* enjoys song. That is why He created the angels, to sing praises and beautiful sounds before Him. We too can gladden Him, through this way.

Meditation:

When you begin to sing, it is good to start off with words and then let those words go, singing just the tune before *Hashem*. Instead of switching tunes, continue and let the *nigun* take you to places spiritually. Let the repetition of the song cause you to become deeper in meditation. Some of my best singing moments were when I sang the same song for twenty minutes before *Hashem*. So, imagine yourself going higher and higher through the song, closer and closer to *Hashem*. Think of how you're removing yourself from worldly things and think about how the only important thing in the world is to be close to *Hashem*. Continue in this way, removing your ego and wanting only to be attached to your holy soul. As you become more proficient in this, you can take others with you on this spiritual journey of song, even if they themselves don't know it; you can fix anything in the world through song.

While Eating

Thoughts:

The Baal Shem Tov taught: the purpose of eating is to rectify [the holy sparks in the food]. (Ohr HaEmes 33b)

Meditation:

Have in mind that your table is taking the place of the *mizbeiach* in the *Bais HaMikdash*. As you eat, bring the food to you instead of bending over towards it. Think how the food is taking the place of the sacrifices in the *Bais HaMikdash*. Imagine the holy table on fire and you are consuming sparks of holiness in complete devotion to *Hashem*, lifting them up and drawing the holiness out of the food. Think that this is not just a physical devotion but that eating is spiritual. Feel the *Shechinah* radiating around you and the table.

Mikvah

Thoughts:

The Baal Shem Tov said that every spiritual level he had reached was due to his diligence in purifying himself by immersing in the *mikvah*. (Likkutim Yekarim 178)

Meditation:

The first time you immerse, have in mind to remove all the impurities that fell upon you due to sin. The second time you should have in mind that, just as a *mikvah* cleanses the contaminated, so does "the holy One blessed be He cleanse *Yisrael*." (Yuma 85b-Mishna)

"מַה מִקְוֶה מְטַהֵר אֶת הַטְּמֵאִים, אַף הַקָּדוֹשׁ בָּרוּךְ הוּא מְטַהֵר אֶת יִשְׂרָאֵל"

The third time think of how *Hashem* gives strength to His creations and sustains you. The fourth time have in mind that your soul is completely pure and that you are in the womb, birthing anew as a completely clean soul. As you emerge, you are like a new person. The fifth time think of all your desires to come close to *Hashem* and all the things you want success in. The sixth time have in mind how all your prayers and thoughts are being elevated to the *Sefirah* of *Binah* and entering the gates of Heaven. The seventh time think of a living or dead *tzaddik* you wish to draw closer too. Imagine the *Sefirah* that their *midos* could be compared to most; then connect to them there and be elevated with them to the *Sefirah* of *Binah*. As you leave the *mikvah*, leave all negativity behind and begin anew your day.

Shefa Through the Worlds

Thoughts:

On the way to the mikvah I thought of a few new *kavanos* to meditate on the name of *YKVK*. This *kavanah* is in order to bring down *shefa* from the world of *Atzulos* to *Beriyah*, *Beriyah* to *Yetzirah*, *Yetzirah* to *Asiyah*.

Meditations:

<u>א-ה-י-ה</u>

א

- ה ה ה ה ה-

ـי י י י י י י ـ

- ה ה ה ה ה

<u>י-ה-ו-ה</u>

ـי י י י י י י ـ

- ה ה ה ה ה-

- ו ו ו ו ו ו-

- ה ה ה ה ה-

<u>י-ד-נ-י</u>

א-

-ד ד ד ד

נ נ נ נ נ נ נ נ נ

נ נ נ נ נ נ נ נ נ

נ נ נ נ נ נ נ נ נ

נ נ נ נ נ נ נ נ נ

נ נ נ נ נ נ נ נ נ

ـי י י י י י י י ـ

(The first set takes you from *Atzulos* to *Beriyah*. Continue this combination of three names through the journey of the four worlds.)

Meditations:

<u>אלף ה-י יוד ה-י</u>

א-

ל ל ל ל ל ל ל ל

ל ל ל ל ל ל ל ל

ל ל ל ל ל ל ל ל

פ פ פ פ פ פ פ פ

פ פ פ פ פ פ פ פ

פ פ פ פ פ פ פ פ

פ פ פ פ פ פ פ פ

פ פ פ פ פ פ פ פ

פ פ פ פ פ פ פ פ

פ פ פ פ פ פ פ פ

פ פ פ פ פ פ פ פ

- ה ה ה ה ה
י י י י י י י
י י י י י י י - ו ו ו ו ו - ד ד ד ד -
ה ה ה ה ה
ַי י י י י י י

א-ל-ף ה-א י-ו-ד ה-א

ַא
ל ל ל ל ל ל ל ל
ל ל ל ל ל ל ל ל
ל ל ל ל ל ל ל ל
ף ף ף ף ף ף ף ף
ף ף ף ף ף ף ף ף
ף ף ף ף ף ף ף ף
ף ף ף ף ף ף ף ף
ף ף ף ף ף ף ף ף
ף ף ף ף ף ף ף ף
ף ף ף ף ף ף ף ף
-ף ף ף ף ף ף ף ף
- ה ה ה ה ה
א-
י י י י י י י י י - ו ו ו ו ו - ד ד ד ד-ה ה ה ה ה
ַי י י י י י י
- ה ה ה ה ה
א-

אלף ה-ה יוד ה-ה

אַ
ל ל ל ל ל ל ל ל
ל ל ל ל ל ל ל ל
ל ל ל ל ל ל ל ל
פ פ פ פ פ פ פ פ
פ פ פ פ פ פ פ פ
פ פ פ פ פ פ פ פ
פ פ פ פ פ פ פ פ
פ פ פ פ פ פ פ פ
פ פ פ פ פ פ פ פ
פ פ פ פ פ פ פ פ
-פ פ פ פ פ פ פ פ
- ה ה ה ה ה
- ה ה ה ה ה
י י י י י י י י - ו ו ו ו ו - ד ד ד ד
- ה ה ה ה ה
- ה ה ה ה ה

Meditations:

ה-ו-ה-י

ה-י ו-י-ו ה-י ד-ו-י

-ד ד ד ד-וווווו-יייייייי
-יייייייי- ה ה ה ה ה
וווווו- יייייייייי-וווווו
יייייייי -ה ה ה ה ה

י-ה ו-א-ו ה-י ד-ו-י

ד ד ד ד-וווווו-יייייייי
-יייייייי-ה ה ה ה ה
וווווו—א -וווווו
ייייייייי-ה ה ה ה ה

ה-א ו-א-ו ה-א ד-ו-י

-ד ד ד ד-וווווו-יייייייי
ה ה ה ה ה
א
וווווו—א-וווווו
-ה ה ה ה
א

ה-ה ו-ו ה-ה ד-ו-י

ד ד ד-וווווו-יייייייי
ה ה ה ה ה - ה ה ה ה ה
וווווו-וווווו
ה ה ה ה ה - ה ה ה ה ה

Lesson 38: Summary

Having revealed to your different aspects of Kabbalah, you have been left with many pearls of wisdom. Inside many lessons were hidden secrets should you look again more closely, you will see gems which are lifechanging. At the same time, we have sharpened the sword of the *Satan* who wishes to protect the higher worlds from those unworthy to enter them. Therefore, I must summarize how you should proceed.

I'd like to remind you that the biggest obstacle in coming close to *Hashem* is one's ego. Those unworthy of closeness to *Hashem*, if they would search themselves, they would find that pride is ramped in their personality. In fact, after learning this *sefer*, it could be we increased this aspect. Therefore, I suggest you work on this more than any other *midah*. Realize that what you have been blessed to know and understand only comes from *Hashem*. Know how little you truly know compared to the great *kabbalists* of old. Reflect the fact that you have much work to do on yourself before you become static in your ways.

It is impossible to grow in Kabbalah without grounding oneself. That would mean lowering your ego to the pathways of a *rebbe* and *rabbi*. Studying foundational Torah such as Chumah, Tanach, Mishnah and the Talmud in the proper order. Practicing *kabbalaistic* mediations without their daily study is insane. Does a soldier go into combat without first going through basic training? If he did, would he be a good soldier?

I opened these new doors for you only so that you should become more enthusiastic about all of Judaism and its importance. That you should realize that you are here for a higher purpose and how important it is to connect to *Hashem* at every moment. At the same time, I have now given a child a knife to play with. What have I done?

I had never intended to reveal so many secrets to you, but I couldn't help myself. The only way to enjoy something beautiful is to share it with others. Please do be responsible and don't shatter more vessels then you fix. One thing I can tell you, even if you know little, even observe little, the main thing is to be humble. To serve *Hashem* with all the love in your heart. With truth and realness. You cannot fool the Master of the World. He knows and sees all.

Lesson 39: Holy Combinations for Reference

שויתי י-ה-ו-ה לנגדי תמיד

י-ה-ו-ה א-ה-י-ה א-ד-נ-י

י-א-א   ה-ה-ד   ו-י-נ   ה-ה-י
א-צ-י   ה-ב-ה   י-א-ו   ה-ו-ה-ת
י-א-ה-ד-ו-נ-ה-י

א-ה-י-ה   י-ה-ו-ה   צ-ב-א-ו-ת
י-ה-ו-ה   א-ד-נ-י

א-י-ד-ה-נ-ו-י-ה
א-י-ה-א-ו-א-ה-א

א-ד-נ-י   י-ה-ו-ה
א-ה-י-ה   י-ה-ו-ה

א   א-ל   א-ל-ה   א-ל-ה-י   א-ל-ה-י-ם
א-ל-ף   ל-מ-ד   ה-א   י-ו-ד   מ-ם

אל-ה-י-ם

א   א-ה   א-ה-י   א-ה-י-ה
א-ל-ף | א-ל-ף ה-א | א-ל-ף ה-א י-ו-ד | א-ל-ף ה-א י-ו-ד ה-א

א-ה-י-ה

ש   ש-ד   ש-ד-י
ש-י-ן   ד-ל-ת   י-ו-ד

ש-ד-י

א   א-ד   א-ד-נ   א-ד-נ-י
א-ל-ף   ד-ל-ת   נ-ן   י-ו-ד

א-ד-נ-י

י-ו-ד   ה-י   ו-י-ו   ה-י

י-ה-ו-ה

י-ו-ד   ה-י   ו-א-ו   ה-י

י-ו-ד   ה-א   ו-א-ו   ה-א

י-ו-ד   ה-ה   ו-ו   ה-ה

251

י-ה-ו-ה   י-ו-ד, י-ו-ד ה-א, י-ו-ד ה-א ו-ו,
             י-ו-ד ה-א ו-ו ה-י
             י י-ה י-ה-ו י-ה-ו-ה

א-ל-ו-ה   א-ל-ף ל-מ-ד ו-י-ו ה-י

             א-ל-ף ל-מ-ד ו-א-ו ה-י

             א-ל-ף ל-מ-ד ו-א-ו ה-א

             א-ל-ף ל-מ-ד ו-ו ה-ה

Asiyah	א-ד-נ-י
	י-ה-ו-ה
	א-ה-י-ה
Yetzirah	א-ד-נ-י
	י-ה-ו-ה
	א-ה-י-ה
Beriyah	א-ד-נ-י
	י-ה-ו-ה
	א-ה-י-ה
Atzilus	א-ד-נ-י
	י-ה-ו-ה
	א-ה-י-ה

Sweetness

א-ד-ט-ד	א-ה-י-ה
א-ז-ב-ו-ג-ה	Name of 8, *Segulah, Tefilah* Answered
א-ו-י	י-ה-ו-ה in the future will be
ה-ב-ה-א	*Kohein Gadol* says on *Yom Kippur*
א-ה-ר-ר-י-א-ל	Name of *Hashem* Clothes for *Shabbos*, good to
or	meditate while getting dressed for *Shabbos*
ז-ה-ר-ר-י-א-ל	
ב-י-ס-ץ	שמחה - *Atbash*
ב-מ-ס-ב ש-צ-צ-ב ס-ב-מ-ו	א-ל נ-א ר-פ-א נ-א ל-ה one letter forward (good for any sickness)
ה-ה-י ה-י-ה י-ה-ה	Written on Moshe's Stick; they are fire!
י-ל-י	Elevate sparks from the *Klipah*; power to heal;

נ-ל-ך   Power to see wonders; no pain while walking large distances

כ-ו-ז-ו ב-מ-ו-כ-ס-ז כ-ו-זו   י-ה-ו-ה א-ל-ה-י-נ-ו י-ה-ו-ה

א-ה-צ-צ-י-צ-י-ר-ו-ן   צ-י-ץ א-ה-ר-ן

א-י-ה א-י-ר-ו-ן א-י-א-ל   Meditate to feel wonders

ה-ר-ב-ח-מ-ן   א-ב-ר-ק *Gematria*

ר-א-ה   Lost on the road; meditate to see the right way to go.

א-י-ט-מ-ו-ן   י-ה-ו-ה מלך *Gematria*

ג-ב-י-ל-ר-ן   Shefa comes to all Klal Yisrael

ע-ז-ו-י   Good Prayer in time of trouble

ה-י-מ-ל   הַ-ו-א יַ-שׁ-ל-ח מַ-ל-א-כּ-ו

ל-פ-נ-י-ך *Hatzlacha*

ז-ג-נ-ז-ג-א-ל   מ-י-כ-א-ל + תגין 21=א-ה-י-ה =

ז-כ-ר-י-א-ל   *Malach* of Memory

ח-ת-ך   פותח אֶת ידך

א-ל-ו-ה   Sleep

א-ר-ט-י-מ-ו-ס   Makes *tumah* run away

י-א-י-א   י-ה-ו-ה אֱ-ל-ה-י-נ-ו יְ-ה-ו-ה אֶחד

י-ו-ח-צ-צ-ב-י-ר-ן + שמע ישראל   Combine and meditate to bring someone back to *teshuvah*

יא-ץ יב-ץ יג-ץ יד-ץ יה-ץ
י-ו-ץ יז-ץ יח-ץ יט-ץ יי-ץ
יכ-ץ יל-ץ ימ-ץ ינ-ץ יס-ץ
יע-ץ יפ-ץ יצ-ץ יק-ץ יר-ץ
יש-ץ ית-ץ   ה' אַוהב צַדיקים Great Name

א-ץ ב-ץ ג-ץ ד-ץ ה-ץ   Great Name

ו ,ז-ץ ח-ץ ט-ץ י-ץ

כ-ץ ל-ץ מ-ץ נ-ץ ס-ץ

ע-פ,ץ

צ-ץ ק-ץ ר-ץ ש-ץ ת-ץ

Guarding Names

ב-ק-י   Guarding

ב-ר-ז-ל   בלהה רחל זלפה לאה

ט-פ-פ-ט-י-ה   Guarding   can use colors while

253

Reb Moshe Steinerman
meditating

י-ו-ב-ב	יַקְרָאֵנִי וְאֶעֱנֵהוּ בַּצָּרָה וַאֲכַבְּדֵהוּ (תהלים צא, טו)
צ-ד-נ-ל-ל-ב-ש	Guarding
צ-מ-ר-כ-ד	Guarding
ר-ה-א ת-מ-פ א-ד-ם ת-מ-י-א	Meditate to save from any troubles

For Tefillah

י-ה-ו-ה א-ד-נ-י י-י-א- י א-ה-י-ה י-א-י-א ה-ד-י-ה ו-נ-א-י ה-י-י ה

י-י-א-י = יִשְׂמְחוּ יֵודוּךְ אֶרֶץ יְבָרְכֵנוּ

Combinations of YKVK

OPENS A PERSON'S HEART	יַ-הַ-נ-הַ
REVEALS HIGH SECRETS, HIGHEST COMBINATION	יַ-הָ-נ-הַ
BIG IN SOCIETY, FOR HATZLACHA	יַ-הַ-נ-הַ
TO BRING HEALING	יַ-ה-ו-הַ
ELEVATE YOUR TEFILLAH	יְ-ה-ו-ה
HAPPINESS, HEALING, GRACE, REMOVE WORRIES	יֹ-הַ-ר-הַ
FOR WEALTH	יָ-ה-נ-הַ
TRAVEL SAFELY & EASILY; HATZLACHA	יִ-הֵ-נ-הָ
OPEN HEART TO UNDERSTAND TORAH LEARNING	יְ-הֹ-וֹ-הַ
TO DRAW DOWN CHESED, KINDNESS	יְ-הֵ-רְ-הָ
FROM THIS COMBINATION, ISRAEL WILL BE RELEASED FROM GALLUS/GOOD FOR ANSWER IN DREAM	יְ-הַ-וְ-הַ
FOR FRIENDSHIP/LOVE	יְ-ה-ו-ה

Nefesh	earthly soul; receives spiritual sustenance	נפש
Ruach	Wind, Spirit in breathing animal/human, *Ruach Hakodesh*	רוח
Neshamah	Soul, Intimacy with *Hashem* as if *Hashem* were breathing on you	נשמה
Chaya	life force	חיה
Yechida	the universal Oneness-G-d	יחידה

דע לפני מי אתה עו

The Four Letters and the Sefiros

Apex of Yud	Keter
Yud	Chochomah
Hey	Binah
Vav =6	The Six Sefiros: Chesed, Gevurah, Tiferes, Netzach, Hod, Yesod
Hey	Malchus

The Supernal Universes

Universe	Inhabitants	Counterpart
Adam Kadmon (First "Man")	Tetragrammatons	Apex of Yud
Atzulos	Sefiros, Partzufim	Yud
Beriyah	The Throne, Souls	Hey
Yetzirah	Angels	Vav
Asiyah	Forms	Hey

Levels of Expression

Universe	Expression	
Asiyah	Otiot	Letters
Yetzirah	Tagin	Orniments
Beriyah	Nekudos	Vowel Points
Atzilos	Ta'amim	Cantellation Notes

The Partzufim

Partzuf		Sefirah	
Atika Kadisha	The Holy Ancient One	Upper Keter	
Atik Yomim	The Ancient of Days		
Arikh Anpin	Long Face	Lower Keter	
Abba	Father	Chochmah	Yud
Imma	Mother	Binah	Hey
Zer Anpin	Small Face (Male)	The Next Six	Vav
Nukva	Female	Malchus	Hey

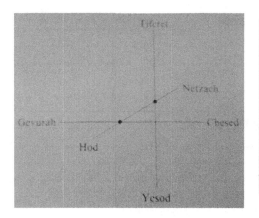

Beginning	Chochmah
End	Binah
Good	Keter
Evil	Malchus
Up	Netzach
Down	Hod
East	Tiferes
West	Yesod
North	Gevurah
South	Chesed

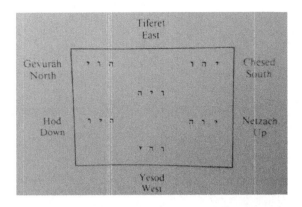

Cholam	ֹ	Begin straight ahead and raise head upward.
Kametz	ָ	Begin at right and move head to left.
Tzereh	ֵ	Begin at left and move head to right.
Chirik	ִ	Begin straight ahead and lower head downward.
Shurek	ּ	Move head directly forward.

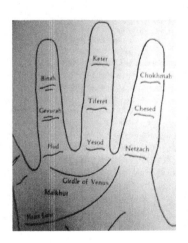

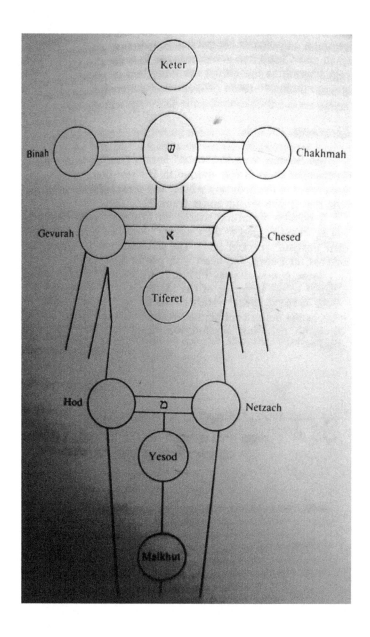

סקילה	י	א	ע״י	א	יוד	הי	ויו	הי
שריפה	ה	ד	ע״י	ה	יוד	הי	ואו	הי
הרג	ו	נ	ע״י	י	יוד	הא	ואו	הא
חנק	ה	י	ע״י	ה	יוד	הה	וו	הה

לג' כלי חכמה	לג' כלי דעת	לג' כלי בינה
יד דוי ואו דא	יוד דוי ויו דוי	אלף, אלף דא, אלף דא יוד
י יה יוד יהוה	יוד דוי ואו דוי	אלף דא יוד דא
יד דא ואו דוי דהה וו דהי	יוד דהה וו דהי	אלף דא יוד דא
		אהיה

לג' כלי חסד דז"א	לג' כלי ת"ת דז"א	לג' כלי גבורה דז"א
א אל אלו אלוה	יוד דא ואו דא	יה
אלוה	י יה יהו יהוה	אלף, אלף למד, אלף למד
אלף למד	יהוה	הי, אלף למד דוי הי יוד, אלף
		למד דוי יוד מם
		יְהֹוָה

לג' כלי נצח דז"א	לג' כלי יסוד דז"א	לג' כלי הוד דז"א
יהוה	יאהדונהי	אלי
צ צב צבט	צין צין דלת צין ולת יוד	א צבא צבאת
צבט א	צין דלת יוד	או ת

מלכות דרחל

אלף דלת צן יוד

א ד נ י

א אד אדנ אדני

נורות מנ"ה דרחל ליסודה ולהמשיך

שביסוד דז"א

יהוה יהוה

יסוד דרחל

שין דלת יוד

ש ד נ י

ש שד שדי

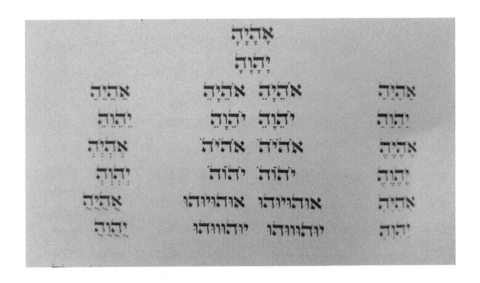

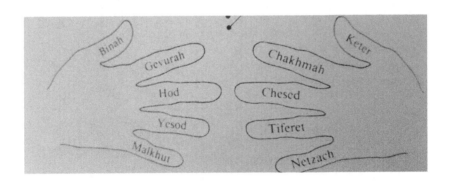

GLOSSARY

ABBA ILA'AH - The higher father
ADAM KADMON - First man, Primal man
ADNA – See Chapter 18
AHAVAS YISRAEL – Love of one's fellow Jew
AIN SOF - Infinite
AM YISRAEL – Jewish Nation
AMIDAH – See definition of *shemonah esrei*
ARICH ANPIN – (lit. "The Elongated Face") *Partzuf Keter* is called *Arich Anpin*. *Arich Anpin* is synonymous with the will. G-d's will to manifest at any particular level is what is responsible for the existence of that level of revelation.
ARIZAL - The most famous Kabbalist of the day was Rabbi Isaac Luria (1534-1572), universally known as the *Arizal*
ASHAM – Sacrifice
ASHREI – Fortunate
ASIYAH - The world of action
ATBASH - The *Atbash* cipher is a very specific substitution cipher where the letters of the alphabet are reversed. This is sometimes used in order to form a new word and show their spiritual relevance.
ATIK YOMIN - The Ancient of Days; the inner dimension of Keter, a level which transcends the entire scheme of the ten Sefirot; an elevated spiritual level that is in absolute oneness with G-d's essence.
ATZILUT(S) - The world of emanation
AVODAS BEIS HAMIKDASH – Service of the Temple
AVODAS HASHEM - Service to G-d
AZAROS - Refers to the leftover blood that would be poured on the western *Yesod* of the *Mizbe'ach*
BAAL TESHUVAH – A person who repents. Usually referring to someone who returns to Orthodox Judaism
BAIS HAMIKDOSH – Holy Temple
BAAL KABBALAH – Expert in *Kabbalah*
BEKAROV – In the future
BERACHA / BERACHOS - Blessings
BERIYAH - The world of creation
BET(S) DIN – Jewish Court
BINAH - Understanding

BITUL TORAH – Wasting time that could have been used to study Torah

B'KEDUSHA - In holiness

BOCHOR / BOCHURIM – Young Single Man/men

BRACHA - Blessing

BRACHA VEHATZLACHA – Blessing for success

CHAS V'SHALOM - It shouldn't happen

CHASHMAL - is used by Ezekiel to describe a mysterious fiery spectacle which he saw in his famous vision of the Heavenly Chariot

CHASSID – Follower or person seeking higher purity

CHATAS - Sin offering

CHATZOS – Midday or Midnight

CHEDER - Religious school for boys

CHENEK - High court penalty of strangulation

CHESED - Kindness

CHIDDUSHIM -original *Torah* insights

CHOCHMAH - Wisdom

CHOSSON - Bridegroom

CHURBAN BEIS HAMIKDASH – Destruction of the Temple

D'VEKUS - Closeness to G-D

DAAS - Understanding

DAVENED - Prayed

DERECH - Pathway

DIN – Judgement from Heaven

DIVREY TORAH – Words of Torah

DOVID HAMELECH - King David

EIN SOF - Endless

EITZ HADAAS – Tree of Knowledge

EITZAH – Advice

E-L CHAI – Connecting to the Sefirah of Yesod, representing the idea of foundation, structure. One of HaShem's holy names

ELIYAHU HANAVI – Elijah the Prophet

EMES – Truth

EMUNAH - Faith

ETZ HADAS – Tree of Knowledge

EVEN SHITIYA –Foundation Stone (which the world was created from)

GABBAI - (Aramaic) (a) the person responsible for the proper functioning of a synagogue or communal body (b) an official of the Rebbe's court, who admits people for yechidus, private meetings

GADOL HADOR – Great Rabbi of the Generation

GAONIM – Great Rabbinical Scholars

GEHENAH - Purgatory, the spiritual realm in which the souls are cleansed from blemishes brought about by their conduct on Earth

GEMARA - (lit. "learning") A reference to the Talmud

GEMATRIA - Numerical value for letters and words

GEULA - Redemption
GEVURAH - Might
GOYIM - Non-Jews
HAKOL KOL YAAKOV – "It is the voice of Yaakov" (*Bereshis* 27:22). Yitzchak then gives Yaakov the *Bechorah,* the birthright to Yaakov instead of Eisav
HALACHA – Jewish Law
HALLELUYAH – Praise G-d
HATZLACHA - Success
HEICHAL HATESHUVAH - The heavenly mansion of return or repentance
HEREG - High court penalty of beheading
HILCHOS LULAV - The laws of one of the Four Species used during the holiday of Succos
HISBODEDUS - Meditation
HISKASHRUS – Connecting to the Sage
HOD – Majesty
HODIYA – Thanksgiving
KAMAYA – Scribal charm written on parchment
LAMENAZEACH – For the conductor; often used by King David in the Psalms as a reference to HaShem
KARBANOS - Ritual sacrifices
KAVANAH - Concentration, intent. The frame of mind required for prayer or performance of a mitzvah (commandment)
KAVANOS – Holy meditational intentions
KAVIM – Measurement used in the Talmudic times
KAVOD - Respect
KEDUSHA – Holiness
KEFIZAS HADERECH – Traveling great distances in a shorter period of time
KELIPOT(S) - Forces of evil
KETER - Crown
KETER MALCHUT - Crown of Kingdom
KETER ELYON - The supernal crown
KETORES - Ritual incense
KIDDUSH – Blessing recited on Shabbos over a cup of wine
KIDDUSH HASHEM – Sanctification of HaShem's name
KLAF – Parchment Paper for scribal work
KLIPAH / KLIPOS - Bad spirits
KOACH – Strength
KOCHOT(S) - The highest type of angels
KODESH HA KODASHIM – Holiest place in the Temple
KOHEN GADOL / KOHANIM GEDOLIM – High Priest(s) who served in the Temple

KTAV ASHURIT(S) - The script of a Torah scroll

LEVITES - A member of the Israelite Tribe of Levi which had special tasks in the Temple

LISHMAH – Performing a commandment for the Mitzvah itself, with complete sincerity

LIST ALL SEFIROS AND WORLDS WITH BRIEF TRANSLATION

LAG B OMER - A Jewish holiday celebrated on the 33rd day of the Counting of the Omer celebrating the end of Rabbi Akiva's students dying. It is also the memorial of Rebbe Shimon Bar Yochai.

MA'ASEH BERESHITH – Works of Creation

MA'ASEH MERKAVAH - Works of the Chariot

MACHLOKES – Argument

MALACH - Angel

MALCHUS – Kingdom

MASKIL – Making wise

MAZAL – Destiny

MESAMEACH – To make happy

MIDAH - Character trait

MILUI - (Full form) of a word, obtained by writing out the spellings of the letters in that word

MISHNA - The first compilation of the oral law, authored by Rabbi Yehudah HaNasi (approx. 200 C.E.); the germinal statements of law elucidated by the Gemara

MISHPAT - Fair and proper judgment

MISNAGDIM - Opponents of Chassidism.

MIZBEACH – The Alter in the Temple

MIZMOR – Psalm

MOSHE RABBENU – Moses, Greatest prophet who ever lived.

MUSAF – "Additional" prayer service recited on Shabbat and festivals, commemorating the additional offerings brought in the Temple on these days

NACHASH – Serpent

NEKUDOS - Vowels

NESHAMAH / NESHAMOS - Soul

NETILLAT YADAIM – Jewish ritual for washing the hands

NETZACH - Conquest

NEVUAH – Prophesy

NIGUN – Melody

OLAM HA'ASIYAH – See Asiyah

OLAM HABA - The World To Come

OR CHOZER - Is related to Divine knowledge of the created world

OR YASHAR - (Lit. "Direct light") light as it is revealed from its source

ORCHIM - Guests

PARDES - [Literally "The Orchard"]

PAROCHES - The decorative cover for the ark containing Torah scrolls

PARTZUF - A Partzuf is a level in which the Sefirot are recognizable as distinct qualities, but nonetheless, unite and connect to work in conjunction, as a unified system.

PESUKEI D'ZIMRA – Verses of song recited in the morning prayers

PIRKEI AVOS – Ethics of our Fathers

POSSUK / PASUKIM – Verse, Verses

RABBEIM - Rabbis

RACHAMIM - Mercy

RATZON - Will

RAV - Rabbi

REMEZ – Meaning "hint" in reference to scriptural interpretations

RIKUD D'KEDUSHA - The holy dance

ROSH HAYESHIVAH – Head Rabbi of a Yeshivah

RUACH HA KODESH – Divine Inspiration

RUCHOS - **Spirits**

SANHEDRIN – The ancient Jewish court system

SEFIROS – The *sefirot* represent the various stages of the Divine creative process, whereby G-d generated the progression of created realms culminating in our finite physical universe. The *sefirot* constitute the interacting components of a single metaphysical structure whose imprint can be identified at all levels and within all aspects of Creation

SEGULAH - A remedy

SEUDAS BRIS – Circumcision meal

SHAILA – Question for a Rabbi

SHALIACH TZIBBUR – Head prayer leader

SHAMAYIM - Heavens

SHECHINAH - The Divine Presence

SHECHTED – Slaughtered

SHEFA - Blessing

SHEIDIM - Demons

SHELAMIM - Sacrifices

SHEMA - A *prayer* that serves as a centerpiece of the morning and evening *prayers*

SHIDDUCHIM – Dating through a matchmaker

SHIR / SHIRA - Song

SHIRAS HAYAM – Song sang at the crossing of the Red Sea

SHLOMO HAMELECH – King Solomon

SHEMONEH ESREI - 18 prayers said three times daily as part of the service

SHOCHET - slaughterer of kosher animals

SHUL – Synagogue

SHULCHAN ARUCH - Code of Jewish Law

SIATTA DISHMAYA - Aramaic phrase, meaning "with the help of Heaven"

SIMCHOS - Joy and celebrations

SKILA - High court penalty of stoning

Chassidus, Kabbalah and Meditation

SPHERES – Referring to the Sefiros
SREIFA - High court penalty of burning
TAGIN – Crowns of the Hebrew letters
TAHARA - Ritual purity
TALMID CHACHAM - Wise man
TALMUD MUVAK – Closest follower of a Rabbi
TAMID - *Tamid* is an abbreviated form for *olat tamid* ("daily burnt-offering") and refers to the daily (morning and evening) sacrifices as set out in Shemos 29:38–42 and Bamidbar 28:1–8
TANACH - Acronym of Torah (Law), Nevi'im (Prophets) and Ketuvim (Writings). Written Torah
TEFILLAH – Prayers
TEFILLIN - Holy Scriptures wrapped in a box with leather straps to attach to the head and arm
TEHILLIM - Psalms
TESHUVAH - Repentance
THE HEICHAL HANEGINA - The heavenly mansion of melody
TIFERET(S) - Beauty
TIKKUN CHATZOT - (Lit. "Midnight service"); a prayer recited by pious Jews at midnight, lamenting the destruction of the Holy Temple
TIKKUN HABRIS – Purity of the Covenant
TIKUN / TIKKUNIM - Repairing
TODAH – Sacrifice of thanksgiving
TORAH LISHMAH – Learning Torah for the sake of Heaven
TORAH SHEBAL PEH – Oral Torah
TORAH SHEBEKSAV – Written Torah
TUMAH - Impurity
TYVOS – Cravings
TZADDIK TZADDIKIM - Lit. Righteous person(s). A completely righteous person often believed to have special, mystical power.
TZELEM ELOKIM – Image of *HaShem*
TZIMTZUM - (lit. "Contraction"); the process of Divine self-contraction and self-limitation which makes possible the concept of limited, worldly existence
VESIKIN – Prayer at sunrise
VESHINANTOM LEVANECHA – To teach one's children
YESOD - Foundation
YETZIRAH - The World of Formation
YICHUD / YICHUDIM – Spiritual Unifications
YIDDELA – Yiddish for Jew
YIDDEN – Yiddish for Jews
YIDDISHKEIT – Yiddish for Judaism
YIMACH SHEMO – May their name be erased
YISRAEL SABA – Israel, The Elder
YISHUV VDAAS – Clear understanding without confusions

Reb Moshe Steinerman

YUNGERMAN – Yiddish for young man

ZEIR ANPIN - (Aramaic., lit. "the small face"); the term used by the *Kabbalah* for the Divine attributes which parallel emotions

ZEMER - Song

Made in the USA
Coppell, TX
21 December 2020

46812208R00154